body images

body images

embodiment as intercorporeality

Gail Weiss

Routledge

New York and London

Published in 1999 by
Routledge
29 West 35th Street
New York, NY 10001

Published in Great Britain by
Routledge
11 New Fetter Lane
London EC4P 4EE

Printed in the United States of America on acid-free paper.

10 9 8 7 6 5 4 3 2 1

Library of Congress Cataloging-in-Publication Data

Weiss, Gail, 1959–
Body images : embodiment as intercorporeality / Gail Weiss.
p.   cm.
Includes bibliographical references and index.
ISBN 0-415-91802-2 (hardcover : alk. paper). — ISBN 0-415-91803-0 (pbk. : alk. paper)
1. Body image. 2. Body schema. I. Title.
BF697.5B63W45   1998
128'.6—dc21   98-3799
                 CIP

For Sam and our five children:
Jason, Robin, Rachel, Simon, and Colin

{contents}

{acknowledgments}

The gestation of this book began before my children were born. I've had my children every two years and it somehow seems suitable that this book is in production just when our twins have turned two years old. Like the birth of the children, the culmination of this particular labor marks both a beginning and an ending. Although I am already immersed in new projects which have taken on lives of their own, I will miss the steady companionship that *Body Images* has provided as so many changes have taken place in my life.

Maureen MacGrogan was the first person I spoke to about this project, and her encouragement and support as my editor, gave me the confidence to proceed. Her patience during the long hiatuses when I fell behind schedule was much appreciated. She understood the difficulties I was facing in balancing the different facets of my personal and professional life and understood the importance of not sacrificing the former for the latter. My departmental colleagues have also been extremely supportive of this project. Special thanks are owed to Bill Griffith, Paul Churchill, and Andy Altman for their solicitude and invaluable advice along the way. As my chair, Bill enabled me to keep this book a priority as I fulfilled my teaching and departmental responsibilities. A sabbatical leave from George Washington University for the spring 1995 semester and two Junior Faculty Summer Grants greatly facilitated my progress on the book.

My participation in the GW Human Sciences program has provided me with wonderful, interdisciplinary colleagues who have also faced the challenge of breaking outside of the traditional limits of their respective fields to do justice to the subjects of their own investigations. Special thanks go to the members of my reading group on the body for acquainting me with authors that I would never have encountered otherwise. Our stimulating discussions have greatly expanded the range of my own interests and have had a direct impact on the arguments made in the pages that follow. My involvement in the 1994 NEH Institute on "Embodiment: The Intersection between Nature and Culture" at UC Santa Cruz, directed by Bert Dreyfus and David Hoy, was also a formative influence on this work.

I feel especially fortunate to be part of a larger community of feminist scholars working on the body. Both Liz Grosz and Judith Butler have served as mentors for me and this book is indebted to their work and to them. Liz's presence here at GW in the fall of 1997 was invaluable as I put the finishing touches on the last chapters. Despite her own frenetic schedule, she was always willing to read portions of this text in draft form on short notice and give me feedback right away. Just having her here was an inspiration.

Dorothea Olkowski, Jeffrey Cohen, Elissa Marder, and Sara Castro-Klaren, have all read or discussed portions of the text with me, and the book has profited from their respective insights. Members of the Merleau-Ponty Circle have listened to me read versions of some of these chapters, and their professional expertise and warm friendship has been a constant source of motivation. Gayatri Patnaik, T.J. Mancini, Phillip Ward, and the staff at Routledge all played crucial roles in bringing this volume to press. The artists who contributed their work to this volume helped me demonstrate that one can write philosophy books with pictures in them. Special thanks go to Peter Brooke for the long hours he spent getting the cover image just right!

Our nannies over the last few years, Emma Addo, Lydia Squire, Ellen Celec, Edith Okumu, and Jessica Cramer have enabled me to stay focused on my work while having the peace of mind of knowing that my children couldn't be in more loving or capable hands. Very few working mothers have this privilege, and my gratitude to them both personally and professionally is enormous. Amanda Walker spent hours typing up the bibliography from my handwritten pages and even helped out on the home front when needed. Her assistance in both facets of my life has been indispensable. Thanks also must go to Valerie Hazel for her work on the index. My students here at GW have always challenged me to think new thoughts and their efforts to come to terms with their own corporeal identities have informed this project from start to finish.

I owe the greatest debt of gratitude to my family. My husband, Sam Brooke, spent many nights and weekends handling all five kids alone so that I could go back to the office and work. He always encouraged me to do what I had to do to make the book as good as it could be, and has never for a moment ceased to support and value my career. Our parents, Harry and Irene Weiss, and Peter and Anne Brooke, have provided us with wonderful models of what family life could and should be and have enabled us to do the same for our children. The fun and craziness we have with Jason, Robin, Rachel, Simon, and Colin remind me daily that there is more to life than being an academic. The insanity at home has actually helped to preserve my sanity throughout this project!

My final thanks go, in advance, to you, the reader, who has chosen this book from among so many possible others. You've kept me silent company as I've worked, and I hope to do the same for you as you read these pages.

{introduction}

[T]he body is and is not ourselves. The body does everything and it does nothing. Neither end nor means, always involved in matters which go beyond it, always jealous of its autonomy, the body is powerful enough to oppose itself to any merely deliberate end yet has none to propose to us if we finally turn toward and consult it.

—Maurice Merleau-Ponty (1973:112)

To write about the body or even the body image is a paradoxical project. This is because these expressions themselves seem to posit both the body and the body image as discrete phenomena of investigation, presumptions that this text challenges from the outset. For Merleau-Ponty, the danger of viewing the body as a singular entity is that we may lose sight of the fact that the body is never isolated in its activity but always already engaged with the world. As far as the body image is concerned, he insists that it is "neither the mere copy nor even the global awareness of the existing parts of the body." Instead, Merleau-Ponty claims that the body image actively integrates parts of the body "only in proportion to their value to the organism's projects" (Merleau-Ponty 1962:100). These projects in turn derive their significance not merely from an individual's intentions, but from the situation out of which they have emerged and within which they are expressed.

Not only are the expressions "the body" and "the body image" problematic insofar as they imply discrete phenomena that are capable of being investigated apart from other aspects of our existence to which they are intrinsically related, but also the use of the definite article suggests that the body and the body image are themselves neutral phenomena, unaffected by the gender, race, age, and changing abilities of the body. Put simply, there is no such thing as "the" body or even "the" body image. Instead, whenever we are referring to an individual's body, that body is always responded to in a particularized fashion, that is, as a woman's body, a Latina's body, a mother's body, a daughter's body, a friend's body, an attractive body, an aging body, a Jewish body. Moreover, these images of the body are not discrete but form a series of overlapping identities whereby one or more aspects of that body appear to be especially salient at any given point in time. Thus, rather than view the body image as a cohesive, coherent phenomenon that operates in a fairly uniform way in our everyday existence, a presumption that underlies many traditional accounts of the body image, I argue in the pages that follow for a multiplicity of body images, body images that are copresent in any given individual, and which are themselves constructed through a series of corporeal exchanges that take place both within and outside of specific bodies.

Some researchers, including philosopher Shaun Gallagher, argue for a distinction between explicit, conscious thought an individual may have about her/his body and a prereflective awareness of how one's body occupies space.[1] On this account, the body image is a function of conscious reflection on my body and its possibilities. The corporeal schema, on the other hand, refers to the dynamic organization of my body which renders it capable of performing physical tasks, an organization which unfolds in the absence of conscious intervention. Although Merleau-Ponty does not argue for such a distinction and uses the words body image and corporeal schema fairly interchangeably, he does suggest that consciously focusing on one's body already presupposes a more primary, prereflective way of experiencing the body. More recently, Michel Foucault has placed into question the possibility of a nonmediated relation to one's body, arguing that we understand our bodies (and are shaped as subjects) through a series of disciplinary practices that socially categorize bodies and submit them to hierarchical differentiations. As far as our body images are concerned, this would seem to imply that they are themselves subject to social construction, indeed, that they cannot be understood as arising out of a private relationship between an individual and her/his own body, but are rather both disciplinary effects of existing power relationships as well as sources of bodily discipline. On the other hand, too strong an emphasis on the social construction of our body images runs the danger of disembodying them by presenting them as merely the discursive effects of historical power relationships. To take such a position is to lose sight of the physiological dimensions that also play such a crucial, continuous role in their construction.

While Merleau-Ponty could be said to do more justice to the kinesthetic aspects of bodily experience than Foucault, and while Foucault provides a much-needed critical analysis of how the prereflective domain is always the normative site of cultural expectations, both authors fail to acknowledge the definitive ways in which bodies are marked by assumptions made about their gender, their race, their ethnicity, their class, and their "natural" abilities. These assumptions, moreover, often tend to go unnoticed until they are violated by a body that refuses to behave as it should. As Judith Butler has noted, we are all familiar with the penalties that come from "doing" one's gender wrong, penalties that range from physical violence and emotional abuse to social ostracism and profound humiliation.[2]

A primary goal of this particular study, is to do equal justice to the physiological, social, and psychical dimensions of body images. More specifically, this analysis seeks to show both how complex and interdependent these aspects of our existence truly are and what a central role body images play in our everyday experience. Rather than approach this investigation through a singular methodology, I have drawn from a wide range of sources, theories, and experiences. First-person accounts, third-person accounts, narrative descriptions, case studies, and theoretical investigations have all occupied my attention at various times in this project. Although much of the research I have done has focused on scholarly sources, I have also profited greatly from nonacademic approaches to bodies and body images, such as those found in newspaper articles, fashion magazines, tabloid headlines, casual conversations with children as well as adults, numerous anecdotal exchanges between myself and other pregnant and lactating women, and writing geared to a more "popular" audience. On the theoretical side, which for better or worse is much more preponderant in this analysis, I refer frequently to the insights of those who are not "official" philosophers but who identify themselves as feminist theorists, psychoanalytic theorists, postcolonial theorists, literary theorists, queer theorists, and cultural theorists. Thus, rejecting the singularity of the concepts, "the body" and "the body image" has led to a corresponding rejection of a more traditional, disciplinary approach to my subject. Instead I have focused on the multiple points of intersection between various disciplines, methodologies, and approaches to bodies and body images, an approach I believe is essential to do justice to the richness and complexity of what I am calling intercorporeal existence. So, although this is a single-authored project for which I take full responsibility, it is a result of an interdisciplinary collaborative exchange that has taken place between and not just within the lines of the text.

Another important goal of this study is to promote continued philosophical discussion of the relationship between bodies and body images, a relationship which has crucial corporeal, social, ethical, and political implications. In chapters one and two, I offer a critical analysis of what I take to be the best accounts available of the body and body image. While chapter one focuses more on Schilder's and Merleau-Ponty's work, chapter two examines feminist critiques of embodied existence as it has been described by Merleau-Ponty and others.

Both Merleau-Ponty and Schilder stress the fact that a body image is neither an individual construction, nor the result of a series of conscious choices, but rather, an active agency that has its own memory, habits, and horizons of significance. Both stress as well the intercorporeal aspect of the body image, that is, the fact that the body image is itself an expression of an ongoing exchange between bodies and body images. Although I believe both theorists offer extremely rich and provocative accounts of both bodies and body images, a serious difficulty in both their analyses is the absence of any discussion of how racial, sexual, age, ethnic, class, moral, and technological differences are marked on our bodies and registered through our body images.

Although I find the work of the feminist and race theorists discussed in chapter two to be crucial correctives to a masculinist bias that appears in earlier accounts of the body and body image, I am also wary of the ways in which feminist as well as nonfeminist accounts of the body image often fail to challenge a longstanding association of the mind with transcendence and the body with immanence.[3] Specifically, I argue that the understandable desire not to be viewed merely as a body or a sexual object, a desire that is discussed so powerfully by so many feminist authors, has often led to a further denigration of the body, rather than a recognition of the limitations of the transcendence/immanence distinction. To avoid the deleterious effects of this identification, for women as well as for bodies themselves, I advocate a nondualistic understanding of corporeal agency which seeks to revalue women's as well as men's bodily capacities and possibilities.

Chapters three and four take up specific influences on the body image that have not received sufficient attention to date. Chapter three focuses on the constitutive roles played by imagination and fantasy in the construction of both individual and cultural body images. In particular, I examine the implications of what Judith Butler has called the morphological imaginary, an imaginary domain that plays a central role in structuring the psyche and which is distinguished by its corporeal dimensions. This leads to a discussion of the ways in which individual fantasies are often the expression of cultural fantasies and myths. These latter in turn regularly take the form of gender, race, and age specific, body image ideals.

In chapter four, I focus on common social practices which demand that we exclude certain aspects of corporeal existence from our body images (e.g. such as the rejection of particular bodily fluids and bodily functions as "disgusting"), and argue that these processes of abjection lead to distortions in our body images that differ only in extreme rather than degree from the distortions produced by a gender-associated disease such as anorexia. A major challenge in addressing the body image distortions that are so markedly exhibited in anorexics, is to provide an account of what these distortions are a distortion from. That is, the very notion of distortion seems to presuppose a kind of norm against which the distortion can be measured, but this is itself a notion I challenge in this chapter. Thus, a central task in chapter four becomes how to account for the serious and life-threatening effects of the distortions in the body images of anorexics without privileging certain bodies and body images over others. A more general goal is to demonstrate that our body images are constructed not only out of the identifications we establish with our own bodies and with others' bodies, but through an ongoing series of disidentifications as well.

Chapters five and six critically examine the interrelationship between bodies and the technologies which are addressed to/made for them. I focus not only on our growing dependence on technologies to inform us about our bodies and to alter our bodily capabilities (e.g. contemporary reproductive technologies), but just as crucially on how the interdependent relationship between bodies and technologies retemporalizes (chapter five) and respatializes (chapter six) our embodied existence. In chapter five, I argue against the demonization of contemporary reproductive technologies as "monstrous," and find that such a view tends to reify women's "natural" reproductive functions in problematic ways. Chapter six focuses on Merleau-Ponty's notion of *écart* as a space of noncoincidence or disincorporation that paradoxically makes the incorporation of technologies into our bodies and body images possible.

The last chapter of this book offers a prolegomena to an embodied ethics. The embodied ethics discussed in chapter seven is grounded in what I call bodily imperatives. Bodily imperatives can be understood as ethical demands that bodies place on other bodies in the course of our daily existence. To develop this account, I draw from the compelling example provided by Simone de Beauvoir's autobiographical narrative of her mother's sudden illness and subsequent death, an account that is deceptively entitled, *A Very Easy Death*. Unlike a Kantian categorical imperative that requires that I dismiss my bodily impulses and inclinations as irrelevant to my ethical projects by attending to reason alone (reason, for Kant as well as his numerous rationalist predecessors being always disembodied), the notion of a bodily imperative insists that we attribute moral significance not merely to intellectual, but also to concomitant physical and emotional responses that arise out of our complex, concrete relationships with other bodies. Although contemporary feminist ethicists have successfully made visible the different, equally legitimate ways in which moral reasoning can be conducted (e.g. an ethic of care as a viable and meaningful alternative to an ethic of justice), I find that the body's role in calling us to respond ethically to one another has continued to be egregiously neglected.

One of the ironies of the embodied ethics Beauvoir provides in *A Very Easy Death*, is that it appears not to be an intentional outcome of her description of her mother's last days, but arises nonetheless in a very nonambiguous way out of Beauvoir's account of the vicissitudes of love and irritation, admiration and disgust, respect and horror, that characterize Beauvoir's daily responses to her mother and, more particularly, her mother's cancerous body. Strikingly, the implicit ethics offered in this text, and its implications which I develop in the course of this chapter, runs counter not only to the explicitly philosophical "ethics of ambiguity" provided by Beauvoir over fifteen years earlier, but also to the characterizations of freedom, responsibility, and being-in-the-world provided by her philosophical peers, Sartre and Heidegger. The embodied ethics proposed in this final chapter argues, above all, that we need to make our bodies just as central to our moral theorizing as they are in our moral practices.

To describe embodiment as intercorporeality is to emphasize that the experience of being embodied is never a private affair, but is always already mediated by our continual interactions with other human and nonhuman bodies. Acknowledging and addressing the multiple corporeal exchanges that continually take place in our everyday lives, demands a corresponding recognition of the ongoing construction and reconstruction of our bodies and body images. These processes of construction and reconstruction in turn alter the very nature of these intercorporeal exchanges, and, in so doing, offer the possibility of expanding our social, political, and ethical horizons.

{1}

Body Image Intercourse

A Corporeal Dialogue between
Merleau-Ponty and Schilder

I cannot understand the function of the living body except by
enacting it myself, and except in so far as I am a body which rises
toward the world.

— Maurice Merleau-Ponty (1962:75)

There is no question that there are from the beginning connecting
links between all body-images, and it is important to follow the
lines of body-image intercourse.

— Paul Schilder (1950:235)

It is arguable that their respective discussions of the body image are
two of the most important contributions Merleau-Ponty and Schilder have
made to phenomenology and psychoanalysis, respectively. Schilder's monu-
mental work, *The Image and Appearance of the Human Body*, is the first full-
length study of the body image as a physiological, libidinous, and socially structured phenomenon.[1] While Merleau-Ponty does not devote an entire text to
the body image, his interest in and discussions of this "corporeal schema"
extend over two decades from his earliest book, *The Structure of Behavior*, to his
final and unfinished work, *The Visible and the Invisible*.[2] Although both
Schilder and Merleau-Ponty develop their own understandings of the body
image by drawing upon the research findings of neurologists such as Head,
Gelb, Goldstein and others who worked with patients suffering from lesions in
the cerebral cortex, what is distinctive about Merleau-Ponty's and Schilder's
accounts is that they extend our understanding of the centrality of the body
image in all aspects of experience for "normal" as well as physiologically
impaired subjects.

It was Sir Henry Head who first introduced the expression "the postural
model of the body" to refer to the body image. This term emphasizes what
many view to be the body image's primary function, namely, to offer what Merleau-Ponty calls "a global, practical, and implicit notion of the relation between

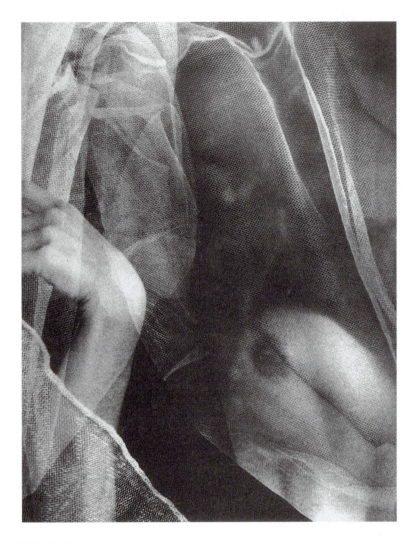

Paisaje de ensueño, Muriel Hasbun (gelatin silver print, 1987)

our body and things, of our hold on them"[3] (Merleau-Ponty 1962:75). As a postural model, the body image informs us from moment to moment and in a largely unthematized way, how our body is positioned in space relative to the people, objects, and environment around us. What this requires is not only a frequent reorientation of one's own mobile body in reference to other, often mobile, bodies (both animate and inanimate), but also the coordination of the body's limbs, organs, muscles, neural pathways, etc. to permit their integrated functioning and the maintenance of an upright posture. Head is also the first to stress the schematic nature of this postural model. Two of the most salient characteristics of the postural schema identified by Head are first, its plasticity, that is, the constant changes the body image undergoes in response to changes in the body and/or the situation. Second, the dynamic organization of the postural model offers a certain equilibrium throughout these changes that enables it to serve as a "standard, against which all subsequent changes of posture are measured" (quoted by Tiermersma 1989:109). In calling attention to the simultaneous adaptability and stability provided by the postural model, Head set the stage for a more comprehensive understanding of the body image and the role it plays in perceptual experience, an understanding which quickly outstripped Head's own view of the postural model as a neural mechanism functioning independently of psychical processes.

Most notably, as both Merleau-Ponty and Schilder stress in their own work, it must be recognized that the body image changes not only in response to actual, physiological changes in the body and/or physical changes in the situation, but is greatly (and often lastingly) affected by psychical and social changes in the body/situation that need not be grounded in or tied to a current state of affairs. As Merleau-Ponty notes, "the normal person *reckons with* the possible, which thus, without shifting from its position as a possibility, acquires a sort of actuality" (Merleau-Ponty 1962:109). While Merleau-Ponty is primarily thinking here about future actions and how they can be corporeally anticipated in and through the body image, Schilder emphasizes the role that fantasies and the imagination play in constructing and reconstructing the body image:

> It is one of the inherent characteristics of our psychic life that we continually change our images; we multiply them and make them appear different. This general rule is true also for the postural model of the body. We let it shrink playfully and come to the idea of Lilliputians, or we transform it into giants.
> (Schilder 1950:67)

Indeed, Schilder goes on to claim that each individual has "an almost unlimited number of body-images," a startling and provocative claim whose implications have been largely undeveloped and one which could be especially useful in feminist theorizing about the body.

Despite many feminists' concerns with the limitations of phenomenology and psychoanalysis in general for an adequate characterization of female corporeality, and despite the fact that both Merleau-Ponty's and Schilder's understandings of the body have been justifiably critiqued for the "invisible" ways in which a masculine body provides the norm for their accounts of embodiment, I am convinced that there is much that is productive in both Merleau-Ponty's and Schilder's accounts of the body image, and it is the productive aspects of their thought, rather than a comprehensive analysis or critique of their positions, that I would like to focus on in this chapter.[4] Specifically, in the sections that follow I will examine Merleau-Ponty's and Schilder's respective understandings of the body image as: a developmental "Gestalt"; developing from a fragmented set of experiences to a more or less coherent phenomenon through the mirror stage; already emerging narcissistically prior to the mirror stage; consistently seeking to establish an always temporary equilibrium; generating its own body image ideal; and, lastly, as revealing its own constitutive otherness or alterity from one moment to the next.

By developing the lacunae and critically extending the implications of these aspects of Merleau-Ponty's and Schilder's accounts of the body image, a richer feminist understanding of how racial, gender, class, age, and cultural differences are *corporeally* registered and reproduced can be achieved. Without an adequate understanding of the crucial role that the body image plays in reflecting and sustaining individual, social, and political inequalities, there is a danger that positive social and political changes will not address the individual's own corporeal existence in the intimate manner necessary to move successfully towards the eradication of sexism, racism, classism, ageism, and ethnocentrism. Although this book does not propose a direct course for such changes, I do believe that the plasticity and stability of the body image can serve to maintain an oppressive "status quo" and that a greater awareness of the "body power" we have at our disposal through this very plasticity and stability can result in new, perhaps subversive, body images that can be used to fight oppression on a corporeal front.

The Body Image as a Gestalt

According to Merleau-Ponty, the body image exhibits an intersensory, spatial, and temporal unity that is not "the straightforward result of associations established during experience, but a total awareness of my posture in the intersensory world, a 'form' in the sense used by Gestalt psychology" (Merleau-Ponty 1962:99–100). This unity is not founded upon an inner or internal unity of the body's organs, muscles, bones, nervous system, and skeletal structure (although these latter are indeed incorporated within the body image) rather, it derives from the world within which the body is always situated and in reference to which the body continually orients and reorients itself: "the body not only flows over into *a world whose schema it bears in itself* but possesses this world at a distance rather than being possessed by it" (Merleau-Ponty 1973:78, my emphasis).

To say that the body bears the schema of the world in itself is to indicate that the body does not impose any sort of pregiven structure upon the world, but is itself structured by its world, which in turn implies that the body image reflects from the start the particularities *and* generalities of a given situation, not merely the idiosyncracies of its own physiological or genetic makeup and psychical constitution. Nonetheless, Merleau-Ponty is careful to avoid any characterization of the world as a "body-constituting" force, since it is the body which "possesses this world at a distance rather than being possessed by it."[5]

The primary means by which the body "possesses" the world are through perception and the bodily motility which makes our perceptual "grasp" on the situation possible, and it is through perception and bodily motility that the body itself "flows over into a world." This reciprocal, reversible relationship between body and world whereby the body "flows over" into a world whose "schema it bears in itself," gives rise to an increasingly complex understanding of the gestalt and the role(s) it plays in perception. For, according to Merleau-Ponty, not only is the body image itself a gestalt but what we perceive are also gestalten, that is, forms, which produce "a certain state of equilibrium, solving a problem of maximal coherence and, in the Kantian sense, making a world possible." Unlike Kant's understanding of form as an a priori, Merleau-Ponty's form:

> is the very appearance of the world and not the condition of its possibility; it is
> the birth of a norm and is not realized according to a norm; *it is the identity of
> the external and the internal and not the projection of the internal in the external.*
> (Merleau-Ponty 1962:60–61, my emphasis)

The schematic organization of both the body image and perceived objects does not predate the phenomena themselves but their schematic organization does not come about on an ad-hoc basis either. Rather, the body image and the perception of discrete objects are progressively developed and refined, with the body image first appearing during the "mirror stage" (from 6–18 months of age) as a corporeal schema which requires, but cannot be reduced to, the infant's awareness of her/his specular image as an image of her/his own body. The developmental nature of perception is in turn clearly implied in the latter's dependency on the efficacy of the body image, since, as Wallon recognized:

> [Perception] presupposes a minimal bodily equilibrium. The operation of a pos-
> tural schema — that is, a global consciousness of my body's position in space,
> with the corrective reflexes that impose themselves at each moment, the global
> consciousness of the spatiality of my body — all this is necessary for perception.
> (quoted in Merleau-Ponty 1964:122)

Regarding the development of the body image, Merleau-Ponty stresses that "the consciousness of one's own body is thus fragmentary [lacunaire] at first and gradually becomes integrated; the corporeal schema becomes precise, restructured, and mature little by little" (Merleau-Ponty, 1964:123). The visual image of the body presented to the child in the mirror cannot, Merleau-Ponty asserts, be equated with the child's own experience of her/his body, and yet, the perception of the specular image as a *discrete, unified* image of the child's body is precisely what facilitates the necessary restructuring and maturation of the child's bodily awareness into a unified postural schema.[6] To understand properly the significance of the mirror stage for the development of the body image (and consequently, as we have seen above, for perceptual development), we must turn to Merleau-Ponty's own account of the mirror stage, an account that displaces (rather than disavows) Lacan's emphasis upon the mirror stage as leading "to the assumption of the armour of an alienating identity, which will mark with its rigid structure the subject's entire mental development" (Lacan 1977:4).

The Mirror Stage

Lacan characterizes the development of the child in the mirror stage as a complex transition from a nonunified body image to the construction of the body image as an orthopaedic totality:

> The *mirror stage* is a drama whose internal thrust is precipitated from insufficiency to anticipation—and which manufactures for the subject, caught up in the lure of spatial identification, the succession of phantasies that extends from a fragmented body-image to a form of its totality that I shall call orthopaedic. . . . (Lacan 1977:4)

Merleau-Ponty, like Lacan, recognizes that there is a process of self-alienation that paradoxically accompanies the move from a fragmented body image to the body image as a *gestalt*. What is paradoxical is that the necessarily alienating acceptance of the specular image as an image of *oneself*, somehow facilitates rather than disrupts the development of a coherent body image out of two, seemingly disparate experiences: seeing one's body "from the outside" in the mirror, and being introceptively aware of one's body "from the inside." For Merleau-Ponty, there are two spatial problems that must be resolved in order for the child to work through this paradox:

> it is a problem first of understanding that the visual image of his body which he sees over there in the mirror is not himself; and second, he must understand that, not being located there, in the mirror, but rather where he feels himself introceptively, he can nonetheless be seen by an external witness *at the very place at which he feels himself to be* and with the same visual appearance that he has from the mirror. In short, he must displace the mirror image, bringing it from the apparent or virtual place it occupies in the depth of the mirror back to himself, whom he identifies at a distance with his introceptive body. (Merleau-Ponty 1964:129)

The first problem is rendered even more complicated for the child because the initial failure to recognize the specular image as an image of oneself must eventually give way to a recognition of the specular image as being *of* oneself, yet not identical *to* oneself.[7] It is precisely this schism between the "of oneself" and "to oneself" that is internalized in the resolution of the second problem and which henceforth becomes an integral (alienating) aspect of the body image. Although this schism is not overcome and remains a source of alienation throughout an individual's life (insofar as the specular image will never be equivalent to one's own, more fluid body image), both Lacan and Merleau-Ponty emphasize that it is this very schism that makes it possible for the child to project and extend her/his own bodily awareness beyond the immediacy of her/his introceptive experiences by incorporating the perspective of the other toward one's own body—a perspective one actively participates in—rather than having it thrust upon one from the outside. Thus, for Merleau-Ponty:

> The specular image, given visually, participates globally in the existence of the body itself and leads a "phantom" life in the mirror, which "participates" in the life of the child himself. What is true of his own body, for the child, is also true of the other's body. The child himself feels that he is in the other's body, just as he feels himself to be in his visual image. (Merleau-Ponty 1964:133–134)

While Lacan invokes the "paranoic alienation, which dates from the deflection of the specular I into the social I" (Lacan 1977:5), I would argue that Merleau-Ponty acknowledges the alienating character of the specular image without viewing it as a source of paranoia since the specular I is not "deflected" into the social I but the two are one in the same. That is, the specular image offers the child a new perspective not only on her/his own body and her/his being-for-others (what we may call an "outside-in" perspective) but *simultaneously* allows the child to project her/himself outside of her/his body *into* the specular image and, correspondingly, into the bodies of others (an "inside-out" perspective).[8] Although the former may indeed be a source of profound alienation, it is the latter, especially, that provides the ground for strong *identifications with others*, identifications that expand the parameters of the body image and accomplish its transition from an introceptive, fragmented experience of the body to a social gestalt.[9] In emphasizing the child's new understanding of visibility and spatiality, Merleau-Ponty displaces Lacan's emphasis on the temporal conflation of a future, complete "I" with the present incomplete sense of self, a fundamental méconnaissance that is, for the latter, the source of the deception that provides the necessary basis for the constitution of the "I." What Merleau-Ponty offers instead is the development of an intracorporeal spatiality accomplished through the mirror stage that provides a more positive and productive account of the formation of the body image (and of the I) as an intersubjective phenomenon that need not be grounded in deception.

These identifications, however, do not offer an alternative to alienation since they are themselves made possible only on the basis of the self-alienation produced by the specular image. According to Merleau-Ponty:

> This forces me to leave the reality of my lived *me* in order to refer myself constantly to the ideal, fictitious, or imaginary *me*, of which the specular image is the first outline. In this sense I am torn from myself, and the image in the mirror prepares me for another still more serious alienation, which will be the alienation by others. For others have only an exterior image of me, which is analogous to the one seen in the mirror. Consequently others will tear me away from my own immediate inwardness much more surely than will the mirror. (Merleau-Ponty 1964a:136)

Strikingly, the self-alienation that arises out of the "schism" between the specular and the introceptive body images, not only serves as a prelude to the "more serious alienation" Merleau-Ponty describes above (and which we will discuss later on), but also makes possible "the acquisition of a new function as well: the narcissistic function." (Merleau-Ponty 1964: 136) While Merleau-Ponty does not provide an account of the significance of this narcissistic function in the development of the body image, it is Schilder who both asks and ultimately answers the crucial question: "What is the relation of narcissism to the image of the body?" (Schilder 1950:196)

The Narcissistic Structure of the Body Image

Schilder, like Lacan and Merleau-Ponty, stresses the developmental nature of the body image and a virtue of his account is his particular concern with the impact of individual experiences and the psychical response to those experiences on the body image as well as his refusal to view the psychical and physiological influences on the body image as independent of one another:

> Concerning the image of the body, we have to suppose that there is a factor of maturation which is responsible for the primary outlines of the postural model of the body. But the way in which these outlines develop, the tempo of development, will be largely dependent on experience and activity; and we may suppose that the finer trends of the body-image will be still more dependent on the life experiences, the training, and the emotional attitudes. There is no reason why one should join either of the extremist groups, for one of which experience, learning, and conditioning are in the foreground (Watson), while for the other experience means little or nothing (Köhler, Koffka, Wertheimer and Wheeler). ... There will be functions which are merely determined by anatomy and physiology. But even in those the psychic influence and the influence of experience will, according to our latest observations, play some part. In other experiences, especially in those concerning the libidinous structure of the postural model, experience will play an outstanding part, but even so experience will be connected with anatomy and physiology. (Schilder 1950:196–197)

Although Schilder bases his account of the libidinous structure of the body image on the experience of primary narcissism whose significance was discussed at length by Freud, he is critical of Freud's understanding of primary narcissism as centered on the body of the newborn. Since, Schilder claims, the newborn is unable to differentiate her or his body from the rest of the world (i.e., since s/he does not experience the body as a discrete entity), it is:

> senseless to say that for the newborn child only the body exists and the world does not. Body and world are experiences which are correlated with each other. One is not possible without the other. When Freud states that on a narcissistic level only the body is present, he must be mistaken. The newborn child has a world, and probably even the embryo has. It is true that on such a primitive level the borderline between world and body will not be sharply defined, and it will be easier to see a part of the body in the world and a part of the world in the body. (Schilder 1950:122–123)

In his essay, "On Narcissism: An Introduction," however, Freud does acknowledge that there are, from the start, not one, but two sexual objects that form the basis for primary narcissism, namely the infant and "the woman who nurses him" (Freud 1957:88). Ultimately, for Freud, the woman who breast-feeds the child plays a very active role in the process by which the infant becomes erotogenically invested in her/his own body, since she is the one who first stimulates the newborn's mouth through the nourishment provided by her breasts, a stimulation that results in a more generalized sexual pleasure that comes from the very act of sucking.

During this oral stage of development then, the narcissistic libido is clearly concentrated in the infant's mouth, and as the child moves on to the anal and phallic stages of development, the intensity of libidinal investment in the mouth will shift first to the anus, then to the clitoris or penis. For Schilder, the object of the narcissistic libido is not the mouth, anus, penis, or clitoris per se, but the *image* of the body that arises out of the sexually pleasurable sensations associated with them. Thus, as the child passes through the various stages of psychogenic development, "the narcissistic libido will be attached to the different parts of the image of the body, and in the different stages of libidinous development the model of the body will change continually" (Schilder 1950:123).

To say that the narcissistic libido has as its object the image of the body rather than the body itself, does not imply for Schilder that this image is at all distinct nor, as we have seen above, does it imply that this image is focused upon the body independently of the world. To talk about an "experience," as far as Schilder (and Merleau-Ponty) are concerned, already implies an intimate exchange between body and world that results in a lack of boundaries between the two. This is true not only of the pre-mirror stage infant, but also, Schilder notes, of adults as well for whom "body and world are continually interchanged. It may be that a great part of experiences will not be finally attributed either to body or world" (Schilder 1950:123).

Pimary narcissism, then, for both Freud and Schilder, never involves an infant's unmediated relationship with her or his own body, but from the start implies a complex series of interactions between the infant and others in an ongoing situation, and the image the infant forms of her/his body through primary narcissistic investments in different bodily zones or regions will already reflect the influences of others and the situation long before the child can recognize her/himself or others as discrete entities (i.e. long before the child enters the mirror stage).[10] As Schilder affirms, "the touches of others, the interest others take in the different parts of our body, will be of an enormous importance in the development of the postural model of the body" (Schilder 1950:126).

Although Schilder is claiming that the body image is the "object" of the narcissistic libido long before the mirror stage, this does not mean that he disagrees with Lacan's and Merleau-Ponty's view of the body image as "fragmented" prior to the mirror stage. Both Schilder and Merleau-Ponty are in agreement that the body image cannot manifest the quality of stability that Head identified so early on, if it does not exhibit an equilibrium; this equilibrium cannot be achieved, however, if too much libidinal energy is concentrated on a single region or zone of the body, for, as Schilder observes: "whenever one part obtains an overwhelming importance in the image of the body, the inner symmetry and the inner equilibrium of the body-image will be destroyed" (Schilder 1950:126).[11]

It is through primary narcissism, then, that the newborn first begins the construction of her/his body image, a process which is never completed, but which continually evolves throughout an individual's life. While Schilder accepts Freud's characterization of the stages of libidinous development, he also emphasizes (as does Freud) that no two individuals proceed through these stages in the same way. And, although Schilder does claim that "in the whole structure of the schema of the body, the erogenic zones will play the leading part" (Schilder 1950:123), the physiological development of the body also contributes greatly to the "building-up" of the body image, not through an internal, biological process but through "continual contact with the outside world" (Schilder 1950:137). Finally, Schilder wants us to realize that the body image of one individual cannot be understood as radically distinct from the body image of other individuals since:

> The child takes parts of the bodies of others into its own body-image. It also adopts in its own personality the attitude taken by others towards parts of their own bodies. Postural models of the body are closely connected with each other. . . . Body-images of human beings communicate with each other either in parts or as wholes. (Schilder 1950:137–138)

Equilibrium as Temporary Stability

Both Schilder and Merleau-Ponty are united in the belief that the body image tends toward a certain equilibrium, but never achieves this equilibrium once and for all. The body image, on both their accounts, must be understood as a dynamic gestalt that is continually being constructed, destructed, and reconstructed in response to changes within one's own body, other people's bodies, and/or the situation as a whole.[12] For the adult, as well as for the child:

> The postural model of the body is stable only for a short time and changes immediately afterwards. Stability of pictures in psychic life probably only connotes a passing phase to which the next phase can be contrasted. But there is no question that in our psychic life there are always tendencies to form units, gestalten, or, to use a comparison from physics, quantums. But whenever a gestalt is created the gestalt tends immediately to change and to destruction. (Schilder 1950:191)

Despite Schilder's suspicion of the "death instinct" in Freud, he does believe that processes of construction are inevitably followed by processes of destruction which he likens to this very death instinct. However, Schilder is also quick to point out that while "it is true that we disrupt the body-image as soon as we have created it . . . the construction processes are always the *basso continuo* even when the disruption of the body-image takes place." Moreover, Schilder characterizes destruction itself as "a partial phase of construction, which is a planning and the general characteristic of life. We destroy in order to plan anew" (Schilder 1950:193). Thus, to the extent that the tendency toward destruction is an exemplification of something like the Freudian thanatos, this drive is not opposed to or even distinct from eros, but is a necessary component of and motivation for its constructive energy.

What motivates the construction/destruction/reconstruction of the body image from one moment to the next, for both Schilder and Merleau-Ponty, are the continual changes that are going on both within the body and within the situation as a whole. That is, the body image has to accommodate a variety of both subtle and dramatic changes in the body/situation (hence, its plasticity), without losing its stability. Maintaining the stability of the body image is a necessary condition for a sense of bodily stability, for, as we have noted, the stability of the body image is precisely what provides us with a reliable sense of where and how our body is spatially positioned as well as a tacit understanding of what our corporeal possibilities are at any given point in time. Merleau-Ponty expresses this feature of the body image by referring to the latter as a "system of equivalents," and an "immediately given invariant" (Merleau-Ponty 1962:141). Although it may function as an invariant due to its omnipresence in our daily life, the body image nonetheless defies rigidity through the continual substitutions it enables such as when legs or sticks function as "arms," a prosthesis serves as a "leg," etc.[13]

Thus, to be "dependable," the body image must be flexible enough to incorporate changes occurring both within and outside of the body, while continuing to seek a certain "equilibrium" which will provide the stability needed not only for effective bodily movement, but also for a relatively unified perceptual experience. For, if the body itself is not experienced as a unity, then it is impossible for the perceptual process itself to provide this unity, given the latter's dependence on the integrated, kinesthetic functioning of the mobile body. "Perception," Merleau-Ponty observes, "presupposes a minimal bodily equilibrium. . . . In fact the effort at equilibrium continually accompanies all our perceptions except when we are lying on our back"[14] (Merleau-Ponty 1964:122). To confirm the crucial role that bodily equilibrium plays in perception as well as the way we experience bodily equilibrium through habitual postures, Schilder cites the results of experiments done by Skramlik who "shows that every habitual posture is so deeply engraved in our mind that postures which are actually different are experienced as similar to this habitual posture" (Schilder 1950:82). These habitual or "primary" postures, for Schilder, not only tend to be those which are physiologically most "comfortable" and maximally effective in achieving perceptual goals, such as an upright posture with the head facing forward in alignment with the rest of the body (a position which often, but not always, ensures the greatest degree of visibility and enhances auditory discrimination), but they also provide a certain degree of psychological (and certainly social) stability insofar as the body tends to be more "relaxed" in a familiar position. Regarding our immediate recognition of these primary postures in both ourselves and others, Schilder asserts:

> We always return to the primary positions of the body. When we think about a person running, we see him changing from one primary position into another primary position. Primary positions are positions of relative rest. The positions in between the two primary positions are neglected and even the movement is neglected as such . . . we may say that we are less interested in what is going on in the field, we are not interested in the continual flow, but more or less in the quantums, the crystallized units of the postural model. We should, however, realize that our own body-image and the body-image of others is not only a body-image at rest but a body-image in movement. (Schilder 1950:270)

Schilder identifies this tendency to return to certain primary postures with a desire to "complete" the body image by rigidifying it, but he also notes that:

> there is a tendency towards the dissolution of the body-image. When we close our eyes and remain as motionless as possible, the body-image tends towards dissolution. The body-image is the result of an effort and cannot be completely maintained when the effort ceases. The body-image is, to put it in a paradoxical

way, never a complete structure; it is never static: there are always disrupting tendencies. With the changing physiological situations of life new structuralizations have to take place, and the life situations are always changing. (Schilder 1950:287)

In a sense, then, it is precisely when the body image becomes too inflexible, that it moves towards its own dissolution. Since the situation is continually changing, socially, emotionally, libidinously, and physiologically, the body image *must* make corresponding changes to maintain its equilibrium. Although Schilder and Merleau-Ponty argue that the body image is always changing in accordance with our own bodily movements and in response to the changing demands of the given situation, Schilder also emphasizes the constructive continuity that is maintained throughout these changes insofar as, in moving from one postural schema to another, "the previous scheme of the postural model remains in the background and upon this previous scheme the new scheme is built up" (Schilder 1950:206–207).

Merleau-Ponty introduces the notion of the "habit body" to refer to these habitual postures which we immediately "fall into" when driving a car, sitting at a typewriter or computer keyboard, walking, etc. and he claims that, "it is an inner necessity for the most integrated existence to provide itself with an habitual body" (Merleau-Ponty 1962:87). That the development of the habit body plays an indispensable, stabilizing role in the perceptual process can be seen in Merleau-Ponty's view of "perceptual habit as the coming into possession of a world" (Merleau-Ponty 1962:153). Nonetheless, a danger that accompanies our continual efforts to achieve bodily equilibrium through a stable body image, can result, as Schilder observes, in human beings' being "bound and tied down by their body-images." Some of the ways in which we resist this rigidification of the body image, Schilder asserts, are through "playing" with the body and the body image, by transforming these latter through clothes, decoration, jewelry, or even self-mutilation[15] (Schilder 1950:206). What Schilder is describing, in effect, is an ambivalent relationship which we have with our own bodies and our body images, whereby we simultaneously seek to construct and destruct stable postural schemas. Hence our fascination with the gymnast who:

> pushes to extremes this play with his own body, and the pleasure we get out of watching his performance is based upon our wish to break through the borderlines of our own body. It is mixed with awe and disgust. We desire the integrity and totality of our own body; we are afraid of every change which may take away a part of this body. . . but we are still continually experimenting with it. (Schilder 1950:206)

In a 1994 interview, Judith Butler also claims that "this desire for a kind of radical theatrical remaking of the body, is obviously out there in the public sphere" (Butler 1994:32). While Schilder, in the example above, focuses on the contortionist's exciting/disturbing expansion of the body's physiological capacities and the vicarious pleasure we may gain from observing such metamorphoses in others (without taking the risks of injury and pain involved in enacting them ourselves), Butler is a bit more suspicious of this desire "for a fully phantasmatic transfiguration of the body" since she views it to be connected with voluntarist conceptions of the body that deny the body's own materiality, a materiality which is never neutral but which is always being constituted and experienced in culturally coded ways (i.e. as gendered, race- and class-identified, etc.). Moreover, Schilder's astute observation that we may prefer the specular satisfaction of seeing others perform such morphological transformations to engaging in them ourselves, focuses exclusively on an individual's own ambivalence toward disturbing her/his bodily integrity rather than the very real *social* risks one takes when one's body transgresses society's normative expectations for one's gender, race, class, age, ethnicity, and profession, to name but a few.

Regarding the consequences of failing to display the "properly" gendered body, Butler notes:

> There are punishments for not doing gender right: a man in Maine walks down the street in a dress, walking the way women are supposed to walk; next day his body is found dead in a ravine. And though we may not have experienced his punishment directly (although much of childrearing is involved in inculcating the rules of gender through the fear of punishment), we nevertheless know something of the terror and shame of being told that we are somehow doing our gender wrong, that we have failed in some way to measure up to the cultural norm and expectation. (Butler 1989:256)

Gender, as Butler powerfully argues, cannot be simply dismissed by separating the body from its gender as if the latter were a Lockean secondary (perceived) quality independent of the actual materiality of the body, rather, gender is itself "a corporeal style, a way of acting the body, a way of wearing one's own flesh as a cultural sign" (Butler 1989:256).

Unfortunately (and this is indeed a serious omission in both accounts), neither Merleau-Ponty nor Schilder even acknowledges, much less develops, the ways in which race, gender, sexuality, age, class, and ethnicity factor into the construction of the habit body (or primary postures). Nor do they offer accounts of how the habit body and our primary postures function as normative standards, standards which are altered through our utilization of the plasticity of the body and the body image to transform them both.[16] Indeed, it is the presence of a distinct set of social and cultural norms that both articulates and gives significance to these primary postures, for, as Elizabeth Grosz notes: "there is no "natural" norm; there are only cultural forms of body, which do or do not conform to social norms" (Grosz 1994:143). Grosz does not view conformity to social norms as itself a problem or something to be avoided, however, rather she argues that the problem revolves around "which particular ones are used and with what effects" (Grosz 1994:143).[17] Although the implications and consequences of choosing some norms over others will be taken up in the chapters that follow, I would like to turn now to a related issue that both Merleau-Ponty and Schilder do touch upon, namely the construction of what we might call a "body image ideal" in order to see how it too functions normatively as an internalized standard against which we continually measure our present body images.

The Ego-Ideal and Its Counterpart: The Body Image Ideal

> The development of the ego consists in a departure from primary narcissism and gives rise to a vigorous attempt to recover that state. This departure is brought about by means of the displacement of libido on to *an ego-ideal imposed from without*; and satisfaction is brought about from fulfilling this ideal. (Freud 1957:100, my emphasis)

A discussion of the construction of an ideal body image and the ongoing role it plays in our experience cannot take place without a corresponding discussion of Freud's conception of an ego-ideal since the two, as we shall see, are ultimately inseparable from (but not reducible to) one another. The "self-love" of primary narcissism (a love which, Schilder has argued, is never unmediated but involves from the outset a body interacting with other bodies within a world), is both reinforced and disturbed by the child's recognition of her/his specular image during the mirror stage. It is reinforced because the unique disclosure of one's corporeality provided by the specular image offers a new source of erotic intensity, namely, through libidinal investment in the image of oneself that reveals one's being-for-others. At the same time, however, the specular image, precisely by disclosing one's being-for-others, introduces the self-alienating dimension we discussed earlier, a dimension that marks the point of departure from primary narcissism, an irrecoverable loss that in turn motivates the formation of the ego-ideal. Merleau-Ponty directly acknowledges the crucial role the specular image plays in the construction of the ego-ideal in the following passage:

> The personality before the advent of the specular image is what psychoanalysts call, in the adult, the ego (soi), i.e., the collection of confusedly felt impulses. The mirror image itself makes possible a contemplation of self. With the specular image appears the possibility of an ideal image of oneself—in psychoanalytic terms, the possibility of a super-ego. *And this image would henceforth be either explicitly posited or simply implied by everything I see at each minute.* (Merleau-Ponty 1964:136, my emphasis)

One of the most salient features of the ego-ideal, as Freud has described it, is its status as a projection of a (lost) perfection, a "substitute for the lost narcissism of his childhood—the time when he was his own ideal" (Freud 1957:116). More precisely, the ego-ideal offers an image of completeness and self-sufficiency which substitutes not for the real thing (since the child never had this completeness and self-sufficiency to begin with) but for an illusion, the illusion that supports primary narcissism.[18] In Heideggerian language, we may say that the ego-ideal offers the (ever elusive) promise of Dasein's grasping itself in its totality, the promise of Dasein's "being-a-whole." For Heidegger, the ontic impossibility of realizing such a totalizing project is due to human temporality, that is, to the ontological structure of human existence. To attain our possibilities once and for all in a given actuality would be, in effect, to die, to no longer be Dasein. As Heidegger observes, "as long as Dasein *is* as an entity, it has never reached its 'wholeness.' But if it gains such 'wholeness', this gain becomes the utter loss of Being-in-the-world" (Heidegger 1962:280).

The perspectival nature of perception also ensures that the ego-ideal can never be presented or grasped as a genuine "object" of perception, for, as Merleau-Ponty notes:

> For there to be perception, that is, apprehension of an existence, it is absolutely necessary that the object not be completely given to the look which rests on it, that aspects intended but not possessed in the present perception be kept in reserve. A seeing which would take place from a certain point of view and which would give us, for example, all the sides of a cube at once is a pure contradiction in terms; for, in order to be visible all together, the sides of a wooden cube would have to be transparent, that is, would cease to be the sides of a wooden cube. (Merleau-Ponty 1967:212–213)

As an image of perfection, wholeness, completeness, the ego-ideal has characteristics that radically distinguish it from any and all perceptual objects. Our inability to understand the ego-ideal on perceptual terms, makes it also difficult, on Merleau-Ponty's account, to understand the level on which it functions in our everyday experience. Clearly, it would be inaccurate to depict the ego-ideal as a wholly unconscious phenomenon, since many of us, to a greater or lesser extent, are able to consciously articulate and even deliberately construct features of our own ego-ideal(s). And yet, the ego-ideal also resists being made into a facticity; its very nature as an "ideal" projection guarantees that in order for it to be efficacious as such, it *cannot* be realized at any given point in time.

To complicate matters further, Freud's understanding of the ego-ideal as developing not independently of the ego but in and through the (bodily) ego, suggests that it, too, should "be regarded as a mental projection of the surface of the body" a projection that "is ultimately derived from bodily sensations" (Freud 1961:26). The ego-ideal, then, must not be seen as disembodied, as a mere phantom, but must be recognized as having its own materiality, a materiality that is directly tied to our corporeal experience and which provides the very means for our libidinal investment in it. Indeed, it is possible to argue that one of the primary material effects of the ego-ideal is the construction of what I will call the body image ideal. As a corporeal enactment of the ego-ideal, all of the normative force of the ego-ideal is directed upon the individual's own body image through its body image ideal.[19]

To begin to understand the normative pressure the ego-ideal (and, correlatively, the body image ideal) continually exerts upon the individual, it is important to recognize that the ego-ideal is never a purely individual phenomenon, since "[i]n addition to its individual side, this ideal has a social side; it is also the common ideal of a family, a class, or a nation" (Freud 1957:101). Although Freud stresses a common basis for individual ego-ideals in this passage, it is also clear on his account that the initial formation of the ego-ideal will be due to one primary social influence in particular, and that the nature of this social influence will vary depending on whether the child is a boy or a girl. For the boy, the ego-ideal will be constructed through his identification with his father, an identification whose strengthening serves to mark his successful resolution of the Oedipal stage.[20] By identifying with the father the young boy in no way sees the father as an equal, rather, he projects onto his father the maturity, authority, and perfection he himself longs to attain (qualities which would enable him truly to be a rival for his mother's affections, a project he has disavowed on the basis of his recognition of himself as lacking).

The two "obstacles" the young girl has to overcome in order to move into the Oedipal stage (the switch in the erotogenic zone from the clitoris to the vagina and the switch from mother to father as love object), make it more difficult for her, on Freud's account, even to reach the Oedipal stage, much less to form the "appropriate" identification and pass into the latency period. And just what is the appropriate identification for the young girl as far as the ego-ideal is concerned? The answer to this question, interestingly enough, is not so clear. Although ultimately, Freud does maintain that the young girl should identify with her mother (as a lover of her father) in order to realize her (heterosexual) "feminine destiny," Freud also emphasizes the importance of the father figure for both the young boy and the young girl in the formation of the ego-ideal. Indeed, the ego-ideal is depicted by him as "a substitute for a longing for the father" (Freud 1961:37).

Despite Freud's claim that the young girl who successfully moves through the Oedipal stage has overcome her hostility for her mother (whom the girl blames for her own castration as well as for the "deception" the mother has practiced in making the girl believe that she was perfect when she, too, is castrated), and has come to identify with her mother, it is evident that the mother can never serve as the model of perfection (so crucial to the ego-ideal as Freud describes it above) that the father represents for the young boy. This is because the girl comes to identify with her mother (if this occurs at all which is by no means guaranteed) by overcoming her denial of her own castration and by recognizing that both she and her mother lack the penis. Hence, the girl's identification with the mother, for Freud, occurs through and in spite of the acknowledgement of a mutual *imperfection*, a lack of completeness which would seem to work against, rather than toward, the formation of the (perfect) ego-ideal. Freud poignantly describes the process leading up to this acknowledgement as follows:

> After a woman has become aware of the wound to her narcissism, she develops, like a scar, a sense of inferiority. When she has passed beyond her first attempt at explaining her lack of a penis as being a punishment personal to herself and has realized that that sexual character is a universal one, she begins to share the contempt felt by men for a sex which is the lesser in so important a respect, and, at least in holding that opinion, insists on being like a man. (Freud 1961:253)

The difficulty of identifying with the mother who shares the ignominy of belonging to this "inferior" sex is enhanced by Freud's assertion "that in the end the girl's mother, who sent her into the world so insufficiently equipped, is almost always held responsible for her lack of a penis" (Freud 1961:254). Freud, recognizing the grave difficulties that stand in the way of the daughter's identification with the mother at the end of the Oedipal stage, does not posit that this identification occurs immediately after the recognition of mother and daughter's mutual castrated status but postulates that the daughter, in her hostility toward the mother, turns to the father as her primary love object, and forms an identification with him. Due to her lack of the penis, this identification cannot be easily maintained, and the daughter instead retains the father as a love object (increasing her hostility for the mother with whom she is a rival for the father's affection), only gradually (if at all) coming to identify with the mother, through transforming her desire to be like the father into a desire first to have a (penis) child with the father and then to have a child by another man.

Generally speaking, Freud characterizes the alteration in the ego that gives rise to the ego-ideal as a kind of "desexualization" whereby object-libido (love/longing for/to be like the father) is transformed into narcissistic libido. Leaving aside for the moment the problematic status of the identification the girl is ultimately supposed to achieve with her mother, Freud suggests that the boy/girl child's strong object-cathexis onto the father, an object-cathexis which in both the case of the young boy and the young girl *cannot* be a complete source of (sexual) gratification, is sublimated through being internalized in the (desexualized) form of the ego-ideal. At times, Freud reminds us that mother-identification also plays a role in the formation of the ego-ideal, and he supports the presence of mother-identification in both the boy and the girl not only because the mother is the first love object for both, but also because of the:

> bisexuality originally present in children: that is to say, a boy has not merely an ambivalent attitude towards his father and an affectionate object-choice towards his mother, but at the same time he also behaves like a girl and displays an affec-

tionate feminine attitude to his father and a corresponding jealousy and hostility towards his mother. It is this complicating element introduced by bisexuality that makes it so difficult to obtain a clear view of the facts in connection with the earliest object-choices and identifications, and still more difficult to describe them intelligibly. (Freud 1961:33)

Nonetheless, the influence of the mother-identification on the ego-ideal appears to be quite negligible for both the boy and the girl since Freud goes on to describe the ego-ideal as having a "double aspect" that can be characterized through the following two precepts: "'You *ought to be* like this (like your father)'" and "'You *may not be* like this (like your father)—that is, you may not do all that he does; some things are his prerogative'" (1961:34). Even if Freud is not willing to grant that identification with the mother (largely pre-Oedipal for the boy and both pre- and post-Oedipal for the girl) plays a significant role in the formation of the ego-ideal, it does seem to be the case that the girl's more problematic identification with the father (problematic as compared to the young boy's especially because it is "destined" to be superseded by an identification with the mother), affects not only the content of her ego-ideal, but also the role this latter plays in her life. As Freud, in an extremely revealing passage, somewhat diffidently notes:

I cannot evade the notion (though I hesitate to give it expression) that for women the level of what is ethically normal is different from what it is in men. Their super-ego is never so inexorable, so impersonal, so independent of its emotional origins as we require it to be in men. Character-traits which critics of every epoch have brought up against women—that they show less sense of justice than men, that they are less ready to submit to the great exigencies of life, that they are more often influenced in their judgements by feelings of affection or hostility— all these would be amply accounted for by the modification in the formation of their super-ego which we have inferred above. We must not allow ourselves to be deflected from such conclusions by the denials of the feminists, who are anxious to force us to regard the two sexes as completely equal in position and worth; but we shall, of course, willingly agree that the majority of men are also far behind *the masculine ideal* and that all human individuals, as a result of their bisexual disposition and of cross-inheritance, combine in themselves both masculine and feminine characteristics, so that pure masculinity and femininity remain theoretical constructions of uncertain content. (Freud 1961:257–258, my emphasis)

By describing the ego-ideal as a "masculine ideal," Freud (not so) unwittingly reinforces the inferiority complex that women have already been subjected to, on his analysis, through the castration complex. That is, as a masculine ideal, based upon what Freud problematically describes as "an individual's first and most important identification, his identification with the father in his own personal prehistory" (Freud 1961:31), the ego-ideal cannot represent the more "mature" stage in the young girl's development that occurs (if and) when her identification switches from her father to her mother. And, since similarity of bodily morphology is precisely what first turns the young girl away from her mother (through her blaming her mother for their disgraceful, castrated state) and then helps to motivate her identification with the mother (through the desire to have a baby with her father as her mother has done), the formation of the ego-ideal as a (desexualized) masculine ideal would not seem to incorporate the girl's/mother's own bodily morphology except insofar as it is construed as lacking (the penis). Thus, the normative force of the ego-ideal in the young girl, as it is played out corporeally in the form of a body image ideal, would appear, on Freud's account, to bring to a crisis the tension between the two contradictory precepts: "You ought to be like your father" and "You must not be like your father." Not only does he wield an authority the daughter (and son) must not dare to usurp or challenge, but for the daughter he also possesses the penis that she must not seek to attain for herself, not now and not ever.

So, while the boy's identification with the father may take the form of internalizing the perfections with which he has endowed this ultimately phantasmatic figure, perfections which he may (unreasonably) hope one day to realize himself, the girl's identification with the father and her internalization of these (illusory) perfections is doomed to failure at the outset since she already knows that she could never achieve her ego-ideal. This does not mean that the boy could ever really be closer to achieving the ego-ideal than the girl since the perfections attributed to this phantasmatic father are based on a denial of the father's own imperfections, and to the extent that the child seeks to attain the ego-ideal regardless, this can only be based on a disavowal of the illusion of perfection that results in the formation of the ego-ideal. But the point is that the boy (for better or worse) can persist in this illusion of perfection longer than the girl, and, in so far as this is the case, the ego-ideal may be more efficacious for him insofar as it represents a positive goal toward which he may strive. The "reasonable" girl, paradoxically (and contra-Freud), may turn out to be precisely the one who recognizes at the outset the untenability of clinging to a masculine ideal and who either rejects this ideal altogether and/or constructs a new ideal that is not quite so masculine!

Racial Epidermal Schemas and White Male/Masculine Body Image Ideals

In *Black Skin White Masks*, Franz Fanon suggests that the problems faced by the young girl in the development of an ego-ideal/body image ideal are negligible in comparison with the difficulties black men and women face in their efforts just to construct a coherent body schema. For these individuals, "consciousness of the body is solely a negating activity. It is a third-person consciousness. The body is surrounded by an atmosphere of certain uncertainty" (Fanon

1967:110–111). This "corporeal malediction," Fanon attributes to the peculiar nature of the "dialectic" that unfolds between the black body and its world, a dialectic that is mediated from the outset by a not so invisible third term, namely, white society with its white values, white norms (both moral and aesthetic), and white expectations. Fanon argues that there is another schema operative not above but *below* the corporeal schema identified by Lhermitte in his work, *L'Image de notre corps*.[21] This schema Fanon calls a "historico-racial schema" and its elements are provided not by "'residual sensations and perceptions primarily of a tactile, vestibular, kinesthetic and visual character,' but by the other, the white man, who had woven me out of a thousand details, anecdotes, stories" (Fanon 1967:111). The additional "task" faced by men and women of color is one of reconciling their own "tactile, vestibular, kinesthetic, and visual" experiences with the structure imposed by this historico-racial schema, a structure that provides the "racial parameters" within which the corporeal schema is supposed to fit. "I thought" Fanon poignantly notes, "that what I had in hand was to construct a physiological self, to balance space, to localize sensations, and here I was called on for more" (Fanon 1967:111).

Fanon goes on to describe his own experience of finding his corporeal schema "assailed at various points . . . crumbled, its place taken by a racial epidermal schema" (Fanon 1967:112). Rather than being able to relinquish responsibility for a schema not of his own making, Fanon discovers that this racial epidermal schema, which constructs him as *The Black Man*, also makes him "responsible at the same time for my body, for my race, for my ancestors" (Fanon 1967:112). And, through assuming this responsibility foisted upon him, Fanon tellingly reveals the only response possible for the "moral" individual who accepts the condemnation of white society for his or her "degraded" state: "Shame. Shame and self-contempt. Nausea" (1967:116). He too internalizes, to use Fanon's language, the "myth of the negro," a myth that proclaims all blacks to be "savages, brutes, illiterates" and he describes the price of "defying" the myth as a black physician, as follows:

> It was always the Negro teacher, the Negro doctor; brittle as I was becoming, I shivered at the slightest pretext. I knew, for instance, that if the physician made a mistake it would be the end of him and of all those who came after him. What could one expect, after all, from a Negro physician? As long as everything went well, he was praised to the skies, but look out, no nonsense, under any conditions! The black physician can never be sure how close he is to disgrace. I tell you, I was walled in: No exception was made for my refined manners, or my knowledge of literature, or my understanding of the quantum theory. (Fanon 1967:117)

The narrative movement of this passage from first to third to first person, visibly demonstrates the invisible social processes at work in the construction of a racially-coded corporeal schema and emphasizes that social objectification should not be viewed as a subsequent influence upon the construction of an individual body image (i.e. coming into play only in the development of an ego-ideal or body image ideal), but is always already operative, and for those societally designated as "racial minorities," the internalization of this racial epidermal schema (whose inscriptive force penetrates the psyche through the skin), results in a (psychophysical) inferiority complex that no body image ideal, however positive, can ever completely overcome. One corporeal consequence, according to Fanon, is that the black man "suffers in his body quite differently than the white man." It is on the basis of this difference, and more importantly, the reasons for this difference, that Fanon critiques Sartre's (fallacious) understanding of the Other when applied to a black consciousness since "the white man is not only The Other but also the master, whether real or imaginary" (Fanon 1967:138).

Fanon, like Merleau-Ponty and Schilder, draws upon both the phenomenological and psychoanalytic traditions to develop his own understanding of the racialized body image. Although his account offers a morphological description of the (unbearable) tension between a body image and the historico-racial schema out of which it develops that is lacking in either Merleau-Ponty or Schilder, he too, quite explicitly focuses on the situation of the male, the colonized black man in particular, leaving the unique situation of black women almost entirely out of account.[22] The difficulties we have discussed above in relation to the young girl's development of an ego-ideal and body image ideal, can only be compounded for the girl of color, for, to the extent that she develops the masculine ego-ideal that Freud envisions, it will almost undoubtedly be based upon a (generic) white man rather than a father-figure representing her own race and/or ethnicity. For, as Fanon observes, "it is in white terms that one perceives one's fellows" (Fanon 1967:163). This failure to account for the unique development of the woman of color's body image, the differences in the historico-racial schema that underlies it, and the consequences of these latter for the internalization of a body image ideal that is both gendered and racialized in problematic ways, will be explored in depth in the next chapters.

As far as the corporeal schema of the white man is concerned, Fanon argues that his "Negrophobia" is not merely a social attitude or psychical disposition, but is rather:

> to be found on an instinctual, biological level. At the extreme, I should say that the Negro, because of his body, impedes the closing of the postural schema of the white man—at the point, naturally, at which the black man makes his entry into the phenomenal world of the white man. (Fanon 1967:161)

As we saw earlier on, it is in the mirror stage that the postural schema moves from fragmentation to an (illusory) image of closure. Thus, the "point of entry" of the racialized Other into the white's world occurs quite early on, during the mirror stage, and this racialized Other presents itself as an absolute Other, a projection of all that is alien to one's own corporeal experience; more precisely, it constitutes that which refuses to be absorbed in the totalizing movement toward corporeal closure. With this re-visioning of Lacan's theory of the mirror stage, Fanon anticipates what he claims a more thoroughgoing investigation will undoubtedly reveal, namely:

> the extent to which the *imago* of his fellow built up in the young white at the usual age would undergo an imaginary aggression with the appearance of the Negro. When one has grasped the mechanism described by Lacan, one can have no further doubt that the real Other for the white man is and will continue to be the black man. And conversely. Only for the white man The Other is perceived on the level of the body image, absolutely as the not-self—that is, the unidentifiable, the unassimilable. For the black man, as we have shown, historical and economic realities come into the picture. (Fanon 1967:161)

While the white man experiences the image of the black man as a phobogenic object, a "stimulus to anxiety" insofar as he is a corporeal reminder of how precarious is the illusion that sustains the "completeness" of the body image and its (perfect) idealizations, Fanon suggests that the black man experiences not whiteness but *his own blackness* as the not-self, as that which resists all attempts to achieve corporeal closure. Whereas the Jew, for Sartre, is overdetermined from within, through her/his internalization of the anti-Semite's normative assessment of her/his psyche, Fanon claims that the person of color is overdetermined from without, on the basis of her/his skin color alone (Fanon 1967:115–116). The Jew can remain (in many but certainly not all cases) invisible in her/his jewishness; the individual of color has no such "choice."[23] It would be more accurate, I believe, given Fanon's own analysis, to see the person of color as overdetermined *both* from within and without insofar as racist attitudes and actions clearly penetrate the skin and are incorporated into both the white *and* the black's body images.

Literary, autobiographical, and philosophical discussions of the debilitating (and even deadly) effects of the internalization of a (racist) historico-racial schema can be found in the works of authors such as Nella Larsen, Richard Rodriguez, and Lewis Gordon. In diverse ways, all three critically extend Fanon's discussion of the consequences of this overdetermination in the form of what Gordon calls "black antiblackness in an antiblack world" (Gordon 1995:104).

In both of her novellas, *Quicksand* and *Passing*, Larsen subtly reveals the simultaneous feelings of fascination and contempt that characterize darker-complexioned blacks' reactions to lighter-complexioned blacks (and vice-versa), blacks to whites and whites to blacks. Through her narrative portrayal of the motivations for, and consequences of, this deep-seated ambivalence, we can achieve a deeper insight into the complex emotional investments that produce a racialized body schema and that in turn shape the formation of a (white) body image ideal.

In her book, *Bodies that Matter*, Judith Butler traces the ways in which (the light-skinned) Irene Redfield's ambivalent sexual desires for (the light-skinned) Clare, in *Passing*, are projected onto her (dark-skinned) husband Brian whom she comes to suspect of having an affair with Clare. Butler argues that the ambivalence that characterizes Irene's/Brian's love/hate for Clare goes hand-in-hand with her/his positing the lovely/lying Clare as "the ideal." Butler describes the "costs" of idealization as follows:

> Idealization, then, is always at the expense of the ego who idealizes. The ego-ideal is produced as a consequence of being severed from the ego, where the ego is understood to sacrifice some part of its narcissism in the formation and externalization of this ideal. The love of the ideal will thus always be ambivalent, for the ideal deprecates the ego as it compels its love. . . . The one I idealize is the one who carries for me the self-love that I myself have invested in that one. And accordingly, I hate that one, for he/she has taken my place even as I yielded my place to him/her, and yet I require that one, for he/she represents the promise of the return of my own self-love. Self-love, self-esteem is thus preserved and vanquished at the site of the ideal. (Butler 1993:180)

The idealization of the Other who "promises the return of my own self-love" is poignantly (and quite problematically we shall see) illustrated in Richard Rodriguez's autobiographical essay, "Complexion." As an adolescent whose "divorce from his body," is produced by the degraded status conferred upon him by his family because of his darker-skinned complexion, Rodriquez recalls that:

> My mother didn't need anymore to tell me to watch out for the sun. I denied myself a sensational life. The normal, extraordinary, animal excitement of feeling my body alive — riding shirtless on a bicycle in the warm wind created by furious self-propelled motion — the sensations that first had excited in me a sense of my maleness, I denied. I was too ashamed of my body. I wanted to forget that I had a body because I had a brown body. I was grateful that none of my classmates ever mentioned the fact. (Rodriguez 1990:271–272)

Years later, after having "compensated" for his epidermal inferiority through a single-minded pursuit of the intellectual (noncorporeal) life, Rodriguez finally breaks "the curse of physical shame," by physically transforming his body through manual labor. The physical pleasure of intense bodily exertion in turn leads Rodriguez to the construction of a less divided body image, one that seeks to enhance, rather than hide, the darkness of his skin which he enjoys exposing to the sun. These days, as a long-distance runner, Rodriguez views his specular image with a mixture of humor, nostalgia, and pride:

> The torso, the soccer player's calves and thighs, the arms of the twenty-year-old I never was, I possess now in my thirties. I study the youthful parody shape in the

mirror: the stomach lipped tight by muscle; the shoulders rounded by chin-ups; the arms veined strong. This man. A man. I meet him. He laughs to see me, what I have become. (Rodriguez 1990:277)

Despite the obvious pleasure Rodriguez takes in looking at his "new body," I would argue that this specular image, which can only now be "jubilantly" assumed, is still the Other, the not-me who laughs back at these narcissistic pleasures, with the mocking laugh perhaps of Cixous' Medusa, the one who laughs last, because the perfection sought is indeed a parody of a youthful (masculine) ideal that cannot be sought without subjection to the "disciplinary practices" that society has prescribed for its attainment.[24] It is striking that Rodriquez's overcoming of what we might call his "epidermal shame" occurs through a (re)assertion of the masculine body image ideal—the taut muscles, tight abdomen, and strong arms that are synonymous, in Western society, with male vitality, vigor, and virility.[25] While Rodriguez is successful in transforming his "bodiless" body image into a more "robust," embodied one, he corporeally destroys racist stereotypes that associate darkness with ugliness through the construction of a body image that parodically supports the identification of physical fitness and youthfulness with masculinity.[26] In the redoubling of the specular confirmation of his "metamorphosis" through this written, first-person narrative, normative standards based on age and gender are powerfully (re)invoked to "trump" those that are based on race—a problematic "solution" whose consequences we will explore further in the following chapters.

Lewis Gordon, in *Bad Faith and Anti-Black Racism*, provides a concrete, philosophical analysis of the "corporeal price" exacted by the black body for identifying with a white body image ideal, an ideal that can only be constructed upon the rejection of *its* absolute, unassimilable Other, the black body viewed as the "epitome of ugliness, horror, and malevolence." According to Gordon:

> The black who regards his body as a black body, as a repulsive body, as, ultimately *pure, unformed matter*, has taken a transcendent position toward his body. His body is frozen under the force of the Look, the force by which his body ends up standing in relation to itself as the Other. The point of perspective becomes separated from itself; the perspective gained in the flight from the black body is the assumption of non-blackness. The black, in such an instance, is able to exist as denial, is able to regard his body as not "really" his. Being ultimately regarded by black and antiblack racists as a body without a perspective, the black body is invited to live in such a way that there is no distinction between *a* particular black body and *black bodies*. Every black person becomes a limb of an enormous black body: THE BLACK BODY. A special form of negation emerges. Liberation from the black body becomes liberation from blackness. (Gordon 1995:105)

Gordon goes on to invoke the Baudrillardian deceptive/seductive specularity that characterizes this "body without a perspective," a truly phantasmatic vision

that operates on many levels at once. The project of transcending one's blackness is not a matter of transcending one's skin color, but, as Rodriguez has
described it above, involves an attempt to transcend one's body altogether, that
is, to attain a disembodied perspective where the body's materiality can be
effaced. It is striking that the internalization of an anti-black perspective can
only be synonymous with an anti-body perspective for, as Fanon shows in his
discussion of the historico-racial schema that underlies the body image, there is
no way one's blackness can be separated from one's corporeality. The anti-black
ego-ideal is not then, and cannot be, a *body image* ideal, because it is a noncorporeal phantasm, a veritable ghost that no white body can embody any more
than any black body can. The inseparability of blackness and whiteness from
their materiality does not mean, however, that their meaning is necessarily
fixed or biologically given. The racial-epidermal schema Fanon has identified
as constitutive in the development of the body image, is itself, as he notes, an
historical construction. Indeed, as Gordon argues:

> blackness and whiteness are projections. But eventually, blackness and white-
> ness take on certain meanings that apply to certain groups of people in such a
> way that makes it difficult not to think of those people without certain affectively
> charged associations. Their blackness and their whiteness become regarded, by
> people who take their associations too seriously, as their essential features—as, in
> fact, material features of their being. (Gordon 1995:95)

While Gordon, working from within a Sartrean perspective, equates essential
features with material features and rejects an understanding of blackness or
whiteness as essential/material, I believe that it is possible to deny the essentiality of skin color without making the corresponding move of denying its materiality. What must be remembered is that the essentiality that is being denied here
has to do with a metaphysical pre-givenness, a fixed referent and/or source of signification that plays a prescribed role in the formation of the body image. A virtue
of both Schilder's and Merleau-Ponty's accounts of the body image is the fact
that no part of the body plays such a role for either of them. In fact, as we have
seen, the body image is itself never pre-given or truly substantive in a metaphysical sense (though it is indeed corporeal), rather, it is constantly changing its own
shape and significance in an individual's life. Attempts to restrict the significa-
tory possibilities of either the body or the body image through too strong an emotional investment in a particular aspect of the body (such as the color of one's
skin) can lead to serious distortions within the body image itself. For, to repeat
Schilder's claim: "whenever one part obtains an overwhelming importance in
the image of the body, the inner symmetry and the inner equilibrium of the
body-image will be destroyed" (Schilder 1950:126).

To understand the impact of the historico-racial schema on the development of the body image and the body image ideal(s) and to understand how
gender, class, age, and cultural norms and expectations are also internalized,

interwoven, and expressed in each, it is necessary to explore further the contributions that other people make to the construction of the body image. Both Schilder and Merleau-Ponty emphasize the importance of others in the processes of construction/destruction/reconstruction that characterize the ongoing development of the body image. Both are especially interested in the nonverbal communication that plays such a crucial role in what Schilder calls "body-image intercourse." Schilder stresses again and again that "the body-image is a social phenomenon," that "there exists a deep community between one's own body-image and the body-image of others," that the "body-images of human beings communicate with each other either in parts or as wholes" (Schilder 1950:217,138). For Merleau-Ponty, as we have seen, to develop a body image is to develop an image of my body as visible to others. There is no body image without this visibility of the body. As a result, the "synthesis" of the specular image and the introceptive feelings I have about my body that occurs (at the end of) the mirror stage is less, Merleau-Ponty claims "a synthesis of intellection than it is a synthesis of coexistence with others" (Merleau-Ponty 1964:140). Let us turn, then, to an exploration of the alterity of the body image, an alterity that motivates the production, for most of us, of "an almost unlimited number of body-images" (Schilder 1950:67).[27]

The Alterity of the Body Image

Given that the body image responds directly to subtle physiological and emotional changes in our own bodies, it may seem as if the body image should be characterized as a personal or even private phenomenon, especially since its largely pre-reflective functioning makes it difficult to thematize for oneself, much less to discuss or somehow "share" it with others. And yet, the "body image intercourse" that Schilder describes, implies that body images are in continual interaction with one another, participating in a mutually constitutive corporeal dialogue that defies solipsistic analysis. This dialogue, for both Schilder and Merleau-Ponty, begins in childhood and precedes the mirror stage. According to Schilder:

> The child takes parts of the bodies of others into its own body-image. It also adopts in its own personality the attitude taken by others towards parts of their own bodies. Postural models of the body are closely connected with each other. We take the body-images of others either in parts or as a whole. In the latter case we call it identification. But we may also want to give away our body-image, and we then project it onto others. The patient projects his own difficulties and his whole body-image into the analyst. (Schilder 1950:137–138)

Through these processes of introjection, projection, and identification, the body image continually incorporates and expels its own body (parts), other bodies and other body images. Moreover, as the phantom limb phenomenon amply demonstrates, the body parts that may be incorporated or expelled in the body image need not be actually present to have an active role in its constitution. Although the experience of a phantom limb can be partially accounted for by attributing it to the body image's memory of the amputated limb, a memory that is essential for the formation of the habit body and which helps to provide the necessary stability that makes integrated and complex bodily movements possible, Schilder argues that there is a strong emotional investment in the missing limb that must be taken into consideration as well. Thus, the role that memory plays in the construction of one's present body image(s) can only be understood if the emotional contexts that situate (and stimulate) these memories are also illuminated and addressed. As Schilder observes:

> We are accustomed to have a complete body. The phantom of an amputated person is therefore the reactivation of a given perceptive pattern by emotional forces. The great variety in phantoms is only to be understood when we consider the emotional reactions of individuals towards their own body. (Schilder 1950:67)

Schilder's reference to the amputee as an "amputated person," is itself revealing because it forces us to acknowledge that the phantom is produced not only to maintain the coherence or completeness of the body image but, in doing so, to maintain the individual's own sense of self. Merleau-Ponty characterizes the body image's resistance to absorbing the reality of the missing limb in terms of a (positive) desire to retain our active engagement in a social world that defines us as individuals:

> What it is in us which refuses mutilation and disablement is an *I* committed to a certain physical and inter-human world, who continues to tend towards his world despite handicaps and amputations and who, to this extent, does not recognize them *de jure*. The refusal of the deficiency is only the obverse of our inherence in a world, the implicit negation of what runs counter to the natural momentum which throws us into our tasks, our cares, our situation, our familiar horizons. To have a phantom arm is to remain open to all the actions of which the arm alone is capable; it is to retain the practical field which one enjoyed before mutilation. (Merleau-Ponty 1962:81)

Taken together, Merleau-Ponty and Schilder provide a striking alternative to clinical accounts of the phantom limb which regard the experience of the phantom solely in negative terms, for instance, as a *failure* of the body image to adapt itself to this profound change in the body. Instead, both Merleau-Ponty and Schilder seem to view the phantom limb experience as an adaptive strategy that seeks to minimize the loss of certain bodily possibilities that invariably accompanies the loss of the limb. "After the amputation," Schilder asserts, "the individual has to face a new situation, but since he is reluctant to do so he tries to maintain the integrity of his body" (Schilder 1950:68). While Merleau-

Ponty and Schilder view the phantom limb as a refusal of the loss of the limb, they also view it simultaneously as an affirmation of one's active engagement in the world.

The tendency of the phantom limb to diminish and disappear over time for most (but not all) amputees, makes it clear that the body image's own memory which guarantees the stability of the postural model of the body from one moment to the next, is itself schematically organized and exhibits the same flexibility as the body image does. Moreover, the tension between the amputee's body and her/his body image which struggles to maintain its integrity by refusing to incorporate the missing limb into its corporeal schema, is not an isolated or unique phenomenon. Rather, for both Schilder and Merleau-Ponty, the phantom limb is only a more extreme form of a phenomenon that all of us experience on a daily basis, namely, the attempt to maintain a certain bodily equilibrium in the face of continual changes in both our body and our situation. Schilder, especially, emphasizes that the continual changes occurring both within and outside of our bodies necessitates the construction of not one, but several body images. To the extent that one may posit an "original shape" to the body image, it must be remembered that "this original shape is based upon continual transformations from the postural model of the child into the postural model of the adult. There is a long series of images" (Schilder 1950:67). This series of images must not be understood linearly, with each new body image replacing the previous one as we move from infancy to adulthood. Rather, previous body images remain accessible and can be re-enacted in a moment as when we return to a childhood "haunt" and find ourselves simultaneously haunted by an earlier body image that was able to negotiate the childhood space with ease. These earlier body images are also projected onto our own children as we watch their fascination with/dread of their bodies and as we find ourselves inhabiting their way of living their bodies as the emotional center of the world.

Thus, it is not just the amputee who refuses to "give up" an earlier body image in order to retain the emotional, physical, and social possibilities that resonated within that earlier situation. In the conclusion of *The Image and Appearance of the Human Body*, Schilder makes this point quite clear and leaves the reader with a rather startling, parenthetical observation:

> Vestibular experiments and observations of amputated people have shown that every body contains in itself a phantom (perhaps the body itself is a phantom) in addition. It is obvious that the phantom character of one's own body will come to a still clearer expression in dreams, which, like phantasies, show a particular variability. (Schilder 1950:297)

To say that the body itself may be a phantom, is to suggest that "the body" is itself a type of projection, a possibility ready to materialize itself in any number of shapes or forms. Moreover, just as the amputee incorporates the phantom into her/his body image in order to preserve bodily integrity, so too, we incorporate the body as a Gestalt, as a "heavy signification" to use Merleau-Ponty's words, into our own body images, in order to ground our own sense of agency and to establish our "real" presence in the world as a material force to be reckoned with. The body image, then, enables us to identify not only with the bodies and body images of others (something we will explore further in the following chapters), but also can express a desire to achieve a stable identity by projecting that very stability onto our own bodies. In *Bodies that Matter*, Judith Butler discusses the role that identifications play in the assumption of a particular sex, and the point she makes about assuming a sex is directly applicable to the identification which materially supports identification with a sex, namely, a sexed *body*:

> Identifications, then, can ward off certain desires or act as vehicles for desire; in order to facilitate certain desires, it may be necessary to ward off others: identification is the site at which this ambivalent prohibition and production of desire occurs. If to assume a sex is in some sense an "identification," then it seems that identification is a site at which prohibition and deflection are insistently negotiated. To identify with a sex is to stand in some relation to an imaginary threat, imaginary and forceful, forceful precisely because it is imaginary. (Butler 1993:100)

The imaginary threat that stimulates the desire for identification with something that will provide us with existential stability, is the threat that this stability will itself be revealed to be a phantasmatic construction, viable only to the extent that it is corporeally sustained at each and every moment of our existence. Butler goes on to observe that the "place" of identification can never be secured:

> Significantly it never can be said to have taken place; identification does not belong to the world of events. Identification is constantly figured as a desired event or accomplishment, but one which finally is never achieved; identification is the phantasmatic staging of the event. In this sense, identifications belong to the imaginary; they are phantasmatic efforts of alignment, loyalty, ambiguous and cross-corporeal cohabitation; they unsettle the "I"; they are the sedimentation of the "we" in the constitution of any "I," the structuring presence of alterity in the very formulation of the "I." Identifications are never fully and finally made; they are incessantly reconstituted and, as such, are subject to the volatile logic of iterability. They are that which is constantly marshaled, consolidated, retrenched, contested, and, on occasion, compelled to give way. (Butler 1993:105)

To say that the body image posits "the body" as a given entity, as the locus for specific desires and forms of identification, is not to deny the materiality of the body or to claim that the body is merely a figment of our (cultural) imagination. "The imagination" is itself a fictive realm, appearing throughout the writings of modern philosophers from Descartes through Kant as a mental faculty, a (non)place where multiple and magical transformations of perceptually-based ideas are always possible. The imaginary, unlike the imagination, does not designate a particular realm or faculty, but permeates our entire perceptual life in so thoroughgoing a fashion that Merleau-Ponty asks the question, "Is vision, the sense of spectacle, also the sense of the imaginary?" He adds:

> Our images are predominantly visual, and this is no accident; it is by means of vision that one can sufficiently dominate and control objects. With the visual experience of the self, there is thus the advent of a new mode of relatedness to self. The visual makes possible a kind of schism between the immediate *me* and the *me* that can be seen in the mirror. The sensory functions themselves are thus redefined in proportion to the contribution they can make to the existence of the subject and the structures they can offer for the development of that existence. (Merleau-Ponty 1962:138)

It should come as no surprise that at least one doctor today is employing mirrors to "treat" the phantom limb, using the visual image of the amputated limb to "counter" the resistant body image and to motivate a new (imaginary) construction, one which will successfully negotiate the tension between the desire to get rid of the irritating (and often quite painful) phantom, and the equally powerful desire to maintain the coherence of the body image.[28] That for most individuals, the phantom limb eventually does disappear (often, as Schilder observes, shrinking first), with or without therapy, should not be understood as the "triumph" of the body (or the specular image of the body) over the body image, but rather, as the construction of a new morphological imaginary, one that offers new sites of projection and identification and new bodily possibilities. And yet, as Elizabeth Grosz reminds us, we must also recognize that it is not the case that "anything goes":

> The body is not open to *all* the whims, wishes, and hopes of the subject: the human body, for example, cannot fly in the air, it cannot breathe underwater unaided by prostheses, it requires a broad range of temperatures and environmental supports, without which it risks collapse and death. On the other hand, while there must be some kinds of biological limit or constraint, these constraints are perpetually capable of being superseded, overcome, through the human body's capacity to open itself up to prosthetic synthesis, to transform or rewrite its environment, to continually augment its powers and capacities through the incorporation into the body's own spaces and modalities of objects, that, while external, are internalized, added to, supplementing and supplemented by the "organic body" (or what culturally passes for it), surpassing the body, not "beyond" nature but in collusion with a "nature" that never really lived up to its name, that represents always the most blatant cultural anxieties and projections. (Grosz 1994:187–188)

While Merleau-Ponty and Schilder provide a rich point of departure for considering the complex, constitutive interrelationships among the body, the body image, libidinous development, neurophysiological organization, the self, other selves, other bodies, objects, and the situation as such, it is feminist theorists who have taken up the task of articulating the social and bodily forces that both constrain and enable the development of the body image. Moreover, it is due to the careful, critical work of feminist theorists of the body such as Iris Young, Judith Butler, Elizabeth Grosz, Luce Irigaray, Patricia Hill Collins, and Susan Bordo that the allegedly "neutral" descriptions of the body image provided by Schilder and Merleau-Ponty, have themselves been revealed as masculinist projections incapable of responding to the different kinds of mirrorings experienced by men and women. Only through an examination of the specula(riza)tions provided by these and other recent theorists can we truly come to grips with the series of political, economic, racialized, sexualized, and gendered cultural/corporeal exchanges that set the terms for, and continually interrupt, body image intercourse.

{2}

Splitting the Subject

The Interval between Immanence and Transcendence

Most frequently, the men see themselves in relation to the task at hand, the women as they appear performing that task. Women are looking into different mirrors. Reflection can be experienced by women either in a mirror or through that human mirror, the indeterminate male observer. This mirrored perspective comes to be their own, as they seek first and within every attribute their own appearance and its value.

—Ellyn Kaschak (1992:106)

In this description of what men and women attend to when watching themselves on video, Ellen Kaschak presents us with a double vision of what are themselves two different kinds of visions: she offers us not only the visions of men and women respectively, but of men and women seeing themselves in action and herself seeing them see themselves. Would a male observor note these same gendered differences in men's and women's respective modes of attention to themselves? To what extent does the gender of the observor (and her relation to her own possibility of seeing herself or seeing herself being seen) affect what is observed? I ask these questions not to discount the observor or her observation, but to note the way in which Kaschak's own observation is itself an intervention, indeed a feminist intervention into what is being observed.

Phenomenology, as Husserl first described it, itself must begin with observations, observations that are not restricted to my own subjective experiences (and this is precisely what differentiates phenomenology from introspection) but which encompass an entire social network of complex human interactions. Husserl never abandoned his hope that philosophy, through its adoption of the phenomenological method, would become a rigorous science. The term "rigor," as employed by Husserl, seemed to refer to at least two primary characteristics that phenomenological inquiry should possess, characteristics that themselves suggest the influence of both Hume and Kant. The first refers to *what* is revealed through phenomenological investigation, the second to *how*

Fragment, Martina Shenal (photo-intaglio)

that investigation is carried out. What is revealed displays its rigor through its neutrality, that is, the non-value-laden quality of the description itself which is, on principle, capable of being replicated by anyone, thereby achieving a Humean and Kantian subjective universality that Husserl, unlike Hume, is quite content to associate with scientific objectivity.[1] The rigor that concerns how the investigation is carried out is attained through a reflexive process whereby one interrogates the modes in which the phenomenon in question is being both intended by and given to one. In Husserl's own words:

> To study any kind of objectivity whatever according to its general essence (a study that can pursue interests far removed from those of knowledge theory and the investigation of consciousness) means to concern oneself with objectivity's modes of givenness and to exhaust its essential content in the processes of "clarification" proper to it. Even if the orientation is not that which is directed toward the kinds of consciousness and an essential investigation of them, still the method of clarification is such that even here reflection on the modes of being intended and of being given cannot be avoided. (Husserl 1965:90–91)

Although the term "objectivity" is in disrepute these days not only in the human sciences but in the natural sciences as well, Husserl's Kierkegaardian understanding of rigor as encompassing the "how" as well as the "what" both anticipates and reinforces feminist attentiveness not only to what is being observed but also to the intentions of the one doing the observing and to the modes through which the phenomenon is "given" in the first place.[2] Despite Husserl's astuteness in this regard, Husserl's, Heidegger's, and Sartre's failure to acknowledge sex, gender, class, and race as influencing how consciousness itself is experienced and intended goes hand-in-hand with their failure to do justice to consciousness as always already embodied. And, while Merleau-Ponty does provide the first systematic phenomenological investigation of the body as a ground for all perception, which by his own account includes all actual and possible human experience, he too, never recognizes the primary impact that sex, gender, class, and race have on how as well as what it is that we experience.

All too often feminists have taken this serious omission/refusal of the "fathers" of phenomenology as a reason to reject phenomenology itself and some have appealed to psychoanalysis to "explain" this omission/refusal as yet another form of male castration anxiety.[3] And yet, Husserl never claims to have exhausted all the modes by which phenomena are intended and given in his phenomenological descriptions; indeed, as I have argued elsewhere, he never abandons his belief in and commitment to the very thing that threatens the rigor of his entire phenomenological inquiry, namely, the zone of indeterminacy that pervades and affects each of our conscious (and bodily) acts.[4]

It is not so far-fetched, I believe, to claim that the interlocking influences of sex, gender, race, and class upon the body image in particular and embodiment more generally, often surface and are experienced within this very zone of indeterminacy, a zone Husserl identifies as a kind of omnipresent horizon that situates and grounds all human activity. In fact, Husserl's own lifelong project is one that is shared by many feminists, namely, to render that which has remained indeterminate (or even invisible) determinate as a phenomenon in its own right, worthy of serious philosophical inquiry. Doing so, as Husserl well recognized, will invoke a new zone of indeterminacy, since to attend carefully to one phenomenon, or one aspect of one phenomenon, means inevitably that other aspects of that phenomenon will escape one's scrutiny.[5]

The influence of the zone of indeterminacy is itself indeterminable in our everyday life. Part of the richness of the image of seeing oneself seeing comes from the constitutive aspects of that "double vision" that themselves remain unseen. In his final unfinished work, *The Visible and the Invisible*, Merleau-Ponty reminds us again and again that the invisible and the visible are chiasmatically intertwined and that there is no visibility without invisibility. A difficulty with Merleau-Ponty's account, however, is that while he claims that this interdependency between the visible and the invisible characterizes perceptual experience from one moment to the next, he fails to acknowledge the ideological stakes that help to determine what remains invisible to those who seek to interrogate the very limits of visibility. In particular, the work of feminist theorists such as Iris Young, Elizabeth Grosz, and Judith Butler, writers who not only employ but also critique phenomenological methodology, is especially illuminating in simultaneously pointing out the promise and the dangers of phenomenology for feminism.

The promise of phenomenology for feminism comes from Husserl's view that no object, attitude, or belief is too mundane for phenomenological investigation; in fact, the realm of phenomenological inquiry is the realm of the life-world itself, and this latter, for Husserl, includes memories and anticipations, possible as well as actual experiences. A significant danger, on the other hand, comes from Husserl's naive belief in the neutrality of that investigation. And, I would argue, while Heidegger, Sartre, and Merleau-Ponty disagree with Husserl on several points (especially regarding the goal of phenomenology as the discovery of essences), all three retain as an essential part of their own respective methods, an (invisible) commitment to a "neutral discourse" that refuses to interrogate its own intentions and forms of givenness.

This particular danger, I believe, is not endemic to phenomenology even though it may seem to threaten the whole phenomenological enterprise as it was originally conceived by Husserl. First of all, Husserl himself argues in the passage I cited earlier that we must include our own modes of being conscious (noetic activity) in our phenomenological descriptions. While he was clearly thinking of Cartesian modes of consciousness such as willing, imagining, believing, dreaming, etc., by extending the very notion of "modes of consciousness" to "modes of embodiment" we can investigate much less visible, but no less significant ways of experiencing the world, such as those provided by our own body images. This latter inquiry, in turn, requires an exploration of how sex, gender, race, class, age, and ethnicity collectively construct our body images, an exploration that is the central focus of this book.

Another danger that feminists must avoid replicating is Husserl's own Cartesian understanding of modes of consciousness as innate, as givens.[6] The very notion of embodiment suggests an experience that is constantly in the making, that is continually being constituted and reconstituted from one moment to the next. To talk about modes of embodiment therefore, is not to invoke a set of Kantian categories, absolute and inviolable, but rather, to talk about modes that are themselves continually changing in significance and appearance over time. The language of "modes," however, is for good reason out-moded, since it hearkens back to a metaphysics of substance that divides the world into essences and "accidents" or inessential modes of being.

It is crucial for both feminism and phenomenology that we continue to see ourselves seeing and to see how others see our seeing in order to bring into focus those aspects of embodiment that are indeed both given and intended, but which haven't been recognized as either.[7] In doing so, we can extend our understanding of both givenness and intentionality as well as our understanding of (the relationship between) feminism and phenomenology.

Engendering the Body Image

In her classic essay, "Throwing Like a Girl," Iris Young offers a critical analysis of the work of two existential phenomenologists, Erwin Straus and Maurice Merleau-Ponty. More specifically, Young reveals the inadequacies in both Straus' and Merleau-Ponty's accounts of embodiment insofar as both they and other thinkers have failed "to describe the modalities, meaning, and implications of the difference between 'masculine' and 'feminine' body comportment and movement" (Young 1990:142). While Straus acknowledges differences between girls and boys in styles of throwing, he seeks to explain these differences biologically. What is surprising about his appeal to biology, according to Young, is that he claims that it is not anatomy but an innate "feminine attitude" that is responsible for the lack of fluidity observed in girls' throwing styles. More specifically, the differences noted by Straus have to do with the girl's tendency to isolate her forearm and to use it alone to throw the ball leaving the rest of the body relatively immobile. The boy, on the other hand, is more likely to make use of his whole body in preparing for and executing the throw. For the girl, the outcome of this process is that "the ball is released without force, speed, or accurate aim," whereas, for the boy, "the ball leaves the hand with considerable acceleration; it moves toward its goal in a long flat curve" (quoted by Young 1990:141).

Young does not dispute Straus' findings of significant differences between boys' and girls' throwing styles, but she does take issue with his explanation for them. Indeed, Young readily agrees that such differences between throwing styles for boys and girls do exist, although clearly there are many girls who do throw "like boys" and a (smaller) number of boys who do throw "like girls."[8] Moreover, Young notes that with respect to physical goal-oriented activity, many other stylistic differences between boys and girls can be found. Whether the task at hand involves throwing, carrying, sitting, or bending and lifting, in each case the observation is similar, namely, boys tend to be much more effective in maximizing their bodily potential in executing physical tasks than are girls.

Although post-Beauvoirian feminists have long been concerned about reifying a "masculine" norm as a goal for women, insofar as it seems inevitably to lead to a further devaluing of whatever gets identified by contrast as "the feminine," Young, Straus, and others clearly imply that the "masculine" style of throwing, carrying, and bending and lifting is preferable to the "feminine" one.[9] Though Young never makes the claim outright, she does imply throughout her essay that the "masculine" style is, indeed, the one that girls as well as boys should be encouraged to emulate because of the psychological as well as physiological advantages that come from utilizing one's whole body while engaged in a particular task. Greater confidence in oneself and one's bodily capabilities, a more accurate understanding of one's physical potential, and a sense of openness to and readiness for the demands of a given situation are positive experiences that both accompany and continue to encourage the development of one's bodily abilities. And yet, although we may readily agree that it is much better to maximize rather than to minimize one's bodily potential, *both* Young and Straus fail to dwell on the *consequences* of this greater valuation of what they describe as "masculine" bodily comportment for both boys and girls.

For Young, living as a woman in contemporary Western industrial patriarchal society involves living a tension between transcendence and immanence, a tension which is reflected in the contradictory modalities that comprise "feminine" bodily comportment. Rejecting Straus' essentialist appeal to an innate (and rather mysterious) "feminine attitude" as the cause of gender differences in throwing styles, Young argues that it is the clash between how girls experience their own bodies and how society experiences and views their bodies that is responsible for many girls' lack of confidence in their bodies, restricted bodily movements, and over-concern about taking bodily "risks" in the performance of new physical tasks. Working from a Sartrian/Beauvoirian understanding of transcendence as a sense of openness to future projects as an existence for-itself and immanence as a sense of rootedness to the past stemming from one's objectification as a being-for-others, Young agrees with Beauvoir that the young girl is societally regarded as more immanent than transcendent and that this is not the case for the young boy. In particular, Young focuses on the ways in which society has typically discouraged young girls from developing their full bodily potential by exaggerating: 1) the threat of physical injury that could come from increased exertion, and 2) the danger of appearing "unfeminine" in the performance of physical tasks.

For instance, while the young boy is often encouraged to engage in "rough-and-tumble" play, the young girl in a similar situation may just as easily be warned not to get her clothes (especially dress) dirty. And, while the skinned knees and torn trousers of the young boy are often viewed as a "badge of honor" that results not only in peer approval and acceptance but also in the tolerant indulgence of parents proud to have such an active boy, the young girl's skinned knees and torn trousers (or dress) often result in disapproval from her more "feminine" peers if not from parents who, if the behavior occurs in an "unsuitable" context, may be slightly ashamed of their "tomboy."[10] Moreover, the source of this disapproval is often twofold: not only does the girl fail at the project of "being a girl" but she fails equally to achieve the status of the boy.[11]

Young claims that it is the *self-referred* quality of "feminine" bodily comportment that gives rise to its contradictory modalities. That is, it is because young girls are socialized to focus so heavily on their bodies, to treat their bodies as objects to be "pruned," "shaped," "molded," and "decorated" that they move with "ambiguous transcendence," "inhibited intentionality," and "discontinuous unity."[12] According to Young:

> The three contradictory modalities of feminine bodily existence—ambiguous transcendence, inhibited intentionality, and discontinuous unity—have their root . . . in the fact that for feminine existence the body frequently is both subject and object for itself at the same time and in reference to the same act. Feminine bodily existence is frequently not a pure presence to the world because it is referred onto *itself* as well as onto possibilities in the world. (Young 1990:150)

What is striking about Young's account in this essay is her own adherence to the Cartesian transcendence/immanence distinction that is taken up, with varying effects, by Sartre, Beauvoir, and Merleau-Ponty. For all three of these latter thinkers, transcendence is much to be preferred over immanence. Sartre views transcendence as a source of human freedom, Beauvoir views transcendence as a "privilege" conferred upon males and denied to females, and Merleau-Ponty departs from the Cartesian tradition by claiming that the body is transcendent rather than immanent, yet he continues to understand transcendence in Cartesian terms, that is, as freely motivated, intentional activity.

According to Beauvoir (and to Sartre, although he never explained it as well as she did), human beings are both transcendent and immanent—we are simultaneously beings-for-ourselves and beings-for-others, and are comprised of both minds (our primary source of transcendence) and bodies (a primary source of immanence). For both Sartre and Beauvoir, being transcendent is identified with *existing* as a conscious being-for-itself and being immanent is associated with *living* one's body as a being-in-itself or as a being-for-others.[13] To refer to one's body before engaging in physical activity would indeed be a move away from "pure" transcendence for Sartre, Beauvoir, and even Merleau-Ponty because one's intentional movement toward one's goal would be interrupted and, for Sartre and Beauvoir especially, being-for-others would threaten to supersede being-for-oneself.[14]

Intertwining Beauvoir's recognition that transcendence is societally associated with males and immanence with females with Merleau-Ponty's radical understanding of the body as a transcendent subject of perception, Young is able to combat Merleau-Ponty's "gender-blind" account of the body with Beauvoir's emphasis on the bodily consequences of gendered social practices, and she is also able to use Merleau-Ponty's understanding of the body as transcendent as a corrective to Beauvoir's more negative (and traditional) view of the body as immanent. And yet, in this essay Young still remains trapped within the confines of the hierarchical transcendence/immanence distinction itself and this is why I find her "explanation" of the contradictory modalities of "feminine" bodily existence in terms of the latter's self-referred character ultimately so unsatisfying. For, in the end, what Young is suggesting is that self-referral is an immanent move which threatens one's transcendent activity because it disrupts the flow of one's action and concentrates one's attention explicitly upon one's body rather than the task to be performed. This, in turn, "inhibits" one's intentionality and leads to discontinuities in one's bodily movements. But does explicit reference to one's body while one is engaged in an action necessarily take away from the "transcendence" of one's intentional activity? And, by implying that this is the case, doesn't Young end up in the unpalatable situation of supporting an entire patriarchal philosophical tradition that seeks to render the body and its contribution to everyday experience invisible?

The problems that give rise to the contradictory modalities of "feminine" bodily existence, as I see it, are not tied to the latter's self-reference as it is described by Young, but rather, have to do with what I would call the "socially-referred" character of bodily existence for many women (and many men). For, there are many tasks which require paying close attention to one's body prior to (and even while) acting and thus self-reference alone does not seem to mark out the specific contradictions that Young identifies with "feminine" as opposed to "masculine" bodily existence.[15] Moreover, I would resist viewing the socially-referred character of bodily existence as inherently negative or as leading inevitably to immanence. This is because all of our (men's as well as women's) actions have a socially-referred character insofar as they arise in response to a social situation.

In particular, I am maintaining that the contradictory modalities of "feminine" bodily existence identified by Young occur not because women focus on their bodies before, during, and even after their action, transforming their bodies into objects in the process, but because many women mediate their own relationship with their bodies by seeing their bodies as they are seen by others and by worrying about what they and these (largely invisible) others are seeing as they are acting. Indeed, Young herself notes that for a particular woman experiencing these contradictory bodily modalities "the source of this objectified bodily existence is in the attitude of others regarding her," yet she quickly moves on from this observation to focus upon how "the woman herself often actively takes up her body as a mere thing" (Young 1990:155). In shifting the focus so quickly from the individual woman to the attitudes of others which motivate her objectified relationship to her body, and then back to the consequences of this objectification for the individual woman, Young deflects attention away from what she calls the source of the objectification, namely, societal attitudes towards women, and in so doing she inadvertently reinforces an interpretation of these contradictory bodily modalities as an individual woman's (rather than societal) "problem."

What makes the social reference of "feminine" bodily existence so problematic, is that the imaginary perspective of these often imaginary others can come to dominate and even supersede a woman's own experience of her bodily capabilities so that the latter becomes conflated with the former much as the child's spectral image in the mirror stage comes to dominate and take priority over the child's kinesthetic experience of her/his body. And, just as Lacan emphasizes the alienating aspect of this identificatory move which both boys and girls undergo in the formation of the (bodily) ego, we can speak in this situation of another form of bodily alienation whose ground is already laid by the earlier one which occurs in the mirror stage. Here, we have a kind of "doubling" of the Lacanian mirror, a doubling in which I am watching this imaginary other watching me. To call this "self-reference" does not acknowledge or do justice to the very real effects of this imaginary other on my action. To call it "social-reference" carries with it a parallel danger, namely that the agent of the action can be rendered invisible altogether, a fate that Irigaray fears has become reality for the "specular woman" who is the source but rarely the author of a great deal of (philosophical) speculation.

Despite the dangers inherent in attributing the contradictory modalities of "feminine" bodily existence to its socially-referred character, I do feel that this displacement of the "self" onto the "social" realm that both supports and constructs the self is necessary and illuminating not only in accounting for what differentiates "feminine" bodily existence from "masculine" bodily existence (insofar as different types of social reference are operative in each) but also in accounting for what differentiates "black" bodily existence from "white" bodily existence, and "jewish" bodily existence from "catholic" or "muslim" bodily existence, to give but a few examples. In addition, appealing to the particular kind of social reference that contextualizes an individual's movements, comportment, and action in a given situation, also avoids identifying social reference with either immanence or transcendence and encourages a focus on the *type* of social reference operative rather than the *fact* of social reference itself.

Social reference, like self-reference, can just as easily increase as decrease one's confidence in one's bodily abilities and potentialities. It can indeed give rise to the contradictory bodily modalities described by Young when it sets limits to, rather than encourages, the full development of bodily motility and spatiality. Realizing the crucial (and usually invisible) role that social reference plays in mediating our relationships with our bodies, allows us to recognize why it is so difficult to eliminate the contradictory modalities discussed by Young. For doing so successfully must be much more than a cognitive process; indeed, it involves a radical modification of our body images and, therefore, of our corporeal styles. Moreover, pointing to the socially-referred character of our bodily comportment enables us to see why it would be overly simplistic to view bodily habit alone as responsible for the body's resistance to change.

Instead of continuing to focus as so many feminists have done on the need for women to change their often negative relationship to their bodies to a more loving and accepting one (a project that may paradoxically, from Young's perspective, encourage women to accept rather than challenge their bodily "limitations"), an emphasis on the socially-referred character of all types of bodily existence reveals the need for societal change in the way "feminine" bodily existence is identified and differentiated from "masculine" bodily existence in the first place. This latter is a project that Young herself begins to undertake in her three later essays on female embodiment, "Breasted Experience," "Pregnant Embodiment" and "Women Recovering their Clothes" (Young 1990).

In her work on embodiment, Young utilizes a phenomenological approach to describe what initially may seem to be fairly everyday and even innocuous experiences in order both to reveal and challenge what Husserl calls "the natural attitude." "The natural attitude," for Husserl, consists of a set of unquestioned presuppositions about our everyday lives which help to define our expectations regarding a particular event or situation, and which provide a context for determining the significance of that event or situation. By calling it "natural" Husserl does not mean to imply that it is the only possible or even the most desirable set of beliefs, attitudes, and values we can have toward that event or situation, rather, he uses the term "natural" to stress both its taken-for-granted and foundational character.[16] Husserl never questions the putative "naturalness" of the natural attitude; such a Foucaultian, genealogical project is beyond the scope of phenomenology as he conceived it. Nonetheless, if, as both Nietzsche and Foucault suggest, "the natural" itself arises out of historical processes of naturalization and normalization that can indeed be traced genealogically, surely these processes should be amenable to phenomenological description as well.

Through her own phenomenological account of the normalizing, disciplinary practices that come to constitute the "natural" throwing style for girls, the "natural" relationship of mother and fetus, and the "natural" relationship between women and their breasts, Young offers what I take to be a subtle critique of the "naturalness" of "the natural attitude." In particular, the trope of the "split subject" which appears again and again in her essays on female embodiment, challenges the presumed intentional unity of the phenomenological subject that undergirds Husserl's, Heidegger's, Sartre's, Beauvoir's, and much of Merleau-Ponty's work.

Throughout Young's inquiry into the varying meanings of female embodiment as they are expressed through throwing styles, fascination with clothes, pregnancy, and female breasted experience, the notion of the "split subject" is continually evoked though it is never named as such. In "Throwing Like a Girl," Young describes the ways in which the female subject is split between contradictory bodily modalities, between a confident "I can" and a diffident "perhaps I cannot." Here, the "splitting" of the subject is understood negatively by Young insofar as it is responsible for many women's unwillingness to maximize their bodily potentialities. Moreover, Young's description of the "self-referred" character of "feminine" bodily existence also suggests that the reference to the self, both prior to and during one's action, "splits" the subject by breaking up the fluidity and unity of one's action and creating an alienated, objectified perspective on that action. Specifically, Young understands the "splitting" of the subject as involving the creation of an artificial separation between a transcendent subjectivity and an objective, immanent body:

> This objectified bodily existence accounts for the self-consciousness of the feminine relation to her body and resulting distance she takes from her body. As human, she is a transcendence and subjectivity, and cannot live herself as mere bodily object. Thus, to the degree that she does live herself as mere body, she cannot be in unity with herself, but must take a distance from and exist in discontinuity with her body. The objectifying regard that "keeps her in her place" can also account for the spatial modality of being positioned and for why women frequently tend not to move openly, keeping their limbs closed around themselves. To open her body in free, active open extension and bold outward-directedness is for a woman to invite objectification. (Young 1990:155)

Young's final point in this passage is crucial for she suggests that the price of refusing to objectify (and monitor) one's own body may be that others do so instead. On this account, self-objectification and contradictory bodily modalities may very well turn out to be worth the risks entailed (i.e. self-alienation, failure to utilize bodily capabilities to the utmost, etc.) insofar as they anticipate and attempt to preclude societal objectification which is all too often a first step toward more violent forms of bodily aggression (e.g. sexual assault). The "split subject," then, arises in response to a patriarchal social system in which women internalize and respond to the (imaginary and real) responses of (imaginary and real) others to their bodies before, during, and after their action. Overcoming the "splitting" of the subject will therefore involve overcoming the inequities that permeate a patriarchal society in which women continually find

themselves subject to the invisible and omnipresent male gaze that is epitomized (and legitimized) historically through the disciplinary regime of the
panopticon.[17]

At this point, it may seem as if, for Young at least, the "splitting" of the subject is always a negative phenomenon, especially for women, inevitably resulting in contradictory bodily modalities and self-objectification. Indeed, Young is
not the only feminist theorist to address the dangers inherent in this type of self-
fragmentation. In her essay "On Psychological Oppression," Sandra Bartky
defines fragmentation as follows:

> the splitting of the whole person into parts of a person which, in stereotyping,
> may take the form of a war between a "true" and "false" self—or, in sexual objec-
> tification, the form of *an often coerced and degrading identification of a person
> with her body*. . . . (Bartky 1990:23, my emphasis)

According to Bartky, fragmentation is one of two key elements to be found in
all cases of psychological oppression. The second is mystification, "the systematic obscuring of both the reality and agencies of psychological oppression so
that its intended effect, the depreciated self, is lived out as destiny, guilt, or neu-
rosis" (Bartky 1990:23). For both Bartky and Young, then, the "splitting" or fragmentation of the subject can be seen as undermining the integrity and agency
of the self. And, through her discussion of the concomitant phenomenon of
mystification, Bartky also helps us to understand how and why so many women
tend to become "trapped" within this "no-win" situation.

In the above quote, Bartky, like Young, condemns in particular, societal
attempts to "reduce" women to their bodies, that is, to regard them as no more
than bodies. It is important to examine more closely, however, why the identifi-
cation/reduction of a person with/to her body is indeed degrading. While I would
certainly not deny that the experience described by Bartky in this essay of being
whistled and hooted at by unknown men across the street is humiliating, and that
it involves a reductive move whereby the men deliberately attempt to make
Bartky aware that she is *a body on display*, I am concerned about the way in
which identifying the humiliation with being made to feel like a "mere body" or
"a nice piece of ass" itself buys into negative stereotypes about the body which
in turn can reinforce rather than change a negative body image. Two questions
or doubts arise for me in reference to this troubling (and all too common) example: 1) Does an explanation of the humiliation in terms of being reduced to one's
body, or, more accurately, parts of one's body really suffice to account for what
is going on here? 2) In what ways does the feeling of humiliation itself intensify
the experience and bodily consequences of objectification?

To feel humiliated when one is receiving unwanted attention directed at
one's body is understandable in a society in which bodies are a constant source
of ridicule and embarrassment. Every week in the aisles of the grocery store,
magazine headlines "shout" at women (and increasingly, men) with bold

urgency about ways to improve our sagging, overweight, aging bodies. Alternately mocking and beguiling, these "miracle stories" of dramatic weight loss and complete bodily transformation beckon, at one time or another, to the most skeptical among us, if only for a phantasmatic moment as we glance at the accompanying (and inevitable) pictures that give testimony to the reality of what can be accomplished if only one is "willing" (read financially able) to try.[18] Yet, I am not convinced that the experience of objectification or even self-objectification is sufficient to bring about psychological oppression. Nor does fragmentation or the "splitting" of the subject seem to be inevitably a negative phenomenon. If, for instance, we are being singled out for our intelligence alone, would this form of objectification (and reduction) be viewed as humiliating and oppressive? Some might claim that having attention drawn to one's intelligence is not even an instance of objectification. But why not? Objectification is indeed a "dirty word" in our society and many feminists (myself included) have rebelled against Sartre's understanding of being-for-others as always involving objectification. My question is, are there ways of understanding both fragmentation and objectification that are non-oppressive or even self-affirming? Addressing this question is especially crucial if we are to understand the impact that the experiences of fragmentation and objectification have on the development and significance of the body image.

Interestingly enough, it is Young, in her essay "Pregnant Embodiment: Subjectivity and Alienation," who offers an example of a *positive, non-alienating* experience of the "splitting" of the subject in pregnancy. This example is also illuminating because of the noticeable changes in the body image that accompany and reinforce the feelings of being a "split" subject. Moreover, in this essay, Young clearly differentiates her position from that of:

> existential phenomenologists of the body [who] usually assume a distinction between transcendence and immanence as two modes of bodily being. They assume that insofar as I adopt an active relation to the world, I am not aware of my body for its own sake. In the successful enactment of my aims and projects, my body is a transparent medium. For several of these thinkers, awareness of my body as weighted material, as physical, occurs only or primarily when my instrumental relation to the world breaks down, in fatigue or illness. . . . Being brought to awareness of my body for its own sake, these thinkers assume, entails estrangement and objectification. . . . Thus the dichotomy of subject and object appears anew in the conceptualization of the body itself. These thinkers tend to assume that awareness of my body in its weight, massiveness, and balance is always an alienated objectification of my body, in which I am not my body and my body imprisons me. They also tend to assume that such awareness of my body must cut me off from the enactment of my projects; I cannot be attending to the physicality of my body and using it as the means to the accomplishment of my aims. (Young 1990:164)

Young suggests that pregnancy offers a paradigmatic example of "being thrown into awareness of one's body." In pregnancy, she notes, "contrary to the mutually exclusive categorization between transcendence and immanence that underlies some theories, the awareness of my body in its bulk and weight does not impede the accomplishing of my aims"[19] (Young 1990:165). To become aware of my body, especially during the second and third trimesters of pregnancy, is to become aware of the movements of another body inside my body, and this is one of the reasons why the pregnant woman comes to experience herself as a "split" subject. Young argues, moreover, that:

> The pregnant subject . . . is decentered, split, or doubled in several ways. She experiences her body as herself and not herself. Its inner movements belong to another being, yet they are not other, because her body boundaries shift and because her bodily self-location is focused on her trunk in addition to her head. This split subject appears in the eroticism of pregnancy, in which the woman can experience an innocent narcissism fed by recollection of her repressed experience of her own mother's body. Pregnant existence entails, finally, a unique temporality of process and growth in which the woman can experience herself as split between past and future. (Young 1990:161)

Ultimately, for Young, the "splittings" described here can and should be positive bodily experiences for the pregnant woman. Nonetheless, Young also maintains that:

> The integrity of my body is undermined in pregnancy not only by this externality of the inside, but also by the fact that the boundaries of my body are themselves in flux. In pregnancy I literally do not have a firm sense of where my body ends and the world begins. My automatic body habits become dislodged; the continuity between my customary body and my body at this moment is broken. In pregnancy my prepregnant body image does not entirely leave my movements and expectations, yet it is with the pregnant body that I must move. This is another instance of the doubling of the pregnant subject. (Young 1990:163–164)

When Young states, in this passage, that pregnancy undermines bodily integrity, I am led to question what she (and I) mean by bodily integrity in the first place. In the context of this discussion, bodily integrity seems to refer to a more unified, bounded experience of the body and the corresponding presence of a unitary, clearly defined body image. *The Random House Dictionary of the English Language* provides three definitions of integrity: "1. soundness of and adherence to moral principle and character; uprightness; honesty. 2. the state of being whole, entire, or undiminished. 3. a sound, unimpaired, or perfect condition" (1973:738). In everyday usage of the term "integrity," these three alternative definitions are often conflated, with the moral connotation predominating. While Young's use of the term "bodily integrity" is appealing to me insofar as it subverts the identification of the moral connotation of integrity with the mind, I also find it rather problematic because she appeals to the notions of wholeness and closure which historically have constituted a regulative norm for bodily experience. Young is herself critical of the dominant model of health which "assumes that the normal, healthy body is unchanging." "Health" she elaborates:

> is associated with stability, equilibrium, a steady state. Only a minority of persons, however, namely adult men who are not yet old, experience their health as a state in which there is no regular or noticeable change in body condition. For them a noticeable change in their bodily state usually does signal a disruption or dysfunction. Regular, noticeable, sometimes extreme change in bodily condition, on the other hand, is an aspect of the normal bodily functioning of adult women. Change is also a central aspect of the bodily existence of healthy children and healthy old people, as well as some of the so-called disabled. Yet medical conceptualization implicitly uses this unchanging adult male body as the standard of all health. (Young 1990:169)

Thinking back to my own preganices, my changing bodily experiences did not so much undermine as *resignify* bodily integrity; newly emerging bodily rhythms, the temporality Young identifies with process and growth gave both consistency and insistency to even the most unsettling and disruptive aspects of my pregnant existence. What was surprising for me, was that this alternative sense of bodily integrity was realized and even reinforced, rather than diminished, *through* (not in spite of) the continual changes I was experiencing in my body. Fluidity and expansiveness, rather than the myths of wholeness and closure (which I don't believe any of us, male or female, ever truly experience) were the tangible signs of this newly discovered bodily integrity. Paradoxically, I would argue that it was precisely through experiencing the "splittings" that Young describes above, that I first discovered what it means to have a sense of bodily integrity. This is not to say that pregnancy is the only way to achieve the kind of bodily integrity I am talking about here. Rather, what I would argue is that bodily integrity is *created* through developing a greater sensitivity to one's bodily changes, capacities, movements, and gestures, whether these latter involve the more noticeable changes of pregnancy, childbirth, and lactation, or the daily changes that *all* bodies (even those of adult males who are not yet old) continually undergo. On this account, it is not the "splitting" of the subject that undermines bodily integrity, but rather the denial of the co-existence of disparate sensations and movements that threatens the consistency of bodily existence, a consistency that is based, more often than not and in true Heraclitean fashion, upon incomparable and even inconsistent bodily experiences.

Contemporary societal "splittings" of the pregnant subject's maternity from her sexuality, on the other hand, *do* seem to me to be serious threats to the bodily integrity of the pregnant woman. For, in denying that pregnant existence is simultaneously sexual existence, our society seeks to restrict the meaning of both sexuality and the pregnant body to opposite, mutually exclusive poles of existence, not to be occupied by the same person at the same point in time. As Young notes:

> There was a time when the pregnant woman stood as a symbol of stately and sexual beauty. While pregnancy remains an object of fascination, our own culture harshly separates pregnancy from sexuality. The dominant culture defines feminine beauty as slim and shapely. The pregnant woman is often not looked upon as sexually active or desirable, even though her own desires and sensitivity may have increased. (Young 1990:166)

Paradoxically, for Young, this denial of the sexuality of the pregnant woman may afford her a greater degree of freedom from sexual objectification by others. Regarded societally as the "expectant mother," she may find it disturbing that for others her sexuality is denied, "split off" from her current pregnant existence, yet this may also provide her with a welcome "break" from unwanted sexual attention. Nonetheless, what Young doesn't go on to add, is that the pregnant woman may now find herself to be the focus of a different kind of attention that can be quite as unsettling and invasive as the sexual attention she may have experienced formerly. Neither her breasts nor her buttocks, but her abdomen is now subject to the penetrating stare of the other. From the abdomen, the usual trajectory of the other's gaze moves to the "ring" finger on her left hand to "verify" the "legitimacy" of her pregnancy. Depending on whether or not the wedding ring is present, the other's gaze may move on to the pregnant woman's eyes to signal social acceptance and personal approval, or be averted altogether in a gesture of dismissal and disapproval. Alternatively, in the absence of the expected wedding ring, the pregnant woman may find herself under extended surveillance by the other who wonders whether it is the swelling of the fingers that accounts for the missing ring, or a less "desirable" state of affairs.[20]

In the essay, "Women Recovering Our Clothes," Young marks, in yet another register, the split between seeing myself and seeing myself being seen and she fantasizes about the possibility of splitting the former experience away from the latter one. Turning to critical analyses offered by psychoanalytic feminist film theorists that reveal the narrative construction of identity played out in contemporary images of women's clothes, a construction that is always facilitated by the "voyeuristic gaze of the other," Young confronts a dilemma:

> It's all true, I guess; at least I cannot deny it: In clothes I seek to find the approval of the transcending male gaze; in clothing I seek to transform myself into a bewitching object that will capture his desire and identity. When I leaf through magazines and catalogs I take my pleasure from imagining myself perfected and beautiful and sexual for the absent or mirrored male gaze. I take pleasure in these images of female bodies in their clothes because my own gaze occupies the

position of the male gaze insofar as I am a subject at all. I will not deny it, but it leaves a hollowness in me. If I simply affirm this, I must admit that for me there is no subjectivity that is not his, that there is no specifically female pleasure I take in clothes. (Young 1990:180)

Can a woman experience narcissistic pleasure in looking at, fantasizing about, and wearing clothes, that is not mediated by an omnipresent male gaze and phallic desire? In addition, can narcissism itself be resignified, so that its connotations of immaturity, self-absorption, and petty vanity are superseded by the three focii of Young's own analysis, namely, touch, bonding, and fantasy? Last, but not least, what role do clothes and clothing images play in the development of the body image?

In her discussion of the erotic, communal, and imaginative possibilities offered to women by clothes, Young succeeds in giving voice to a nonphallic, specular pleasure that refuses to be circumscribed by the omnivorous male gaze. Following Irigaray, Young claims that "touch immerses the subject in fluid continuity with the object, and for the touching subject the object touched reciprocates the touching, blurring the border between self and other" (Young 1990:182). "By touch" she adds,

> I do mean that specific sense of skin on matter, fingers on texture. But I also
> mean an orientation to sensuality as such that includes all senses. Thus we
> might conceive a mode of vision, for example, that is less a gaze, distanced from
> and mastering its object, but an immersion in light and color. Sensing as touch-
> ing is within, experiencing what touches it as ambiguous, continuous, but never-
> theless differentiated. (Young 1990:182)

While Merleau-Ponty emphasizes the chiasmatic relationship between touching and touched, a relationship marked by a reversibility in which that which touches is simultaneously touched in turn, he nonetheless reminds us of the nonreducibility of these disparate experiences. In an important sense, for Merleau-Ponty, the touching/touched experiences are always dual, never singular. "But" he asserts,

> this incessant escaping, this impotency to superpose exactly upon one another
> the touching of the things by my right hand and the touching of this same right
> hand by my left hand, or to superpose, in the exploratory movements of the
> hand, the tactile experience of a point and that of the "same" point a moment
> later, or the auditory experience of my own voice and that of other voices—this is
> not a failure. For if these experiences never exactly overlap, if they slip away at
> the very moment they are about to rejoin, if there is always a "shift," [bougé] a
> "spread," [écart] between them, this is precisely because my two hands are part
> of the same body, because it moves itself in the world, because I hear myself
> both from within and from without. I experience—and as often as I wish—the

transition and the metamorphosis of the one experience in to the other, and it is only as though the hinge between them, solid, unshakeable, remained irremediably hidden from me. But this hiatus between my right hand touched and my right hand touching, between my voice heard and my voice uttered, between one moment of my tactile life and the following one, is not an ontological void, a non-being: it is spanned by the total being of my body, and by that of the world; it is the zero of pressure between two solids that makes them adhere to one another. (Merleau-Ponty 1968:148; 1964:194)

Later on, in a "Working Note" (dated May 1960), Merleau-Ponty complicates our understanding of this "hinge" or "hiatus" which both separates and brings together the experiences of touching and being touched. "Something else than the body" he argues,

is needed for the junction to be made: it takes place in the *untouchable*. That of the other which I will never touch. But what I will never touch, he does not touch either, no privilege of oneself over the other here, it is therefore not the *consciousness* that is the untouchable—"The consciousness" would be something positive, and with regard to it there would recommence, does recommence, the duality of the reflecting and the reflected, like that of the touching and the touched. The untouchable is not a touchable in fact inaccessible—the unconscious is not a representation in fact inaccessible. The negative here is not a *positive that is elsewhere* (a transcendent). . . . The negativity that inhabits the touch (and which I must not minimize: it is because of it that the body is not an empirical fact, that it has an ontological signification), the untouchable of the touch, the invisible of vision, the unconscious of consciousness (its central *punctum caecum*, that blindness that makes it consciousness i.e. an indirect and *inverted* grasp of all things) is the *other side* or the *reverse* (or the other dimensionality) of sensible Being; one cannot say that it is *there*, although there would assuredly be points where it *is not*—It is there with a presence by investment in another dimensionality, with a "double-bottomed" presence the flesh, the *Leib*, is not a sum of *self-touchings* (of "tactile sensations"), but not a sum of tactile sensations plus "kinestheses" either, it is an "I can"—The corporeal schema would not be a *schema* if it were not this contact of *self* with *self* (which is rather non-difference) (common presentation to . . . X). (Merleau-Ponty 1968:254–255)

I quote these rather long and "murky" passages, to illustrate Merleau-Ponty's own shifting understanding of tactility and his fascination with what he alternatively calls the "hinge," the "hiatus," and the "junction," that phantasmatic non-place where touching and touched, body and world come together in and through their differentiation. Refusing, as does Young, to privilege one person's touching over that of another, Merleau-Ponty invokes a nontranscendent untouchable that is neither consciousness nor the unconscious, self or other, body or world, touching or touched.

How, exactly, does this chiasmatic encounter between touched and touching grounded upon the nonground of the untouchable come to be expressed in the body image or corporeal schema as an "I can"? Is the body image of the touching body different than the body image of the touched body? Is the body image itself a "split" phenomenon? And if so, what are its (bodily) effects? If, as Young is suggesting above, clothes offer us a tactile experience that is ambiguous, continuous, *and* differentiated at once, how might this experience provide a counterpoint to a Merleau-Pontian understanding of the body image?

We have already noted Young's challenge to Merleau-Ponty's positive conception of the body image as a confident "I can" through her discussion, in "Throwing Like a Girl," of both the societal and self-imposed constraints placed upon women's bodies in contemporary patriarchal societies. In "Women Recovering Our Clothes," I would argue, Young is seeking to discover, like Merleau-Ponty, that which is "untouchable" within our tactile experience, that which cannot be reduced to, or superseded by, a dialectic between self and other. In this same Working Note of May 1960, Merleau-Ponty further explores the meaning of tactility and visibility through the phenomenon of specularity which underlies them both. He suggests that the "fission" (écart) between touching and touched, seeing and being seen, actually produces (rather than undermines) a strong sense of self. "The flesh" he notes,

> is a mirror phenomenon and the mirror is an extension of my relation with my body. . . . To touch oneself, to see oneself, is to obtain . . . a specular extract of oneself. I.e. fission of appearance and Being—a fission that already takes place in the touch (duality of the touching and the touched) and which, with the mirror (Narcissus) is only a more profound adhesion to Self. (Merleau-Ponty 1968:255–256)

Without the duality of touching and touched, seeing and (being) seen, Merleau-Ponty implies, narcissism would itself become an impossibility. And, although all narcissism may indeed be mediated by the presence and perspective of others, this need not mean that the specular confirmation offered by the mirror is reducible to how we are seen by these others. Nor, as Young subtly points out, need we experience the perspective of others through the alienating model of the voyeuristic gaze.

In "Women Recovering Our Clothes," Young describes a nonantagonistic, mutually affirming relationship between women that can be achieved through such banal narcissistic experiences as trying on clothes *together*, looking, perhaps, in the same dressing room mirror, sharing the possibility of self-transformation in the process:

There they chat to one another about their lives and self-images as they try on outfits. . . . Women buy often enough on these expeditions, but often they walk out of the store after an hour of dressing up with no parcels at all; the pleasure was in the choosing, trying, and talking, a mundane shared fantasy. (Young 1990:184)

For Young, the untouchable nonrealm invoked by Merleau-Ponty, a non-realm that is neither consciousness nor the unconscious, is itself a site of fantasy. "Clothing images" Young asserts, "are not always the authoritative mirror that tells who's the fairest of them all, but the entrance to a wonderland of characters and situations" (Young 1990:184). By focusing in on the lack of coincidence between touching and being touched, and, more specifically, on the imaginative possibilities that arise in the gap between touching (oneself and others through) clothes and being touched by them, Young seeks liberating fantasies for women that are nonvoyeuristic and nonoppressive, fantasies that allow us to revalue the mundane narcissistic pleasures of "dressing up," of wearing a favorite outfit, of window shopping with friends.

In her final essay on female embodiment, "Breasted Experience," Young leads us further away from a purely narcissistic interpretation of being concerned with one's appearance by concentrating on the need for an expansion of our *societal* imagination. She argues here that society must endeavor to create positive images of the one-breasted woman, images that would offer an alternative to the current practice of hiding mastectomy (another type of "splitting" of the subject) through surgical implants and/or breast "reconstructions."

Before moving on to consider Young's description of female breasted experience and how it affects our body images, let us examine more closely what she has to say about fantasy. Contrary to Judith Butler's emphasis upon the *morphological imaginary*, a phrase which itself highlights the materiality of this traditionally immaterial (in both senses of the word) domain, Young seems to accept the classic equation of fantasy with that which is unreal or desubstantialized even while she argues for the important role that fantasy plays in women's lives:[21]

Part of the pleasure of clothes for many of us consists of allowing ourselves to fantasize with images of women in clothes, and in desiring to become an image, unreal, to enter an intransitive, playful utopia. There are ways of looking at oneself in the mirror that do not appraise oneself before the objectifying gaze, but rather desubstantialize oneself, turn oneself into a picture, an image, an unreal identity. In such fantasy we do not seek to be somebody else. Fantasizing is not wishing, hoping, or planning; it has no future. The clothing image provides the image of situations without any situatedness; there is an infinite before and after; thus the images are open at both ends to an indefinite multitude of possible transformations. (Young 1990:186)

Although I appreciate the care with which Young distinguishes fantasy from wishing, hoping, or planning, I am troubled by the way in which the body disappears altogether in this description of both fantasy and the phantasmatic image. To claim, as Young does, that "the clothing image provides the image of situations without any situatedness" implies that the clothing image is itself disembodied, a phantom that frees us from our own corporeality. Once again, and despite earlier arguments to the contrary, it seems as if Young is accepting a more immanent view of the body, as if the body is a material prison that our fantasies can allow us to escape. In contrast, what I would emphasize is that when I am trying on clothes before the mirror, the clothing images that I create and fantasize about, are images of my clothed *body*. Furthermore, I would argue, the self-transformations I explore through these fantasies offer so much narcissistic pleasure precisely because they are not unreal or desubstantialized, but rather, because they are materialized through my body and because they hold out the possibility of *resituating* myself within my existing situation.

Reinforcing her disembodied view of fantasy, images, and the imagination, Young goes on to identify women's fantasies of themselves and other women in clothes with aesthetic freedom, "the freedom to play with shape and color on the body, to don various styles and looks, and through them exhibit and imagine unreal possibilities." "Women" she adds,

> often actively indulge in theatrical imagining, which is largely closed to the everyday lives of men or which they live vicariously through the clothes of women. Such female imagination has liberating possibilities because it subverts, unsettles the order to respectable, functional rationality in a world where that rationality supports domination. The unreal that wells up through imagination always creates the space for a negation of what is, and thus the possibility of alternatives. (Young 1990:186)

There are several problems with this account of what Young calls "female imagination" that are brought to the fore in this particular passage.[22] First of all, Young not only tacitly sets up the body as an adversary to be overcome through aesthetic freedom which will allow us to "exhibit and imagine unreal possibilities," but she also suggests that "female imagination" is at odds with "respectable, functional rationality," inadvertently supporting, rather than subverting, traditional stereotypes about women's "inherent" irrationality. If this "irrational" (at least from the standpoint of rationality) female imaginary "creates the space for a negation of what is," how are we to understand this space and the alternatives it is supposed to offer if we are ourselves "desubstantialized," turned "into a picture, an image, an unreal identity?" That is, how can self-transformation (much less social transformation) be realized in such a non-material fashion?

Unlike the depiction of fantasy as irreal that is presented in "Women Recovering Our Clothes," in "Breasted Experience," Young does present a more *cor-*

poreal fantasy of the new possibilities that can and should be made available to women who have had a breast removed. Rather than attempt to deny (as many physicians and concerned friends and family have done) that a woman's breasts are central to her bodily existence, Young maintains that "for many women, if not all, breasts are an important component of body self-image; a woman may love them or dislike them, but she is rarely neutral" (Young 1990:189). Just as Beauvoir, in *The Second Sex*, points out the contradictions that permeate the "many-faced myth" of Woman, so too, Young explores the contradictions that constitute what she calls the "breast ideal":

> What matters is the look of them, how they measure up before the normalizing gaze. There is one perfect shape and proportion for breasts: round, sitting high on the chest, large but not bulbous, with the look of firmness. The norm is contradictory, of course. If breasts are large, their weight will tend to pull them down; if they are large and round, they will tend to be floppy rather than firm. In its image of the solid object *this norm suppresses the fleshy materiality of breasts,* this least muscular, softest body part. (Young 1990:191, my emphasis)

The bra, Young argues, aids in the dematerializing normalization of women's breasts, both by "lifting and curving the breasts to approximate the one and only breast ideal" and by hiding the presence of the nipples, those "no-nos" that "show the breasts to be active and independent zones of sensitivity and eroticism" (Young 1990:195–196).

Plastic surgery also facilitates the realization of patriarchal culture's phantasmatic breast ideal, not only through breast reconstructions after mastectomy, but through the increasingly popular surgical procedures of breast reduction, breast augmentation, and breast "lifts." For women with the money and desire to undergo the necessary (and extremely painful) medical procedures, the "perfect breasts" may indeed seem to be a practical option, however many of the women who do undergo these operations are not prepared for the long-term bodily effects, which can include inability to lactate and nurse a baby, lack of sensitivity in the breasts, infections, bruising, and recurrent pain (Young 1990:201).

Women who lack the money for cosmetic surgery, but who nonetheless desire "perfect breasts," can try any number of physical regimes and/or can mail away for special apparatuses advertised in the grocery store magazines, all of which promise to transform breasts one is (and, they imply, ought to be) ashamed of into objects of pride. It is patriarchal culture, Young asserts, that "constructs breasts as objects, the correlate of the objectifying male gaze" (Young 1990:200). Not only the breasts, but abdomens, buttocks, thighs, calves, upper arms, and other body parts are often isolated and subjected to rigorous disciplinary practices, practices which are presented as forms of "body maintenance," in order to allow the body to approximate its particular gendered ideal.[23] In the end, Young implies, the possibility of distinguishing between a female and a social imaginary is obliterated since, "there is little choice of what body to value; the normalized body is reinforced by the transformative possibilities of medical technology. Why wouldn't a woman "choose" perfect breasts when the opportunity is there?" (Young 1990:201).

Young finds breast enlargement to be, on the whole, more problematic from a feminist standpoint than breast reduction. This is because the latter operation is often done to decrease back pain, and/or to allow women to participate comfortably in everyday physical activities. By implication, Young suggests that breast augmentation lacks these more "worthy" motivations, and that the women who undergo it transform their own breasts into commodities that they (literally) purchase in order to achieve the phallocentric breast ideal.

And yet, what Young doesn't acknowledge is that breast reduction is as problematic as breast enlargement as far as sexual objectification is concerned. Both the woman whose breasts are perceived to be (by herself as well as others) "too small," and the one whose breasts are viewed as "too large," suffer enormously for these bodily "inadequacies." While the attainment of the "perfect breasts" through plastic surgery or some other nonmedical means may seem to play into sexual objectification, these operations may just as often appear to the women who undergo them as ways of *relieving* sexual objectification, that is, ways of drawing attention away from their breasts through their "normalization."[24]

Breast loss, according to Young, is indeed a trauma not only because of the split the surgeon's knife creates in the body, but also because of the corresponding (and usually less expected), rupture experienced in one's self and body image. Precisely because the breasts are identified by phallocratic society as the *visible* site of a woman's sexuality, the loss of a breast is societally interpreted as a corresponding loss in sexuality.[25] Moreover, the socially-referred character that we earlier discussed in relation to women's bodily experiences, all but guarantees that individual women who have undergone mastectomies will internalize the societal notion that one's sexuality and sexual appeal are diminished with the removal of one's breast. "Julia,"[26] a heterosexual woman who has undergone a mastectomy and who gives an autobiographical account of her feelings about it in Wendy Chapkis' book, *Beauty Secrets: Women and the Politics of Appearance*, reveals the strength of these societally-induced fears:

> Then came the mastectomy and my sense that that was it for casual sex. Feeling that men wouldn't be able to deal with it. That I wouldn't be able to deal with it. *I couldn't even fantasize.* I felt that if my relationship ever ended, and I wanted to get intensely involved with someone new, then of course I would deal with it. But there would always be something that One Would Have To Deal With. (Chapkis 1986:154, my emphasis)

"Julia's" inability to fantasize highlights the intimate relationship between the imaginary and the functionings (and disfunctionings) of the body. "Julia" "recovers" her sexuality after having sex with an old lover (albeit with her shirt on) who helps her to realize that she is still sexually attractive. In a way, it is not surprising that the affirmation of her sexuality, to be effective for her, cannot come from the reassurances of her partner but must come from someone outside the relationship, someone who is not beholden to her in any way. Moreover, the sexuality that is affirmed does not eradicate "Julia's" preoccupation with something that has to be dealt with; her decision to keep her chest hidden from this particular lover makes it clear that the sexuality that has been recovered is recovered *despite* her mastectomy rather than through a joint exploration of the new erotic possibilities the mastectomy may offer.

Phallocentric perceptions regarding the desexualizing character of mastectomy are internalized not only by heterosexual women, but by many lesbians as well. Although "Cathy," another woman who offers in Chapkis' book a personal account of the effect of her mastectomy on her life, attributes the extensive support she received after her operation to her lesbian community, she too, narrates her and her lover's fears about the effect the mastectomy would have on her sexuality. Not surprisingly, "Cathy" discovers "that straight people were much more threatened by me with one breast than were lesbians. Men in particular seem threatened by 'unwhole' women" (Chapkis 1986:26). Her surgeon, in fact, was very upset by her decision not to get implants or wear a prosthesis. "The oddest thing about this conversation," "Cathy" notes,

> was that there was nothing I could say to silence him. He gently told me that he had seen "many a marriage flounder on the shoals of a mastectomy." If I said "I don't need this discussion because I am a lesbian" it would sound as if lesbians don't care about how they look. I felt totally trapped listening to him go on and on. (Chapkis 1986:26)

From "Cathy's" perspective, the primary motivation for buying a prosthesis is "to keep people from being threatened by anyone looking physically different" (Chapkis 1986:26). And, she pragmatically points out, this is hardly a good enough reason to go out and spend the six or seven hundred dollars necessary to own one. Nonetheless, "Cathy" also acknowledges that:

> Constantly confronting sexism is exhausting. You can't do it non-stop. So you make compromises. But I make compromises to make myself comfortable, not other people. It is either their reactions or my feelings. I'm not willing to try to make other people less uncomfortable with the fact that I have had cancer and have one breast. Why the hell should I take care of them? I'm the one whose feelings should be protected. (Chapkis 1986:27)

A photograph that appears in the middle of "Cathy's" story, shows a naked woman with one breast, arms outstretched to the sunny sky above, head back soaking in the rays and warmth of the sun. She appears relaxed, triumphant, and joyful, and where the scar marking her "missing" breast would be, an undulating garland of flowers appears. "Deena," the woman photographed, is the very picture of confident sensuality and contentment, and she best illus-trates, I think, the positive body images that Iris Young would like to see real-ized for all one- (and two-) breasted women. Unlike "Julia" and "Cathy," we are not made privy to "Deena's" story; we do not know how she has managed to overcome the substantial cultural obstacles that prevent so many women from loving themselves, loving others, and being loved with one breast. We also do not know if her confidence and contentment will stay with her throughout her life, as she deals with the inevitable responses of others to what our culture regards as her "unfortunate tragedy." Nonetheless, what makes "Deena" such a powerful and riveting figure, is her proud affirmation of her one-breasted body, an affirmation that is achieved in and through the splitting of her breast from her body, a splitting that allows rather than denies her new bodily possibilities. In this photograph, "Deena" lives out what for many of us is a utopian fantasy. In her erotic embodiment of this fantasy, "Deena" alters the morphology of our own imaginaries, and thereby expands the power and range of our body images.

The criticisms of Young's work that I have raised above are not intended to and cannot take away from the landmark contribution her essays on embodi-ment have made to feminist phenomenology. These essays open up a rich ter-rain completely ignored by Schilder, Merleau-Ponty, and others who have explored the development and significance of the body image. What Young succeeds in demonstrating, above all, is that there is no such thing as *the* body image, though she accomplishes this in a much different way than Schilder. For, what Young emphasizes is that it is always *her* or *his* body image that we are talking about, fantasizing about, and altering through our bodily discourse with one another. Throughout these essays, Young lovingly engenders the body image, embracing its fluidity, multiple possibilities, and resistance to constrict-ing cultural forces. What Young amply demonstrates is that the "splitting" of the subject through contradictory bodily modalities, pregnancy, the inevitable disparity between seeing myself and being seen, and mastectomy is unable to negate our bodily possibilities once and for all; rather, depending on our own responses to these experiences, it may even enhance them.

Mask/Reality, Martina Shenal (gum bichromate print, 1986)

{3}

Morphological Fantasies

Imaginary Schemas, Corporeal Fluidity,
and Sexual Difference

The body manifests the stigmata of past experience and also gives
rise to desires, failings, and errors. These elements may join in a
body where they achieve a sudden expression, but as often, their
encounter is an engagement in which they efface each other,
where the body becomes the pretext of their insurmountable
conflict.

— Michel Foucault (1984:83)

But biology cannot be regarded as a form whose contents are historically provided, nor as a base on which cultural constructs are
founded, nor indeed as a container for a mixture of culturally or
individually specific ingredients. It is an open materiality, a set of
(possibly infinite) tendencies and potentialities which may be
developed, yet whose development will necessarily hinder or
induce other developments and other trajectories. These are not
individually or consciously chosen, nor are they amenable to will
or intentionality: they are more like bodily styles, habits, practices,
whose logic entails that one preference, one modality excludes or
makes difficult other possibilities.

— Elizabeth Grosz (1994:191)

The internalization of representations of the female body by
women is fundamental to the formation of feminine identity, but
this process is not straightforward and unproblematic. It is by map-
ping the way in which the body circumscribes subjectivity that feminists can begin to describe how gender is constitutive of identity,
while, at the same time, never determines it completely.

— Lois McNay (1991:129–130)

Images of the Body Image

As we attend to the respective insights of phenomenologists, psychoanalysts,
and feminist theorists regarding body images, it is important to take stock of the
different images of the body image their discourses present to us. From a phenomenological perspective, what is especially striking about body images is the

fact that they are at once exceedingly personalized and extremely anonymous or prepersonal in their functioning. Body images are always images of a *particular* body, a body that is different from all others and that is lived in idiosyncratic ways. And yet, body images actively structure our movements and gestures without our consciously being aware that they are doing so. Their anonymity ensures their efficacy, but it also helps to mask the central role that our body images play from one moment to the next in our everyday life.

Psychoanalysis offers us an account of the development of the body image in terms of a series of libidinal investments (and divestments) directed toward specific body parts, zones, and regions. Through their participation in the same libidinal economy, body images are able to communicate with one another, a communication whose effects can best be seen in the processes of identification, projection, and introjection that characterize what Schilder calls body-image intercourse.

Feminist theorists such as Young, Butler, Grosz, and Irigaray challenge both phenomenological and psychoanalytic portrayals of the body image by disrupting the (unwritten) assumption that the anonymity of the body image makes it a gender-neutral phenomenon, and by contesting the universality of a libidinal economy in which female sexuality can only be understood as "lacking." In addition, their work as well as the work of Susan Bordo and numerous others, points us toward a more satisfactory understanding of the complex interconnections that continually occur among body images, body image ideals, images of the female body (especially those that are presented to us through advertisements, films, the newspapers, and other forms of mass media), and the cultural imaginary that actively supports them.[1] Through systemic critiques of the hidden presuppositions that guide both the construction and the significance of these various images, feminist theory offers us a way of expanding the cultural imaginary to include what are as yet only phantasmatic possibilities for corporeal and intercorporeal transformation.

Images, claims Michèle Le Doeuff, "are not, properly speaking, 'what I think,' but rather, 'what I think with,' or again 'that by which what I think is able to define itself'" (quoted in Morris 1988:83). In this chapter, I explore what Le Doeuff calls the "profundity" of our body images, an expression that Meaghan Morris associates with the ability of images "to serve as agents of definition in a particular discursive process" (Morris 1988:83). With respect to our body images, in particular, I am using the term profundity to refer to their own depth and corporeal intensity as these are revealed through a feminist lens. Although Merleau-Ponty, Schilder, Lacan and others have stressed the importance of the imaginary in shaping and defining our respective bodily realities, they have failed to offer a critical analysis of the imaginary as an ongoing site of cultural contestation. It is only through this latter analysis, moreover, that we can develop an adequate understanding of how the imaginary both produces and is produced by its own images.

To interrogate the relationship between the body image and the imaginary, is, in a sense, "to boldly go where no man has gone before"; it is to enter an uncharted territory in which the very terms "the imaginary" and "the body image" are themselves up for grabs. The women who serve as both theoretical and practical guides in this project, are themselves well aware of the pitfalls and dangers that confront such an endeavor. For, to open up and test the limits of the binary cultural fantasies that define male and female, masculine and feminine, heterosexual and homosexual, white and black, young and old bodies is, at the same time, to undermine radically all attempts to ground our identities upon them. To the extent that the inexorable search for identity can and must continue, the goal is to discover new, more fluid foundations, ones that genuinely make possible the kind of "eidetic variation" that was once sought (albeit in a less corporeal register) by Husserl.

Exploring the corporeal possibilities that have been foreclosed by a given culture's own imaginary, itself helps to bring into being a new imaginary—one that does justice to the richness of our bodily differences. Changing the body image, I maintain, must involve changes in the imaginary which situates the body image within a vast horizon of possible significances. To change the imaginary, we must in turn create new images of the body, dynamic images of non-docile bodies that resist the readily available techniques of corporeal inscription and normalization that currently define "human reality." We must also recognize that these new images may be no more "liberating" than the old ones; newness is itself no guarantee of anything. Rather, what is at stake here is a reconceptualization of the "immateriality" of fantasy and the "intransigence" of reality; as fantasies are materialized and "reality" becomes phantasmatic, alternative metaphysics become possible; metaphysics which adequately account for the processes of construction, destruction, and reconstruction that are constitutive of human corporeality.

Dreams, Imagination, and Images

In his 1954 preface to Ludwig Binswanger's 1930 essay, "Dream and Existence," entitled, "Dream, Imagination and Existence," Foucault argues that:

> The imaginary world has its own laws, its specific structures, and the image is somewhat more than the immediate fulfillment of meaning. It has its own density, and the laws which govern it are not solely significant propositions, just as the laws of the world are not simply decrees of will, even a divine will. Freud caused the world of the imaginary to be inhabited by Desire as classical metaphysics caused the world of physics to be inhabited by Divine Will and Understanding: a theology of meanings, in which the truth anticipates its own formulations and completely constitutes them. The meanings exhaust the reality of the world which displays that reality. (Foucault 1993:35)

By failing to do justice to the morphology of the imaginary and to the density of its images, "[p]sychoanalysis," Foucault succinctly states, "has never succeeded in making images speak" (Foucault 1993:36). Turning to Husserlian phenomenology, and, in particular, to an incipient theory of expression that Foucault locates in Husserl's 1914 revision of the Sixth Logical Investigation, Foucault maintains that "[p]henomenology," unlike psychoanalysis, "has succeeded in making images speak; but it has given no one the possibility of understanding their language" (Foucault 1993:42).[2]

In this early, critical assessment of the respective limitations of psychoanalysis and phenomenology, Foucault offers an account of two different kinds of images, those that "trap" the imagination and those that "fulfill" it. Although this leads, in my view, to a false dilemma insofar as it relies upon a problematic distinction between alienating, subjective images and objective, stylistic expressions that is ultimately untenable, Foucault's discussion of the relationship between the image and the imagination is valuable insofar as it seeks to dismantle the referential relationship that is ordinarily posited between the image and reality.[3] Through a poignant reworking of Sartre's famous example of the absent Pierre from *Being and Nothingness*, Foucault argues against a traditional understanding of the imaginary as designating an "absent presence" or irreal in order to demonstrate that, on the contrary, it is "through the imaginary that the original meaning of reality is disclosed" (Foucault 1993:69).

What is the "original meaning of reality" that the imaginary reveals? The answer, Foucault suggests, is to be discovered through the dream, which:

> unveils, in its very principle, the ambiguity of the world which at one and the same time designates the existence projected into it and outlines itself objectively in experience. By breaking with the objectivity which fascinates waking consciousness and by reinstating the human subject in its radical freedom, the dream discloses paradoxically the movement of freedom toward the world, the point of origin from which freedom makes itself world. The cosmogony of the dream is the origination itself of existence. (Foucault 1993:51)

Surprisingly surrealist in his depiction of the dream as uniquely revelatory of human existence, and simultaneously existentialist in his understanding of human existence as world-production made possible through human freedom, Foucault chastizes psychoanalysis for exploring "only one dimension of the dream universe, that of its symbolic vocabulary, which from beginning to end transmutes a determining past into a present that symbolizes it" (Foucault 1993:56). For Foucault, the dream does not offer us a new world, or even a symbolic understanding of an existing world, rather, the dream is "the world at the dawn of its first explosion when the world is still existence itself and is not yet the universe of objectivity" (Foucault 1993:59). Through the analyses of dreams, fantasies, and deliriums, Foucault argues, we can see how space and time themselves combine and symbolize "each other to constitute a universe" (Foucault 1993:62).

In what is perhaps the most famous passage from this early essay, Foucault maintains that:

> we must reverse our familiar perspective. Strictly speaking, the dream does not point to an archaic image, a phantasm, or a hereditary myth as its constituting elements; these are not its prime matter, and they do not constitute its ultimate significance. On the contrary, every act of imagination points implicitly to the dream. The dream is not a modality of the imagination, the dream is the first condition of its possibility. (Foucault 1993:66–67)

As the originary condition of the possibility of the imagination, the dream inaugurates an existential order and significance which, Foucault is suggesting, is both prior to and constitutive of "reality" as well as "objectivity." Although it is beyond the scope of my analysis to explore the ramifications of these bold claims, claims which themselves seem quite at odds with the more cautionary, discursive truths that characterize the later Foucault, I cite them here in order to set the stage for a discussion of the productive power of the imagination, and more specifically, to explore this latter's material effects as they are registered in the morphology of the body image. Most notably, by tracing the productive power of the imagination to the dream rather than to a preexisting "reality," Foucault paves the way for a non-substance-based (but nonetheless material) metaphysics, such as the metaphysics of fluidity later developed by Luce Irigaray.

When the imagination becomes entrapped in its images, as in morbid fantasies and hallucinations, Foucault argues that "the dimension of the imaginary has collapsed" (1993:72). According to Foucault, the goal of psychotherapy in such cases must be to "free" the imagination from its (deathly) fascination with images, that is, to enable the imagination to dream once more (Foucault 1993:73–74). Such dreaming, he implies, would disrupt the hold of any one image or set of images upon the imagination by hearkening back to the preobjective origins of human existence, where significations are not yet fixed, but are nonetheless present in all of their multiplicity, contradictions, and fluidity.

In a move that anticipates Julia Kristeva's emphasis on the semiotic power of poetic language, Foucault maintains that the poetic imagination does not become enmeshed in its images, rather, the very multiplicity of the images it generates enables the poetic imagination to avoid being overly invested in any one of them. The creativity of this poetic imagination, Foucault asserts, stems from its destructive power; more specifically, its power to destroy or consume its images rather than to promote or reunite them (Foucault 1993:72).[4] It is precisely when our images become fixed, he suggests, that they must be destroyed before they bring about the destruction of the imagination itself.[5]

At the end of "Dream, Imagination and Existence," Foucault argues that what Binswanger has:

> brought to light regarding dreams is the fundamental moment where the move-
> ment of existence discovers the decisive point of bifurcation between those
> images in which it becomes alienated in a pathological subjectivity, and expres-
> sions in which it fulfills itself in an objective history. The imaginary is the
> milieu, the "element," of this choice. (Foucault 1993:74–75)

Is there a "decisive point of bifurcation" between these two kinds of images, however? And, are these our only two choices, pathological subjectivity or Hegelian objectivity? In contrast to the fixed images that alienate and ultimately seek to destroy the imagination, Foucault here invokes a different kind of image, one which "fulfills" the movement of existence by bringing it to the "fullness of presence" of objective expression. Although earlier on in the essay, Foucault offers a rudimentary genealogy of objectivity through a description of the existential trajectory whereby human freedom establishes a world, a trajectory both enacted and revealed through the dream, now Foucault problematically depicts this self-same objectivity, in the form of objective expression, as the "natural," teleological and nonalienating fulfillment of existence, albeit one that is accomplished in and through the imaginary. On what grounds, exactly, are we to distinguish the alienating images that produce a pathological subjectivity from the expressive images that, he notes, achieve their "meaning in a 'style,' if one may understand by that term the originative movement of the imagination when it becomes 'the Visage willing to exchange'" (Foucault 1993:74)?

Surprisingly, it is Binswanger who, twenty-four years before the publication of Foucault's preface, offers us a way out of this dilemma through his Kierkegaardian affirmation of:

> the "passion of inwardness" by virtue of which subjectivity must work itself
> through objectivity (the objectivity of communication, intelligibility, submission
> to a transsubjective norm) and out of it again. . . . (Binswanger 1993:101)

Rather than attempting to distinguish between different kinds of images, and to locate in these images the power to destroy or fulfill the imagination, Binswanger stresses the creative agency by means of which one establishes oneself as a subject capable of transforming dreams into an inner life-history:

> An individual turns from mere self-identity to becoming a self or "the individ-
> ual," and the dreamer awakens in that unfathomable moment when he decides
> not only to seek to know "what hit him," but seeks also to strike into and take
> hold of the dynamics in these events, "himself"—the moment, that is, when he
> resolves to bring continuity or consequence into a life that rises and falls, falls
> and rises. Only then does he *make* something. That which he makes, however, is

> not life—this the individual can not make—but history . . . . What he actually
> makes is the history of his own life, his inner life-history. . . . (Binswanger
> 1993:102)

Paradoxically, it is by reading Foucault's 1954 preface to Binswanger's "Dream and Existence" through Binswanger's 1930 essay, and not the other way around, that Foucault's emphasis upon objective expression as imaginative fulfillment can be displaced, in favor of a more satisfactory understanding of the imaginative movement whereby life is transformed into existence. Moreover, through an exploration of the morphological structure of the imaginary, a morphology that is itself shaped by cultural practices, social norms, familial expectations, and religious values, we can attain a much richer and more accurate grasp of the constitution of an inner life-history that is, in the final analysis, always *his* or *her* life-history, in short, the life-history of a corporeal subject imaginatively/materially marked by sexual difference. To embark upon this analysis requires moving beyond the rudimentary, existential accounts provided by Foucault and Binswanger in these essays, accounts which emphasize an individual's freedom to "make" history but do not adequately acknowledge the cultural forces that both constrain and enable that freedom.[6] Far from offering us the "original meaning of reality," the imaginary, Judith Butler argues, must itself be understood as a hegemonic cultural production, a production which "constitutes itself through the naturalization of an exclusionary heterosexual morphology" (Butler 1993:91).

Alternative Imaginary Schemas

At the end of the second chapter of *Bodies that Matter*, Butler calls for a "displacement of the hegemonic symbolic of (heterosexist) sexual difference and the critical release of alternative imaginary schemas for constituting sites of erotogenic pleasure" (Butler 1993:91). What is at stake in the production of these alternative imaginary schemas, however, is far more than the constitution (and reconstitution) of sites of erotogenic pleasure. For, Butler suggests, the very articulation of such subversive imaginary schemas (of which the "lesbian phallus" is a prime example) destabilizes the heterosexist presumptions that delimit the significative possibilities of our bodies within the Symbolic domain. This destabilization occurs, not through the simple replacement of one imaginary schema with another (as if that was even possible, or, ultimately, desirable), but through a complex process according to which we imaginatively inhabit the performative exclusions that produce the fiction of a unified subject.

After a brief discussion of morphology and the possibilities and fears that this term invokes when it is used in reference to corporeal transformation, I will examine in some depth Butler's account of how the body is itself constructed through an imaginary schema and will show why this (Lacanian) claim does not at all entail that the body is an imaginary construction. Next, I will explore the corporeal implications of Butler's provocative suggestion that through the creative deployment of alternative imaginary schemas, both "anatomy—and sexual difference itself—[can be opened up] as a site of proliferative resignifications" (Butler 1993:89). To begin my examination of the resignificatory potential of alternative imaginary schemas I will turn to Irigaray's nonphallic depiction of female sexuality. The final section of this chapter critically engages Grosz's "exploration of the lived and social dimensions of sexual difference," an exploration which affirms sexual specificity but denies that such specificity can be reduced to (or explained in terms of) either biological *or* cultural factors (Grosz 1994:192). But first, a digression.

Morphology. The term itself conjures up certain images, corporeal images which, for me at least, resist explicit characterization or definition. The very word "morphology" has a fluidity that defies discrete boundaries, borders, and barriers. Lacking the concreteness of the term "anatomy," morphology also invokes a *logos*, a way, as Heidegger notes, of letting "something be seen"; logos, he suggests (following the Greeks), is itself a discourse which "lets us see something from the very thing which the discourse is about" (Heidegger 1962:56). While philology offers us a discourse about language and biology offers us a discourse about life, what kind of discourse is morphology about? Given that the term "morphe" itself is most frequently translated as "shape" or "form" (in a material sense), it would seem that morphology should offer us a discourse about shapes, or even, perhaps, a discourse about shaping—how shapes are formed. But what kinds of shapes count as morphes? What is the status of the materiality of these shapes? That is, must these shapes themselves be material, materialized, or even materializable to figure within a discourse of morphology?

Morphing as Phantasmatic Transformation

Power Rangers have been the toy of choice for preschool boys and many preschool girls since 1994. Looking at (and often stepping on) the Power Rangers scattered about my house (Zachary, Tommy, Trini, Billy, Kimberly, Jason—yes, I know them all), reminds me of another, contemporary connotation of morphing, namely, transformation. Push a button on the belly of these Power Rangers and their heads and torsos flip to reveal a new bodily morphology; no longer recognizable as human, they become cyborgs with superhuman powers, ready and able to fight evil wherever it can be found.

Attending a talk at my children's preschool entitled "The Effects of Power Rangers on our Children," I was curious to hear what, exactly, the effects were presumed to be. The talk began with the presupposition that Power Rangers are bad and that they represent a danger to children. There were two claims, in particular, that seemed to sum up the essence of many parents' and teachers' objections to them: 1) The karatelike fighting of the Power Rangers (against their evil foes) is violent and encourages the children to be violent as well; 2) Their ability to morphe from human kids into superhuman cyborgs makes children think that they, too, can become Power Rangers one day. In the words of one teacher, "at least with the Super Teenage Mutant Ninja Turtles, no child ever thought she or he could become one. They are readily identifiable as creatures of 'pure fantasy.' Power Rangers, on the other hand, blur the distinction between fantasy and reality and this is especially problematic for young children."

A less serious objection had to do with the banal plots of the Power Ranger television series (this drove the parents who watched the show crazy, but did not seem to bother their children at all). Another, more serious objection, had to do with the female Power Rangers who *seem* to share equal status with the males, but who actually end up looking to the males for protection and guidance, thereby reinforcing rather than challenging stereotypical depictions of the "helpless" (and hapless?) teenage girl. For mothers and fathers who hoped that these female Power Rangers would indeed be a positive alternative to the ubiquitous Barbie (herself morphologically transformed in 1995 into Disney's "ethnic" Pocahontas), this was indeed a disappointment.[7]

Turning for a moment to the second objection, I would like to explore further the "dangers" these morphological creatures allegedly embody for the children who love them. Looming largest, in many parents' minds, is a danger of identification. Because the Power Rangers go from being "real teenagers" to superhuman cyborgs, the children may themselves think that they can become superhuman creatures, able to vanquish enemies with ease, all the while remaining invulnerable to pain or death. The Power Rangers, so the argument goes, are not a "pure" fantasy, and this lack of purity is itself dangerous. Purity, as it is invoked in this context, is associated with an imagining that remains opposed to reality, that is, a Disney-like fantasyland that offers a palliative escape from reality. And yet, most nonacademics are happily unaware of the fact that the "real" status of the "pure" fantasy epitomized by Disneyland has itself come under attack, most notably by Jean Baudrillard, who has argued that:

> Disneyland is there to conceal the fact that it is the "real" country, all of "real" America, which *is* Disneyland (just as prisons are there to conceal the fact that it is the social in its entirety, in its banal omnipresence, which is carceral). Disneyland is presented as imaginary in order to make us believe that the rest is real, when in fact all of Los Angeles and the America surrounding it are no longer real, but of the order of the hyperreal and of simulation. It is no longer a question of a false representation of reality (ideology), but of concealing the fact that the real is no longer real, and thus of saving the reality principle. (Baudrillard 1983:25)

For Baudrillard, the purity of reality and the purity of fantasy are both phantasmatic. Moreover, there is no metaphysical basis for distinguishing between reality and fantasy to begin with. If any distinction between Disneyland and what lies outside Disneyland can be made, it is that Disneyland is a simulation that grasps itself as a simulation; the "Real World," on the other hand, is a dissimulating simulation insofar as it presents itself as (and in so doing constructs the illusion of) Reality.[8]

Although I will refrain from addressing the potentially deadly effects of these dissimulating simulations that Baudrillard is concerned with, dangers which, he argues, are most tangibly embodied in the imminent threat of worldwide nuclear destruction, I would like to consider the specific corporeal dangers evoked by the second objection to Power Rangers. What interests me especially about this objection is the concern it manifests for the effect of Power Rangers on the child's body image. For, if those who make this objection indeed feel that children may be "duped" into believing that they, too, will one day be able to morphe into cyborgian creatures, then this belief will inevitably influence the significance of embodiment for that child.

In particular, accepting the possibility of radical bodily transformation (and positively identifying with this possibility), involves a corresponding destabilization of the body as a *given*. Imagining oneself as a future Power Ranger is to imagine a morphological transformation that will overcome one's bodily deficiencies and limitations, enabling one, to be sure, to fight "the enemy" with ease and confidence, but it will also allow one to explore and test out new and unforeseen *bodily* capabilities. The point is that to become a Power Ranger (and to believe in the possibility of becoming a Power Ranger) requires a belief in the power of corporeal transformation. And, while educators and parents might be justifiably concerned about the ideological effects of this particular type of transformation, the belief in transformation itself should not be targeted as the problem. Encouraging children to explore the alternative imaginary schemas opened up by changes in bodily morphology is perhaps one of the oldest, and potentially most subversive tactics available for undermining social constraints on what bodies can and can't do. Unfortunately, for those of us who are no longer able (or willing) to believe that such radical bodily transformation is possible, less magical (and less entertaining!) tactics will have to suffice.[9]

The (Sexed) Morphology of the Imaginary

In *Bodies that Matter*, Butler explores how cultural prohibitions, such as the incest taboo, the taboo against auto-erotic love, and the interdiction against homosexuality, prohibitions presumed to be universal by both Freud and Lévi-Strauss, play a constitutive role in the formation of the bodily ego. Butler focuses on the prohibition against homosexuality, in particular, and, maintains that for Freud, "the ego-ideal which governs what Freud calls the ego's 'self-respect' requires the prohibition against homosexuality" (Butler 1993:65).[10] Prohibitions, she argues, attain their efficaciousness by means of the pain produced by guilt. She asks, is this "guilt-induced bodily suffering" which arises in response to the disciplinary techniques that "install" these prohibitions on particular bodies "analogous to the way in which we achieve an 'idea' of our own body?" (Butler 1993:64). Ultimately, she suggests that there is more than an analogy at stake. The materiality of pain produces its own "delineating effects," effects which include "'ideas' of the body without which there could be no ego, no temporary centering of experience" (Butler 1993:64). Butler describes this process as follows: "gender-instituting prohibitions work through suffusing the body with a pain that culminates in the projection of a surface, that is, a sexed morphology which is at once a compensatory fantasy and a fetishistic mask" (Butler 1993:65).

To summarize her rather complex argument as it is articulated both in *Gender Trouble* and in *Bodies that Matter*, Butler is claiming, first, that the "great" prohibitions articulated by Lévi-Strauss and Freud are linked by their shared repudiation of homosexual desire (e.g. the child's pre-Oedipal, incestuous desire for the phallic mother), and, second, that this repudiation is itself a disavowed loss which is melancholically incorporated into the bodily ego (Butler 1990:68).[11] Because the loss is itself unnameable (a condition established by the ubiquity of the prohibition), it cannot be metaphorically signified. Instead of metaphorically expressing the loss, "incorporation *literalizes* the loss *on* or *in* the body and so appears as the facticity of the body, the means by which the body comes to bear "sex" as its literal truth" (Butler 1990:68).

What Butler is suggesting here is that the facticity of the body, a facticity defined through the body's erotogenic zones, surfaces, orifices, "parts," and circumscribed boundaries, is itself (discretely *and* discreetly) produced through the melancholic structure of the bodily ego. More specifically, the unacknowledged loss of homosexual desire functions, *through its exclusion*, to produce its opposite, namely, a bodily morphology structured through a heterosexual matrix, a matrix in which identifications are predicated upon difference, not sameness.[12] Rather than viewing a sexed morphology as somehow originary or determinative of a specific gender identification then, "gender-instituting" prohibitions produce the bodily pain of guilt which in turn results in the projection of a specific bodily ego with a particular, sexed morphology, a morphology that is "sexed" as either "male" or "female." "Suffice it to say," Butler concludes, "that the boundaries of the body are the lived experience of differentiation, where that differentiation is never neutral to the question of gender difference or the heterosexual matrix" (Butler 1993:65).

According to Butler then, the heterosexual matrix that structures the bodily ego and produces the sexed morphology of the body, is itself an imaginary schema. Indeed, the very power and ubiquitousness of this matrix is due to the fact that it manifests itself within an imaginary domain, a domain that exists across time, space, social classes, races, ages, ethnicities, bodies, and cultures.[13] To say that the bodily ego and the body is constructed in accordance with this imaginary schema, as Butler does, is not, however, to argue (as many of Butler's critics have done) that the body must then be understood as an imaginary, or even purely social construction.[14] For, although Butler argues that "we might understand the psyche . . . as that which constitutes the mode by which that body is given, the condition and contour of that givenness," she also cautions against viewing the materiality of the body:

> as a unilateral or causal *effect* of the psyche in any sense that would reduce that materiality to the psyche or make of the psyche the monistic stuff out of which that materiality is produced and/or derived. (Butler 1993:66)

Through the critique of social constructionism that Butler offers in the introduction to *Bodies that Matter*, and through passages like the following, she continues to affirm simultaneously the body's irreducible materiality and the ways in which that materiality is always already invested with cultural significance:

> It must be possible to concede and affirm an array of "materialities" that pertain to the body, that which is signified by the domains of biology, anatomy, physiology, hormonal and chemical composition, illness, age, weight, metabolism, life and death. None of this can be denied. But the undeniability of these "materialities" in no way implies what it means to affirm them, indeed, what interpretive matrices condition, enable and limit that necessary affirmation. That each of those categories have a history and a historicity, that each of them is constituted through the boundary lines that distinguish them and, hence, by what they exclude, that relations of discourse and power produce hierarchies and overlappings among them and challenge those boundaries, implies that these are *both* persistent and contested regions. (Butler 1993:66–67)

Just as Foucault offers a genealogy of the subjectivation of subjects, so too, Butler traces the ways in which the materialities of bodies are materialized, "that is, how they come to assume the *morphe*, the shape by which their material discreteness is marked" (1993:69). To view the materiality of the body as a cultural *acquisition*, as Butler does, does not mean that the materiality of the body is purely a cultural *creation*.[15]

But in what sense is the materiality of the body acquired, and what role do imaginary schemas play in this process? For Lacan, imaginary morphology is always a narcissistic and idealizing projection. Archetypically exemplified in the child's identification with her/his specular image, this imaginary morphology provides the body with an (illusory) unity that makes the ego (itself an imago) possible. Although I will not pursue a discussion of this notion of imaginary morphology for Lacan (numerous Lacanians and feminist psychoanalytic theorists have already done this), what interests me about Lacan's account is the way in which he foregrounds the projective quality and productive effects of the imaginary itself. If, as Lacan, Schilder, and Merleau-Ponty have suggested, we understand the body image as a morphological projection, one that is informed by, but not reducible to, the specular image of the body, what are the productive (and, possibly, destructive) effects of this particular imaginary morphology on the body?

In Butler's own critical appropriation (some, including herself, might even call it a misappropriation) of Lacan, she makes two points in particular that I find especially illuminating in addressing the questions raised above. First, Butler claims that societal prohibitions can themselves be understood as projected morphologies. In the failure of these prohibitions (e.g. the incest taboo and the taboo against homosexual desire) to:

> produce the docile body that fully conforms to the social ideal, they may delineate body surfaces that do not signify conventional heterosexual polarities. These variable body surfaces or bodily egos may thus become sites of transfer for properties that no longer belong properly to any anatomy. (Butler 1993:64)

The temporality invoked in the very notion of a projection, more specifically, the imbrication of the future with the present and past which marks a projection as a projection in the first place, opens up a phantasmatic space of possibility in which that which is projected can end up being assimilated, modified, rejected, or even, as Trevor Hope notes, retroactively installed as prior to the projection (Hope 1994).[16] By following through the contingent, corporeal implications and deviations of these projected, prohibited morphologies, Butler steers clear of the Scylla of biological determinism on the one hand and the Charybdis of cultural (including linguistic) determinism on the other.

The second point that she makes is integrally connected to the first one. Butler notes that the primary, imaginary identification with the specular image of the body that occurs in the mirror stage "*gives form* or *morphe* to the ego through the phantasmatic delineation of a body in control" (Butler 1993:260). "That primary act of form-giving," she goes on to add, "is then displaced or extrapolated onto the world of other bodies and objects, providing the condition of their appearance" (Butler 1993:260). For Butler, the ongoing morphological elaboration of the ego, initiated through this "primary act of form-giving," belies any conception of the ego as a self-identical substance. Rather, on her interpretation of Lacan, the ego must be understood as an *identificatory relation*:

> indeed, the cumulative history of such relations . . . a sedimented history of imaginary relations which locate the center of the ego outside itself, in the externalized *imago* which confers and produces bodily contours. (Butler 1993:74)

To the extent that all identifications are themselves projections, identificatory relations are always morphological *idealizations*, idealizations which may reinforce as well as subvert the prohibitions out of which they have emerged.

The paradox of the ego as both arising out of the "phantasmatic delineation of a body in control" even as it displaces the "primary act of form-giving" onto other bodies and objects, enables us to see how new imaginary schemas are continually projected, schemas which do not replace one another, but which coexist more or less uneasily. These schemas, on Butler's Lacanian account, do not originate with the ego, rather, they are precisely what morphologically constitutes it as such:

> That complex identificatory fantasies inform morphogenesis, and that they cannot be fully predicted, suggests that morphological idealization is both a necessary and unpredictable ingredient in the constitution of both the bodily ego and the dispositions of desire. It also means that there is not necessarily one imaginary schema for the bodily ego, and that cultural conflicts over the idealization and degradation of specific masculine and feminine morphologies will be played out at the site of the morphological imaginary in complex and conflicted ways. (Butler 1993:86–87)

By displacing the hegemony (and unassailability) of the Lacanian Imaginary through the postulation of a plurality of idealizing imaginary schemas extending both within and outside of the ego (transversing both the Innenwelt and the Umwelt), Butler opens up a tremendously fecund domain in which it is no longer possible to maintain the morphological distinctness of heterosexuality vis-a-vis homosexuality, or even of masculinity vis-a-vis femininity. Rejecting the simplistic notion of a single identification that consolidates (and reifies) the ego and univocally characterizes one's sex, gender, and desire, she pushes us to acknowledge:

> the structuring presence of cross-identifications in the elaboration of the bodily ego, and to frame these identifications in a direction beyond a logic of repudiation by which one identification is always and only worked at the expense of another.[17] (Butler 1993:87)

For Butler, insofar as the projected, idealizing morphologies which structure the bodily ego melancholically incorporate the very prohibitions which motivate them, the cross-identifications which arise in and through this process offer the possibility of resignifying the "givenness" of anatomy, sexual difference, and race (Butler 1993:89). This is because they undermine the binary logic that separates the natural from the cultural, the female from the male, the homosexual from the heterosexual, the black from the white. Moreover, I would argue that the morphological indistinctness that blurs the boundaries between these oppositional pairs is itself a distinguishing characteristic of our lived bodily experience, one that is belied whenever we are interpellated through a fixed subject position. And, given the reciprocal, chiasmic relationship that exists between these identifications and the imaginary which enables their construction, destruction, and reconstruction, the destabilization of the former signifies that there is a corresponding destabilization of the latter. As Butler notes, "if these central identifications cannot be strictly regulated, then the domain of the imaginary in which the body is partially constituted is marked by a constitutive vacillation" (Butler 1993:90).

It is by means of the vacillation within and among these imaginary schemas, in fact, that Butler locates the possibility of disrupting the hegemony of the (heterosexist) Symbolic order as well as the hegemony of what Hope refers to as the "homosocial Imaginary" (Hope 1994). Despite our attempts to understand anatomy through the binary logic of sexual difference (i.e. one's body is sexually coded from, and even before birth, as either male or female), Butler declares that anatomy "is also that which exceeds and compels that signifying chain, that reiteration of difference, an insistent and inexhaustible demand" (Butler 1993:90).

As our own (cross-)identifications traverse racial, gender, class, ethnic, and age boundaries, not just anatomy, but sexual difference itself is simultaneously renegotiated. This renegotiation may, and often does take the form of reinscribing (reinstituting) these boundaries, but it can also break through these boundaries to define alternative corporeal cartographies. The project of remapping the established (heterosexist) terms of sexual difference is one that Luce Irigaray takes up, her goal being to avoid reproducing the binary, oppositional logic through which sexual difference is currently grasped and expressed. This project, she argues, requires nothing less than the creation of a new, more fluid metaphysics, one that does justice to the corresponding fluidity and volatility of our corporeal existence.

Irigaray's Metaphysics of Fluidity

A central trope in Irigaray's work is the specular image that, contrary to a conventional understanding of the mirror as (mimetically) mirroring back just what "is there" to begin with, reflects only what the one who is seeing the reflection (and who may or may not be the one mirrored) wants to see. Working from within a Lacanian framework in which the subject's imaginary (and imaginative) identification with a coherent, specular image is inherently alienating insofar as it belies the incoherence and turbulence of our own corporeality, Irigaray argues further that the specular image is itself a function of a phallocratic society that delineates the contours of women's bodies and their desires and expects/compels them to "mirror" this image back in return. Butler makes a similar point, observing that:

> the body in the mirror does not represent a body that is, as it were, before the mirror: the mirror, even as it is instigated by that unrepresentable body "before" the mirror, produces that body as its delirious effect—a delirium, by the way, which we are compelled to live.[18] (Butler 1993:91)

Nowhere is the mirror's production of the body "before" the mirror more horrifyingly enacted than in the Grimms brothers' classic fairy tale, "Snow White and the Seven Dwarves." In her reworking of this fairy tale in her prize-winning collection of poems, *Transformations*, Anne Sexton reveals the delirious/deadly effects of women's specularization through a sardonic invocation of the "happily ever after" which promises to obliterate any and every distinction between Snow White and her evil Stepmother:

> And thus Snow White became the prince's bride.
> The wicked queen was invited to the wedding feast
> and when she arrived there were
> red-hot iron shoes,
> in the manner of red-hot roller stakes,
> clamped upon her feet.
> First your toes will smoke
> and then your heels will turn black
> and you will fry upward like a frog,
> she was told.
> And so she danced until she was dead,
> a subterranean figure,
> her tongue flicking in and out
> like a gas jet.
> Meanwhile Snow White held court,
> rolling her china-blue doll eyes open and shut
> and sometimes referring to her mirror
> as women do.[19]
> (Sexton 1971:9)

In her depiction of a Snow White who arises out of the ashes of the dead Queen to become, ultimately, indistinguishable from her former nemesis, Sexton offers us an alarming picture of a living death, the static existence of the mute china doll who is condemned to an "eternal recurrence" of the same phantasmatic existence.[20] This poem itself suggests that "domestic bliss," for women, is a function of a culturally fixed, imaginary schema. In her own work, Irigaray takes up the morphological challenge of articulating alternative imaginary schemas to counter this frozen image, schemas which are already, she suggests, operative within many women's experiences, and which must be individually acknowledged and culturally validated in order to "break the patriarchal ice."

One way Irigaray accomplishes this, is through an imaginary reconfiguration of the notion of *place*, both the place where sexual difference is thought to be decisively established (i.e. genitalia) as well as the (non-)place that woman is supposed to occupy within the Symbolic order. For Irigaray, women, despite their conscious (or unconscious) intentions, continually fail to occupy the place that has been designated for them. And, this is not due to a *lack* on their part (e.g. from a psychoanalytic perspective, their symbolic castration), but rather to their own corporeal excess, their own (sex-specific) *jouissance*. Female sexuality, in particular, Irigaray claims, is characterized by fluidity and multiplicity, a fluidity and multiplicity that I am arguing gives rise to multiple body images which continually engage in reciprocal exchanges with one another, blurring the boundaries between them.

If, as Edward Casey argues, the relationship between place and person is always reciprocal, women's failure to "remain in (their) place," will have definite corporeal consequences. For, according to Casey:

> When places change aspect or fade in significance, I change or fade with them: *their* alteration is *my* alteration. But my own changes may be funded back into the very places that have been so formative of my identity in the first place.

And, he adds,

> Given this reciprocity of person and place, place-alienation is itself two-way: I from it, it from me. When caught up in this double-sided otherness, I feel, almost literally, "beside myself." I feel myself to be other than myself and not just somewhere other than where I am in world-space (e.g. my exact address, my cartographic location, etc.). Even though I am literally here in a particular place, my place is not *this* place. By the same token, this place is no longer *my* place: indeed, my place has become other to (and other than) me. *The entire situation, and not just my psyche, is schizoid.* (Casey 1993:307–308, my emphasis)

For Irigaray, this schizoid situation is inevitable in a patriarchal society that deprives women of their own "place," that turns women into dispossessed persons who live a "borrowed existence" through the munificence of their (parasitic) "hosts" and who are expected to take their assigned places with gratitude. As she observes:

> If traditionally, and as a mother, woman represents *place* for man, such a limit means that she becomes *a thing*, with some possibility of change from one historical period to another. She finds herself delineated as a thing. Moreover, the maternal-feminine also serves as an *envelope*, a *container*, the starting point from which man limits his things.

And, if a woman refuses to "remain in her place":

> she continuously undoes his work—distinguishing herself from both the envelope and the thing, ceaselessly creating there some interval, play, something in motion and un-limited which disturbs his perspective, his world, and his/its limits. But, because he fails to leave her a subjective life, and to be on occasion her place and her thing in an intersubjective dynamic, man remains within a mas-

ter-slave dialectic. The slave, ultimately, of a God on whom he bestows the characteristics of an abolute master. Secretly or obscurely, a slave to the power of the
maternal-feminine which he diminishes or destroys. (Irigaray 1993:10)

In these passages, Irigaray is arguing for a genuine "intersubjective dynamic" between men and women that will allow us to escape from the master-slave
dialectic. To accomplish this, she advocates an "exchange" of places whereby
each must *be* a "place" and a "thing" for the other. This invocation of place and
thing are provocative but also very problematic. Insisting that man should be a
"place" for woman, Irigaray implies that this will strike balance into an historical situation where women have always been expected to provide a place (as
home/womb) for man. To the extent that Irigaray is suggesting that each of us
should be a horizon of significance for the other, it is clear that this claim does
not and should not apply only to relationships between the sexes. If we can
extend this claim to characterize same-sex relations as well as relations between
individuals of different races, ages, and social classes, her position becomes
much more appealing and much more powerful.

By contrast, it is less clear how to work productively with Irigaray's suggestion that man should also, "on occasion" be "her thing" for the notion of thing
invoked here seems quite negative. For me, it immediately suggests a Sartrian
being-in-itself (*être-en-soi*), a brute, material presence that is incapable of con-
ferring meaning upon the situation since the latter can only be produced by an
intentional subject, a being-for-itself (*être-pour-soi*). This image of an immanent "thing" even if "exchanged," cannot, I would argue, get us away from the
cultural, psychical, and corporeal limitations of a (Hegelian) master-slave
dialectic, a complicated relationship whereby the master attempts to dominate
the slave, but ultimately requires the slave to confirm him in his dominance,
something that requires the slave's own subjectivity, and which therefore
undermines the sovereign subject-position of the master. While Hegel's subversive reading of the subjectivity of the slave as being necessary to confirm the
subjectivity of the master challenges a simple, dualistic interpretation of this
relationship as a dominant master victimizing a dominated slave, it is also crucial to realize that the slave's refusal to confirm the master in his dominance
could easily cost the slave her/his life.

To arrive at a genuine, intersubjective dynamic that escapes the fixed roles
occupied by master and slave in the master/slave dialectic, we need to move
beyond the passive connotations of a "thing," even if we are talking about
things that are exchanged. Place, on the other hand, is potentially a more
promising image so long as it is understood that in exchanging places, the "reciprocity between person and place" which Casey discusses, guarantees that the
places, and not just the persons, will be irrevocably altered in significance. And,
as I've mentioned above, it is also important to avoid a heterosexist formulation
of this exchange (which itself arises, but is not excused by Irigaray's proposing

this model as a way of negotiating sexual difference), since this limits its useful-ness for relationships between people in which sexual difference plays only a minor role.[21]

While Irigaray argues for a fluid conception of female sexuality, one that does justice to women's own corporeal fluidity, and while she radically reworks a Freudian/Lacanian psychoanalytic model by positing a female libido mod-eled on excess rather than lack, her way of developing these points subjects her time and time again to the accusations of essentialism and homophobia. Those who are sensitive to the sublety of Irigaray's logic have often defended her from these charges, emphasizing that it is precisely because Irigaray takes the (female) body seriously that she stresses the corporeal, erotic, psychical, and political significance of sexual difference. Tina Chanter eloquently states Iri-garay's project as follows:

> in her attention to the question of sexual differences and their psychoanalytic construction, Irigaray sees the need to reexamine the function and significance of the sex/gender distinction within feminist discourse. She does so in a way that brings the body back into play, not as "the rock of feminism" but as a mobile site of differences. Irigaray's attention to the body, far from amounting to a refusal of culture and history, allows her to scrutinize critically the assumptions that femi-nists make when they suspend questions of sexual difference to achieve political change. To accuse her of essentialism not only rejects her interrogation of cer-tain assumptions about sameness that habitually underlie feminist struggles for equality in the political arena, it also refuses to acknowledge the challenge Iri-garay issues to conventional conceptions of the enigmatic divide between nature and culture. (Chanter 1995:46)

A central question for my own inquiry concerns the specific transformations within the body image that Irigaray's alternative understanding of sexual differ-ence makes possible. To take up this question, I will turn to Grosz's work on corporeal existence, since Grosz, much more than Irigaray, focuses on the intercorporeal exchanges and transformations that continually resignify *both* women's and men's sexed bodies.

The (Imaginary) Fluidity of Sexual Difference

A singular danger in arguing that sexual difference plays a formative, and there-fore, foundational role in human existence (particularly in intersubjective rela-tions), is that one is usually thought to be starting from an essentialist concep-tion of the two sexes. A virtue of Elizabeth Grosz's embodied account of sexual difference is that there is never any one difference that characterizes it: sexual difference itself is always multiple, overdetermined, and therefore perpetually contested. Moreover, by employing a Deleuzian perspective to balance what Grosz calls the "inside-out" standpoint of psychoanalysis, Grosz stresses that this multiplicity, overdetermination, and contestability is not merely a function of changes in how sexual difference is elaborated within and across cultures throughout the centuries, but rather, stems from a view of the body as itself:

> the site or sites of multiple struggles, ambiguously positioned in the reproduc-
> tion of social habits, requirements, and regulations and in all sorts of production
> of unexpected and unpredictable linkages. Through Deleuze and Guattari's per-
> spectives, the body, bodies, flows in bodies rather than "subjects," psychic beings,
> are what produce. Admittedly, this implies the de-massifications of the categories
> of sex, class, race, and sexual preference, so that even within these categories a
> whole range of forces is always in play. Identities and stabilities are not fixed.
> (Grosz 1994:181)

For Grosz, these "de-massifications of the categories of sex, class, race, and sexual preference," do not result in their being dismantled altogether. Rather, they
are continually being reassembled and rearranged in relation to one another, in
accordance with different corporeal agendas; these latter agendas are themselves altered in turn by the shifting demands that our bodies seek to meet
through them, demands that are ethical in nature and which I will characterize
in chapter seven as bodily imperatives. Indeed, Grosz argues that:

> Sexual difference entails the existence of a sexual ethics, an ethics of the ongo-
> ing negotiations between beings whose differences, whose alterities, are left
> intact, but with whom some kind of exchange is nonetheless possible. (Grosz
> 1994:192)

What Grosz is calling for here is more of an ethics of sexual *differences* rather
than an Irigarayan ethics of *sexual difference*. The former suggests that there are
an infinite number of ways for sexual differences to be established and
expressed, the latter invokes (however unintentionally) a more monolithic,
binary conception of sexual difference.

I have called this section, the (imaginary) fluidity of sexual difference, in
order to call attention both to the fixed, decidedly unimaginative ways in which
bodies have traditionally been marked as sexually different, and at the same
time, to suggest in a more positive vein that preserving the fluidity of sexual difference (and racial, class, age, and other differences) requires the construction
of alternative imaginary schemas and the creation of multiple body images that
correspond to them. A key element of this project, for Grosz, will involve a
recognition of the *alterity* that characterizes not only relations between the
sexes but our relations with our own bodies. As she notes:

> Bodies themselves, in their materialities, are never self-present, given things,
> immediate, certain self-evidences because embodiment, corporeality, insist on
> alterity, both that alterity they carry within themselves (the heart of the psyche
> lies in the body; the body's principles of functioning are psychological and cul-

tural) and that alterity that gives them their own concreteness and specificity (the alterities constituting race, sex, sexualities, ethnic and cultural specificities). Alterity is the very possibility and process of embodiment: it conditions but is also a product of the pliability or plasticity of bodies which makes them other than themselves, other than their "nature," their functions and identities. (Grosz 1994:209)

To resignify the static terms of sexual difference as it has been culturally depicted, I would argue, requires the development of fluid, corporeal schemas that both depend upon and produce new forms of corporeal alterity. By claiming that alterity is both a condition and a product of the "pliability or plasticity of bodies which makes them other than themselves, other than their 'nature,' their functions and identities," Grosz implies that fluidity and differences/otherness go hand in hand. On her account, to seek to abolish or somehow transcend sexual difference (even for concrete, political purposes such as the need to secure "equal rights" for women), actually impoverishes rather than enhances the diversity and richness of our intercorporeal exchanges. As far as the alterity that marks the body image itself is concerned, Grosz, argues that:

the body image is capable of accommodating and incorporating an extremely wide range of objects. Anything that comes into contact with the surface of the body and remains there long enough will be incorporated into the body image — clothing, jewelry, *other bodies*, objects. They mark the body, its gait, posture, position, etc. (temporarily or more or less permanently), by marking the body image: subjects do not walk the same way or have the same posture when they are naked as when they wear clothing. And the posture and gait will, moreover, vary enormously, depending on what kind of clothing is worn. (Grosz 1994:80, my emphasis)

Taking together Foucault's and Binswanger's emphasis on the continual interplay between images and the imaginary, Casey's understanding of the reciprocal exchanges that characterize the relations between places and persons, Butler's argument that we can never establish an identification without at the same time performing a set of exclusions (namely of that which falls outside of that identification), exclusions which are melancholically incorporated (and psychically disavowed) by the subject, Irigaray's celebration of corporeal "excess," and Grosz's claim that "alterity is the very process and possibility of embodiment," we can begin to chart a path towards the development of new morphological fantasies, fantasies that will take us not beyond differences per se, but which depend upon differences, corporeal differences, for their very existence. Such a path cannot and must not involve reducing the numerous differences among these respective authors and their respective projects to a single, overarching perspective; rather, it requires an exploration and acknowledgement of these differences as well as a corresponding acknowledgement of the differences between their own accounts and my own particular investigation.

What I am arguing for here is the development of new morphological fantasies in order to combat self-imposed as well as socially-imposed limitations on our own body images. Moreover, I am maintaining that these fantasies themselve require the development of alternative imaginary schemas, the preservation of corporeal fluidity, and a recognition of the bodily power and pervasiveness of sexual, racial, and other differences, differences that serve to set bodies apart from, and thereby place them in relation to, one another. To the extent that these latter differences are pernicious, and oppressive to the individuals who are marked by them, conceptual, or even cultural solutions will not suffice; instead, what is required above all are *corporeal* solutions, new body images and new ways of imagining bodies whose very diversity resists univocal labels or definitions. For, as Drucilla Cornell observes:

> To reduce someone to objectified fantasies imposed upon them by someone else's imaginary is to deny that person their own imaginary and thus denies that they should be the ultimate source of the interpretations and reincarnations of their own sexuality. (Cornell 1995:207)

While I am claiming that body images are themselves always characterized by a series of intercorporeal exchanges that break down the boundaries both between the body images of one individual and the body images of that individual and other individuals, it is also clear that these fluid, multiple body images produce a sense of bodily (and moral) integrity that will be undermined if these body images and the imaginary which contributes to their production are regulated by others or dictated, more generally, by a hegemonic Symbolic order. This is not to say, on the other hand, that our body images are ever purely our "own" constructions, for they are not. Instead, what I am emphasizing and what Cornell is emphasizing in the above passage, is the need to recognize and affirm the power of individual agency in the construction, deconstruction, and reconstruction of the very terms of our corporeality.

{4}

The Abject Borders of the Body Image

On the days when I am not tortured by hunger, the dread of becoming fat again moves to the center. Two things, then, torture me: First, hunger. Second, the dread of getting fatter. I find no way out of this noose. . . . Horrible feeling of emptiness. Horrible fear of this feeling. I have nothing that can dull this feeling.

—Ludwig Binswanger (1958:253)

In the medical model, the body of the subject is the passive tablet on which disorder is inscribed. Deciphering that inscription is usually seen as a matter of determining the "cause" of the disorder; sometimes (as with psychoanalysis) *interpretation* of symptoms will be involved. But always the process requires a trained—that is to say, highly specialized—professional whose expertise alone can unlock the secrets of the disordered body. For the feminist analyst, by contrast, the disordered body, like all bodies, is engaged in a process of making meaning, of "labor on the body." From this perspective, anorexia (for example) is never *merely* regressive, never *merely* a fall into illness and chaos. Nor is it facilitated simply by bedazzlement by cultural images, "indoctrination" by what happens, arbitrarily, to be in fashion at this time. Rather, the "relentless pursuit of excessive thinness" is an attempt to embody certain values, to create a body that will speak for the self in a meaningful and powerful way.

—Susan Bordo (1993:67)

This illusion of unity, in which a human being is always looking forward to self-mastery, entails a constant danger of sliding back again into the chaos from which he started; it hangs over the abyss of a dizzy Assent in which one can perhaps see the very essence of Anxiety.

—Jacques Lacan (1953:15)

These three statements issue from quite divergent sources and represent three different perspectives on the challenges any given individual may face in striving to achieve "normal" psychical development. "Ellen West," an

Selves Portrayal, Priscilla A. Smith (1985)

early twentieth-century anorexic who is the subject of Ludwig Binswanger's case study, does not succeed in overcoming her contradictory desires despite repeated and prolonged psychotherapy and ends up commmitting suicide. Susan Bordo explicitly addresses the antinomies that characterize anorexic existence and advocates a move away from medical models in favor of both cultural diagnoses and cultural solutions to the anorexic's body image distortions. Jacques Lacan, in the quote cited above, suggests that the attainment of a unified sense of self is extremely difficult for each and every one of us, not only for anorexics or for others who are deemed to be "abnormal" in some way or another. In this chapter, I will use anorexia as a paradigm case to discuss the more general issue of distorted body images. Before turning to a consideration of anorexia as it has been interpreted by Susan Bordo and others, I will begin by addressing the (problematic) presuppositions that are involved in identifying a given body image as distorted in the first place. Lacan's work on the "mirror stage" reveals the serious challenges that *any* subject faces in the process of constructing a coherent body image, and along with Julia Kristeva's work on abjection, it aids us in understanding why we need new models to distinguish between "normal" and "abnormal" body images. At the end of this chapter, I propose one such model that I believe provides an original and potentially productive way of thinking about and treating anorexia.

In his famous essay on the "mirror stage," to recall our discussion from chapter one, Lacan argues that as the young child comes to identify with her/his specular image in the mirror, the "form of its totality" that is acquired obscures a certain constitutive loss, or, more accurately, series of losses that make the coherence of the body image possible. According to Judith Butler:

> The mirror stage is not a *developmental* account of how the idea of one's own body comes into being. It does suggest, however, that the capacity to project a *morphe*, a shape, onto a surface is part of the psychic (and phantasmatic) elaboration, centering, and containment of one's own bodily contours. This process of psychic projection or elaboration implies as well that the sense of one's own body is not (only) achieved through differentiating from another (the maternal body), but that any sense of bodily contour, as projected, is articulated through a necessary self-division and self-estrangement. (Butler 1993:71)

While Lacan devotes much attention to the (alienating) identity that arises out of the child's identification with her/his specular image, both Butler and Kristeva concentrate on what fails to be subsumed within that identity, on what is left out of the totalizing process that transforms momentary and diverse bodily sensations into a unified body image.[1] For Kristeva, that which is "lost" or which resists incorporation into the body image is also precisely what makes the coherent body image possible because it marks the boundary between the body image and what it is not. There is a permanent danger that this boundary will be dissolved, however, since the boundary is only reinforced on one side, the

Symbolic side. The "other side" is the unnameable, abject domain that continually threatens to overrun its carefully established borders. The fragility of the border in turn undermines the stability and coherence of the body image; as Kristeva notes: "The more or less beautiful image in which I behold or recognize myself rests upon an abjection that sunders it as soon as repression, the constant watchman, is relaxed" (Kristeva 1982:13).

This abject specter, which continually haunts the ego and seeks to disrupt the continuity of the body image, is all the more terrifying because it is a ghost incarnated in flesh, blood, spit, mucus, faeces, vomit, urine, pus, and other bodily fluids. Hence, the boundary between the body image and what it is not is not (merely) a symbolic one; rather, it must also be understood as a corporeal refusal of corporeality. As Elizabeth Grosz observes:

> Abjection involves the paradoxically necessary but impossible desire to transcend corporeality. It is a refusal of the defiling, impure, uncontrollable materiality of the subject's embodied existence. It is a response to the various bodily cycles of incorporation, absorption, depletion, expulsion, the cycles of material rejuvenation and consumption necessary to sustain itself yet incapable of social recognition and representation. It is an effect of the child's corporeal boundaries being set through the circulation of (socially unacceptable) drive energies and the rhythms of incorporation and evacuation necessary for existence. (Grosz 1989:72; Gross 1990:88)

Abjection is necessary because some aspects of our corporeal experience must be excluded to enable the coherent construction of both the ego and the body image, but it is also impossible because, as Grosz, Butler, and Kristeva all suggest, that which is excluded is not eliminated altogether but continually "erupts" and therefore disrupts the privileged sites of inclusion.

To the extent that processes of abjection and the corresponding construction of an abject domain, are part and parcel of the formation of our body images, it is all the more necessary to examine the specific roles abjection and the abject domain play in what are often referred to as "distorted" body images, that is, body images that refuse or resist normalization in a Foucaultian sense. These aberrant body images which are usually at odds with societal attitudes, individual and social expectations, and which can severely limit an individual's physical capacities are paradigmatically exemplified in the case of "Gertrude," a seventeen-year-old female anorexic patient cited by Dr. Hilde Bruch, who worries while she is undergoing a "re-feeding" program that has brought her weight to just over ninety pounds, that she might be gaining too much, i.e., getting fat (Bruch 1978:16).

Although the starving anorexic who is convinced she is overweight serves as a striking example of an individual with a distorted body image, it is evident that distorted body images can be found in a much larger population, including schizophrenics, individuals with multiple personality disorders (who may have several incompatible body images), individuals who have sustained severe nerve damage and/or who are suffering from neurological disturbances, and individuals whose bodies transgress our socially entrenched corporeal norms such as dwarves, "giants," and those all too numerous others whom society designates as "freaks."[2]

To begin to discuss the problem of distorted body images, we must first address the rather tricky issue of what the distortion is a distortion *from* since the very notion of distortion, like the notion of "the Other" that Beauvoir discusses in *The Second Sex*, suggests some kind of deviation from a norm, a standard that is itself identifiable as such. Locating the Archimidean point against which the distortion can be measured does not seem to be a viable way to proceed, however, because the body image is itself continually changing in response to physiological changes in the body, as well as in response to the physical and social demands that we face, as individuals, from one moment to the next in our daily lives.

In his classic study of the body image, *The Image and Appearance of the Human Body*, Paul Schilder claims that each of us has an infinite number of body images. Distortion, then, cannot be attributed to the presence of a multiplicity of body images, since this multiplicity itself characterizes the "normal" case. And, if we take seriously Butler's claim that "[i]dentifications are multiple and contestatory" then, I would argue, it seems to make sense that there will be multiple, contestatory body images that accompany them (Butler 1993:99). Susan Bordo challenges the viability of the normal/pathological distinction from yet another perspective, arguing that, with respect to the distorted body images produced by eating disorders, "the anorectic does not 'misperceive' her body; rather, she has learned all too well the dominant cultural standards of *how* to perceive" (Bordo 1993:57).

Rather than attempting the impossible task of providing a single explanation or "diagnosis" of the phenomenon of body image distortion, I would like to focus instead on the relationship between body image distortion and abjection to see if shedding more light on the latter can lead to a greater understanding of not only distortion, but also the construction of body images that are taken to be "normal." Focusing on corporeal processes of boundary construction and destruction is especially crucial, for, I suggest, it is through the setting up and breaking down of boundaries that both distorted and nondistorted body images come to play a normative role in identity formation.

While Kristeva is especially interested in the question, "Where then lies the border, the initial phantasmatic limit that establishes the clean and proper self of the speaking and/or social being?" (Kristeva 1982:85), and posits the origin of abjection in the child's simultaneous longing for and horror of its pre-individuated connection with the maternal body, I am interested not in the ultimate source of the abject (indeed, unlike Kristeva, I do not think that the domain of the abject can be traced to a single corporeal relationship or site), but in the process of abjection itself, a process described by Kristeva as an act of expulsion, a self-purging whereby with the food I vomit, I also "expel *myself*, I spit *myself* out, I abject *myself* within the same motion through which 'I' claim to establish myself" (Kristeva 1982:3). Expelling (parts of) myself to establish myself as a member of the Symbolic order, I create corporeal boundaries between myself and what is not myself, and, in so doing, actively constitute myself as an idiosyncratic entity. On this account, abjection is necessary to create the boundaries that will individuate the self, but to recognize the need to create these boundaries is also to recognize the fragility of the self that is so constituted, and so not only the abject, but the very process of abjection must also be buried, repressed, denied.[3] According to Grosz:

> Abjection is the underside of the symbolic. It is what the symbolic must reject, cover over and contain. The symbolic requires that a border separate or protect the subject from this abyss which beckons and haunts it: the abject entices and attracts the subject ever closer to its edge. It is an insistence on the subject's necessary relation to death, to animality, and to materiality, being the subject's recognition and refusal of its corporeality. The abject demonstrates the impossibility of clear-cut borders, lines of demarcation, divisions between the clean and the unclean, the proper and the improper, order and disorder. (Grosz 1990:89)

For Grosz, Butler, and Kristeva, as we have noted, the attempt to establish corporeal borders will inevitably fail, not only because of (imperialistic) desires to see (and perhaps conquer) what lies beyond the "borderlands," or because of the seductive force of the abject itself, but because of the phantasmatic status of the "I" that simultaneously requires and disavows the need for borders to assure itself of its own autonomy and discreteness. In *Unbearable Weight: Feminism, Western Culture, and the Body*, Susan Bordo emphasizes that the very project of demarcating the "I" from what it is not relies upon a dualistic metaphysics, a metaphysics that devalues the corporeality of the body by contrasting its alleged passivity and "brute" materiality with the transcendent, mental activity associated with the "I," activity which has traditionally been identified with human reason, will, vitality, and spirit. And, Bordo reminds us: "This duality of active spirit/passive body is also gendered, and it has been one of the most historically powerful of the dualities that inform Western ideologies of gender" (Bordo 1993:11).

While it is crucial to recognize the repudiation of one's own corporeality that accompanies these psychic processes of boundary construction constitutive of the subject as such, Butler points out that the ongoing attempt to establish these borders, once and for all, also functions to demarcate those who "count" as subjects from those who do not:

> This exclusionary matrix by which subjects are formed thus requires the simultaneous production of a domain of abject beings, those who are not yet "subjects,"

but who form the constitutive outside to the domain of the subject. The abject designates here precisely those "unlivable" and "uninhabitable" zones of social life which are nevertheless densely populated by those who do not enjoy the status of the subject, but whose living under the sign of the "unlivable" is required to circumscribe the domain of the subject. This zone of uninhabitability will constitute the defining limit of the subject's domain; it will constitute that site of dreaded identification against which—and by virtue of which—the domain of the subject will circumscribe its own claim to autonomy and to life. In this sense, then, the subject is constituted through the force of exclusion and abjection, one which produces a constitutive outside to the subject, an abjected outside, which is, after all, "inside" the subject as its own founding repudiation. (Butler 1993:3)

How are we to understand this "force of exclusion and abjection," much less the precipitating role it plays in the formation of the subject and its body images? In a 1980 interview, Kristeva offers a poignant description of abjection as:

an extremely strong feeling which is at once somatic and symbolic, and which is above all a revolt of the person against an external menace from which one wants to keep oneself at a distance, but of which one has the impression that it is not only an external menace but that it may menace us from the inside. So it is a desire for separation, for becoming autonomous and also the feeling of an impossibility of doing so—whence the element of crisis which the notion of abjection carries within it. Taken to its logical consequences, it is an impossible assemblage of elements, with a connotation of a "fragile limit." (Kristeva 1988:135–136)

If (the process of) abjection is necessary for the development of a coherent body image, the repudiation of what lies beyond the "fragile limit" that marks the border between the "I" and what is "not-I" will give rise to its own body image distortions as certain bodily fluids, bodily activities, and body parts, are disavowed and refused a "legitimate" place in the construction of a corporeal identity. For Kristeva, as well as for Grosz (but for strikingly different reasons), the "price" of such de-legitimization is far too high. Kristeva stresses the creative "juices" that flow from this abjected domain, in the form of 1) the revolutionary possibilities of poetic language, and 2) the maternal reenactment of (what Kristeva takes to be) the "original narcissistic crisis" through pregnancy and childbirth. As Kelly Oliver observes in her discussion of the subversive significance of maternity and poetic language for Kristeva: "Like poetic language, pregnancy is a case where identity contains alterity as a heterogeneous other without completely losing its integrity" (Oliver 1993:183). And yet, there is a darker side to these attempts somehow to resolve or come to terms with the abject, for, as Butler observes, they may end up reinforcing the hegemony of the Symbolic order that they are supposed to belie.

In her essay entitled, "The Body Politics of Julia Kristeva," Butler describes Kristeva's celebration of poetic language and pregnancy as follows:

> for Kristeva, poetry and maternity represent privileged practices within paternal-
> ly sanctioned culture which permit a nonpsychotic experience of that hetero-
> geneity and dependency characteristic of the maternal terrain. These acts of *poe-
> sis* reveal an instinctual heterogeneity that subsequently exposes the repressed
> ground of the Symbolic, challenges the mastery of the univocal signifier, and dif-
> fuses the autonomy of the subject who postures as their necessary ground. The
> heterogeneity of drives operates culturally as a subversive strategy of displace-
> ment, one which dislodges the hegemony of the paternal law by releasing the
> repressed multiplicity interior to language itself. (Butler 1990:85–86)

Butler goes on to offer a powerful critique not only of Kristeva's reification of poetry and maternity as successful subversive strategies but, more fundamental-ly, of Kristeva's understanding of the abject as founding rather than being found or constructed within the Symbolic order. Butler argues that Kristeva focuses exclusively on the prohibitive effects of repression (of the abject), and does not acknowledge, as does Foucault, the generative effects of repression which can include the very production of "the object that it comes to deny." Privileging the maternal body as a means of celebrating the (abject) corporeal heterogene-ity that, for Kristeva, both precedes and is disavowed by the Symbolic order, results, Butler claims, in Kristeva's failing to see that:

> The female body that is freed from the shackles of the paternal law may well
> prove to be yet another incarnation of that law, posing as subversive but operat-
> ing in the service of that law's self-amplification and proliferation. (Butler
> 1990:93)

In her essay, "Ours to Jew or Die," Kristeva herself recognizes the danger of positing "an object of hatred and desire, of threat and aggressivity, of envy and abomination" (all terms which at various times have been used to describe the maternal body by Kristeva as well as by others), an abject object, in this case the Jew, which "gives thought a focus where all contradictions are explained and satisfied" (Kristeva 1982:178). The anti-Semite, according to Kristeva, by pro-jecting this abject object outside the Symbolic law ensures that the Jew is not protected by it; moreover, not content with the punishment meted out by the Symbolic order to those who transgress it, the anti-Semite seeks to destroy the Symbolic law in order to construct a new law, beyond the Symbolic, a law purged of the threats the abject other continually poses to the Symbolic order. This new law, unlike the "constraining and frustrating symbolic one . . . would be absolute, full, and reassuring" (Kristeva 1982:178). This desire to move beyond all limits, for Kristeva, self-destructs on its own limits, namely, its reliance on what she calls "the deadliest of fantasies" (Kristeva 1982:180). This deadly fantasy is, indeed, a fantasy of death—the death of the abject other which is viewed as necessary to maintain the corporeal integrity of the self.

As an external projection of one's own abjected corporeality, the expulsion of the abject other from the Symbolic order seeks to purge the self so that it may be reborn without the taint of defilement. For Kristeva, such a desire itself reinforces, rather than denies, the power the abject wields *within* the Symbolic order's own carefully defined boundaries. "The abject," she claims:

> is perverse because it neither gives up nor assumes a prohibition, a rule, or a law; but turns them aside, misleads, corrupts; uses them, takes advantage of them, the better to deny them. It kills in the name of life—a progressive despot; it lives at the behest of death. . . . (Kristeva 1982:15)

Regardless, then, of whether one seeks the origin of abjection within or outside of the Symbolic order, it is clear that the abject is a force that must constantly be reckoned with from within the Symbolic domain. For Kristeva:

> abjection is coextensive with social and symbolic order, on the individual as well as on the collective level. By virtue of this, abjection, just like *prohibition of incest*, is a universal phenomenon; one encounters it as soon as the symbolic and/or social dimension of man is constituted, and this throughout the course of civilization. But abjection assumes specific shapes and different codings according to the various "symbolic systems." (Kristeva 1982:68)

In *Bodies that Matter*, Butler explores some of the diverse shapes and codings abjection takes on in order to reveal the constitutive role the processes of abjection and exclusion play in the formation of the subject. Naming the abject other, compelling the abject other to exist as "the abject," excluding the abject other from certain privileges, regions, and social practices, are strategies we employ, Butler argues, to distance ourselves from the recognition of our own self-alienation and self-repudiation. Through these forces of abjection and exclusion, the abject is provided with a concrete identity and occupies a place, whether that place be a prison, a refugee center, a ghetto, a concentration camp, or another yet to be constructed "zone of uninhabitability"; in short, a place where society can dispose of its "excrement."

In her essay entitled, "What Does Cannibalism Speak? Jean de Léry and the Tupinamba Lesson," Sara Castro-Klaren furthers our understanding of how the abject other is projected "outside" the subject through the abjection of its own unresolved physical and psychical "horrors." Specifically, Castro-Klaren explores "how anthropophagy and the orgies observed among the Caribs and the Tupi speak, as they construct the 'savage,' of the dark night of the soul of the subject" (Castro-Klaren 1993:26). She appeals to Kristeva's notion of the abject to interpret the fascination/horror of the "civilized" European (e.g. Columbus, Léry, and their audiences) for the cannibalistic practices of these "savages," practices which were rarely witnessed firsthand but whose recountings were compelled by expectant ethnographers who eagerly interrogated those natives willing to "confess" them. According to Castro-Klaren, Léry's own, highly respected and widely influential ethnographic study of the Tupi, reveals more about Léry and sixteenth-century French Christianity than it does about the Tupi:

> Three months of precarious exile (October 1557–January 1558) among the Tupi, away from the inimical French Catholic settlers in the bay of Guanabara, arrested and traversed by twenty years in a France bled and scorched by religious wars, are transformed into a text that surreptitiously and yet obviously deals with the hottest issue of the day: the transubstantiation of bread and wine into the flesh and blood of the only son of God. Anthropophagy among the Tupi is the substitute construct for theophagy among the Christians. The representation of the Tupi as orgiastic cannibals enables Léry, the survivor of at least three major famines . . . in which civilized men were allowed to eat human flesh, to collect his thoughts on the great prohibitions. He collects them, he reinscribes them as memory of the journey to "over there" and projects upon them the business of the other "over here." The unspeakable status of incest, offerings of the flesh of the firstborn, sex outside a guilt complex, cannot and do not therefore fall within the realm of the subject. As Kristeva puts it, abjection transforms the "anxiety of the borderline subject into the site of the Other." (Castro-Klaren 1993:34–35)

If, as Kristeva, Grosz, Butler, and Castro-Klaren all agree, the construction of the abject other ultimately represents our (unsuccessful) attempts to repudiate our own abjection, what effects do these attempts and the existence of this abject other have upon our own body images and upon our own understanding of the phenomenon of distortion? Grosz's somatic reading of abjection provides us with some important clues. "Abjection," she observes,

> is the body's acknowledgement that the boundaries and limits imposed on it are really social projections—effects of desire, not nature. It testifies to the precarious grasp of the subject on its own identity, an assertion that the subject may slide back into the impure chaos out of which it was formed. (Grosz 1990b:90)

Despite their helpful analyses of the phenomenon of abjection and the role both the abject other and abjection play in the processes of identity formation, Kristeva, Butler, and Grosz all seem to leave us with an "unlivable" dilemma that we nonetheless continue to live out from one moment to the next. We cannot dispense with the abject without dispensing with our own identities since the latter are founded upon the former. On the other hand, we can hardly "embrace" the abject without its ceasing to be the abject, a process which will, inevitably it seems, force the creation of a new abject object to take the place of the old one.[4] The refusal of identity is not an option either, since the refusal of identity is itself the taking up of an identity position, and, in either case, we will always find identities (and abject objects) projected upon us regardless of our wishes, needs, or desires.

Precisely because our own body fluids and body parts are implicated in these processes of abjection and exclusion, the coherence of the body images we develop can, as Lacan first noted, only be a precarious fantasy, one that we maintain with difficulty. If certain bodily functions, desires, and practices are, by social (and sometimes even physical) necessity, expelled from participation in the construction of the body image, then, to return to our original question, on what basis are we to distinguish distorted body images from body images that are not distorted? It would seem that the normalized body image, one that complies with the imperatives of the Symbolic order, can only arise on the basis of bodily distortions (and perhaps contortions), performative exclusions which mark the threshold of the abject. And yet, insofar as that which has been abjected continually overruns its carefully circumscribed borders, it appears that these abject sites of our corporeality continue to seep into our own body images, threatening their coherence, and disrupting our attempts to contain our bodily excesses and deficiencies.

To distinguish distorted body images from nondistorted body images is, then, a much more difficult task than one may at first suppose. Perhaps what is needed is a new vocabulary for these body images that resist normalization, body images that refuse to cohere, or that somehow do manage to cohere in what looks, from an outsider's perspective, to be an impossible configuration. What does seem to be clear is that when bodies are at odds with their own body images, when that which is needed to sustain the body (e.g. relationships with other people, food, drink, clothing, shelter) becomes the abject other, distortion may turn out to be the only viable strategy for survival, and paradoxically, an affirmation predicated on a negation of life.

Susan Bordo, in particular, emphasizes the moral connotations that accompany this repudiation of (aspects of) embodied existence, arguing that "food refusal, weight loss, commitment to exercise, and ability to tolerate bodily pain and exhaustion have become cultural metaphors for self-determination, will, and moral fortitude" (Bordo 1993:68). In such a cultural climate, she maintains, it is hardly surprising that eating disorders are on the rise, especially among young women, nor is it surprising to find that self-starvation itself has deep spiritual dimensions which are in turn nourished by the traditional mind/body dualism that associates the mind with transcendence and the body with immanence.

"Within such a framework," Bordo asserts, "interpreting anorexia requires, not technical or professional expertise, but awareness of the many layers of cultural signification that are crystallized in the disorder" (Bordo 1993:67). Chief among these "layers of cultural signification," for Bordo, is what she calls an "amazingly durable and flexible strategy of social control," namely, "the discipline and normalization of the female body." Indeed, Bordo goes on to claim that this is "perhaps the only gender oppression that exercises itself, although to different degrees and in different forms, across age, race, class, and sexual orientation" (Bordo 1993:166). The predominant techniques through which this discipline and normalization are accomplished, she suggests, are "diet, make-up, and dress—central organizing principles of time and space in the day of many women" (Bordo 1993:166).

A danger of Bordo's account as well as the account of Morag MacSween, who also offers a feminist social constructionist perspective on anorexia, is that in attempting (quite successfully, I believe) to draw our attention to the limitations of medical models that tend either to ignore or minimize the substantial, motivating role that cultural norms and expectations regarding the "perfect" female body play in eating disorders, they lose sight of the fact that it is medicine and not culture that we must look to to treat these eating disorders and the body image distortions associated with them.[5] That is to say, while Bordo and MacSween are correct in arguing that as long as doctors refuse to acknowledge the cultural forces that encourage women to starve themselves in the pursuit of an elusive, ascetic body ideal, they will fail to understand why these disorders are so prevalent as well as how to eradicate them, it is nonetheless extremely problematic to claim, as Bordo does, that interpreting anorexia does not require "technical or professional expertise." For anorexia nervosa is indeed a corporeal dis(-)ease and not merely a tragic, contemporary cultural symptom of our postmodern times which anyone is equally free and qualified to interpret.

If, as Bordo suggests, anorexia nervosa is indeed a psychopathology only to the extent that psychopathology is itself the "crystallization of culture," it is nonetheless the case that it is not culture that is killing anorexic women and men, but their agonistic relationships with their own bodies. While Bordo would certainly recognize the validity of this point, her argument is that "[o]ur bodies, not less than anything else that is human, are constituted by culture" (Bordo 1993:142). Moreover, she also maintains that "female bodies have historically been significantly more vulnerable than male bodies to extremes in . . . cultural manipulation of the body" (Bordo 1993:143). Working from a feminist social constructionist perspective, Bordo traces this female corporeal vulnerability not to anatomical differences between males and females, but to cultural forces themselves, forces which have defined women (and, more specifically, thin women) as the object of masculine desire. MacSween reinforces this point when she claims that "[i]t is not the body itself which makes women 'passive vessels,' but how that body is *socially constructed*" (MacSween 1993:50).[6]

The question thus becomes, why has slenderness become the aesthetic ideal for women (as well as for men, as Bordo repeatedly acknowledges)? Why is slenderness what our patriarchal culture has come to associate with its body image ideal? These are indeed important questions, questions that Bordo addresses creatively and incisively in her work, but her answers, while complicated and historically nuanced, tend to be generated out of only one of the multidimensions she originally argues for, namely culture itself. While a feminist cultural analysis can certainly aid us in addressing these questions, it is woefully inadequate when it comes to resolving the issues themselves, that is, treating the diverse corporeal effects of these multi-faceted symptoms. Even setting the issue of treatment aside, it is clear that one cannot even begin to interpret the lived, bodily dimensions of anorexia unless one has either direct (either as a doctor, nurse, therapist or social worker) or indirect access to information obtained in clinical work with anorexics.

By abjecting the "fat" body from the culturally constructed aesthetic domain, people and not just body parts are designated as the abject other, doomed to exist in those uninhabitable, unlivable regions that Butler reminds us are, in point of fact, densely populated. Indeed, these regions are not just inhabited by those who are considered or consider themselves to be overweight. In fact, I would argue, they are currently in danger of being overpopulated insofar as none of us can forever live up to what Audre Lorde calls the "mythical norm." And for women, by definition, it is impossible even to try. This is because this mythical norm consists of those who are "white, thin, male, young, heterosexual, christian, and financially secure" (Lorde 1990:282). Despite the fact that this norm is also impossible for men of color, homosexual men, poor men, old men, and non-Christian men to achieve as well, in America and in much of Europe, this mythical norm indeed serves to define a cultural body image ideal. And, to the extent that this mythical norm functions as an imaginary, identificatory pole that regulates our satisfaction/dissatisfaction with our own specular images, it is clear that the elaboration of a coherent body image is itself an arduous task.

Returning to the question which I raised earlier in this chapter, namely, how do we account for "distorted" body images such as that of the anorexic, it is evident that the answer cannot be reduced to the contradictions between her own body image and the perceptions of others (i.e. her view of herself as overweight, and others' view of her as emaciated), since such an explanation only takes us back to the Sartrian tension between being-for-others and being-for-itself, a tension that characterizes not only the anorexic's existence but everyone who is nonanorexic as well.[7] Nor do I think it can be answered by appealing to the enormous social pressure (real as it is) that the hegemonic cultural body ideal of the tall, thin body, places upon us.[8] Paradoxically, I would argue, the deadly distortions in the anorexic's body image stem from its excessive *coherence*, a coherence that can only be maintained through her disidentification with and repudiation of her own multiple body images.

To develop this point further, what I am claiming is that although there are very real contradictions in the anorexic's body image (and, although they take different forms, they are also present in the body images of other individuals which are viewed as pathologically distorted), the contradictions themselves should not be viewed as the cause of the distortions. This is because, as I have tried to show throughout this text, we all have contradictions in our body images, contradictions that on a Lacanian analysis stem from the irresolvable gap between our own diverse and fluid bodily sensations on the one hand, and our identification with the unified, integrated specular image which subjectivates us. While Lacan does not acknowledge the (nonpsychotic) possibility of an individual's possessing multiple body images, he does recognize that the Gestalt that arises out of the identification of the subject with the specular image, attains its coherence at the expense of our lived corporeality:

> The fact is that the total form of the body by which the subject anticipates in a mirage the maturation of his power is given to him only as *Gestalt*, that is to say, in an exteriority in which this form is certainly more constituent than constituted, but in which it appears to him above all in a constrasting size (un relief de stature) that fixes it and in a symmetry that inverts it, in contrast with the turbulent movements that the subject feels are animating him. Thus, this Gestalt— whose pregnancy should be regarded as bound up with the species, though its motor style remains scarcely recognizable—by these two aspects of its appearance, symbolizes the mental permanence of the *I*, at the same time as it prefigures its alienating destination; it is still pregnant with the correspondences that unite the *I* with the statue in which man projects himself, with the phantoms that dominate him, or with the automaton in which, in an ambiguous relation, the world of his own making tends to find completion. (Lacan 1977:2–3)

This strange pregnancy, which is not distinctive to women, but is characteristic of "the species" as a whole, itself symbolizes the crucial disjunction between the corporeality of the subject and the specular image through which that subject is constituted. More simply, Lacan's metaphorical use of pregnancy as a characteristic of the species (and not of women in particular) further dissociates this Gestalt from the actual bodies of women (and men). By identifying the specular image with a statue, with "phantoms that dominate" and with an automaton in which "the world of his own making tends to find completion," Lacan points simultaneously to the enabling and the oppressive potentialities that accompany the gestation of the subject.

The turbulence that characterizes our lived bodily experience, a turbulence which, for Lacan, is psychically rejected in favor of a projected (imaginary) identification with the specular image, can, as he well recognized, never be denied altogether. Indeed, I would maintain that this turbulence is expressed and even accentuated in the transitions we continually make between one body image and another. For the nonpathological subject, I am suggesting, it is the very multiplicity of these body images which guarantees that we cannot invest too heavily in any one of them, and these multiple body images themselves offer points of resistance to the development of too strong an identification with a singularly alienating specular (or even cultural) image. That is, these multiple body images serve to destabilize the hegemony of any particular body image ideal, and are precisely what allows us to maintain a sense of corporeal fluidity.

By contrast, I am claiming that it is precisely the lack of *destabilization* in the anorexic's body image that is the source of its deadly destructiveness. Thus, rather than view the anorexic as an incoherent or contradictory subject, I am claiming that she is *too* coherent, psychically and corporeally dominated by what Ellen West, the pseudonymous anorexic subject of Ludwig Binswanger's famous case study, repeatedly identified as her *idée fixée*, namely, the "dread of getting fat." Indeed, the "mocking" phantoms that accompany her desire to be an ethereal or "fleshless" body, phantoms that remind her that she can never realize her ideal, do not destabilize the dominance of this idea but actually reinforce its hegemony. The power of their ghostly presence is incarnated in Ellen's poem "The Evil Thoughts," a poem which does not succeed in exorcising these "demons," but which only seems to strengthen their force and ubiquity:

> One time we were your thinking,
> Your hoping pure and proud!
> Where now are all your projects,
> The dreams that used to crowd?
>
> Now all of them lie buried,
> Scattered in wind and storm,
> And you've become a nothing,
> A timid earthy worm.
>
> So then we had to leave you,
> To dark night we must flee;
> The curse which fell upon you
> Has made us black to see.
>
> If you seek peace and quiet,
> Then we'll come creeping nigh
> And we'll take vengeance on you
> With our derisive cry.
>
> If you seek joy and gladness,
> We'll hurry to your side;
> Accusing you and jeering
> We'll e'er with you abide!
> (Binswanger 1958:244)

The dread of getting fat, in Ellen's life, continually wins out over a competing "wish for harmless eating," and, designated as untreatable by her doctors, she returns home to die. The final day of her life shows the futility of protest against these phantoms who cannot be nourished by any earthly sustenance:

On the third day of being home she is as if transformed. At breakfast she eats but-
ter and sugar, at noon she eats so much that—for the first time in thirteen
years!—she is satisfied by her food and gets really full. At afternoon coffee she
eats chocolate creams and Easter eggs. She takes a walk with her husband, reads
poems by Rilke, Storm, Goethe, and Tennyson, is amused by the first chapter of
Mark Twain's "Christian Science," is in a positively festive mood, and all heavi-
ness seems to have fallen away from her. She writes letters, the last one to a fel-
low patient here to whom she had become so attached. In the evening she takes
a lethal dose of poison, and on the following morning she is dead. "She looked as
she had never looked in life—calm and happy and peaceful." (Binswanger
1958:267)

Ellen's "idée fixée," an obsession which can only be vanquished through the
annihilation of the body itself, is a perfect example, both literal and symbolic,
of a corporeal reduction of an anorexic's universe, a reduction that is facilitated
by a singularly oppressive body image. This lack of fluidity and/or multiplicity,
indeed the hegemonic nature of this particular body image, offers no way
to live the corporeal contradictions that haunt Ellen West. The failure of
Ellen's physicians to treat her disease, stems from their inability to teach her
more about these contradictions than she already knows. Indeed, Ellen's very
eloquent and clearsighted appraisal of her "impossible" existence makes it
clear that neither medical, cognitive, nor cultural explanations can begin to do
justice to the surprising coherence that marks the distortions of an anorexic's
experience.

To arrive at an "embodied understanding" of anorexia and other eating disorders, as Bordo seeks to do, requires beginning with their lived, bodily dimensions rather than with a medical, cognitive, or even cultural diagnosis of them.
And, I am arguing, this involves focusing less on the cultural and bodily contradictions that appear in this particular disease, contradictions which are all too
apparent not only to outsiders but often to the anorexic herself, but on the need
to respond *corporeally* to these contradictions through the creation of multiple
body images. These body images will inevitably be in tension with one another, but, by communicating with one another through the "body image intercourse" discussed by Schilder, they allow us to negotiate productively the turbulence of our corporeal existence, a turbulence that cannot and should not be
abjected from our body images, since it is precisely what enables us to meet the
vicissitudes of our bodily life. Of course, the effectiveness of this process will
also depend upon a medical, cultural, and philosophical commitment to mul-
tiply our aesthetic body ideals beyond the hegemony of the anticorporeal, fat-
free body, an image that continues, in many contemporary societies, both to
define and regulate the abject borders of our body images.

{5}

The Durée of
the Techno-Body

The implosion of space into time, the transmutation of distance
into speed, the instantaneousness of communication, the collaps-
ing of the workspace into the home computer system, will clearly
have major effects on the bodies of the city's inhabitants. The subject's body will no longer be disjointedly connected to random others and objects through the city's spatiotemporal layout; it will
interface with the computer, forming part of an information
machine in which the body's limbs and organs will become interchangeable parts. Whether this results in the "crossbreeding" of the
body and the machine—whether the machine will take on the
characteristics attributed to the human body ("artificial intelligence," automatons)—or whether the human body will take on the
characteristics of the machine (the cyborg, bionics, computer prosthesis) remains unclear. Yet it is certain that this will fundamentally
transform the ways in which we conceive both cities and bodies,
and their interrelations. What remains uncertain is how.

—Elizabeth Grosz (1995:110)

Almost daily, we are bombarded with news of innovative technologies
capable of repairing bodily injuries (e.g. laser surgeries), replacing body parts
(e.g. prostheses), and now cloning animal bodies to create genetically identical
but anatomically distinct beings. These innovations have met with ambivalent
responses from the public at large, who usually hears of them via the media,
from the scientists who have developed them, and from academics who have
theorized about them. On February 23, 1997, the front page of that icon of
respectability, the *New York Times*, was emblazoned with a headline that
seemed more in keeping with its tabloid döppelganger, the *National Enquirer*:
"Scientist Reports First Cloning Ever Of Adult Mammal/Researchers Astound-
ed/In Procedure on Sheep, Fiction Becomes True and Dreaded Possibilities
Are Raised."[1] In the days that followed, more and more articles appeared in
newspapers and magazines confirming the initial report, providing evidence of
similar procedures that have been successfully performed with monkeys, and
raising questions about that most horrifying/tantalizing possibility—could
humans be next?[2]

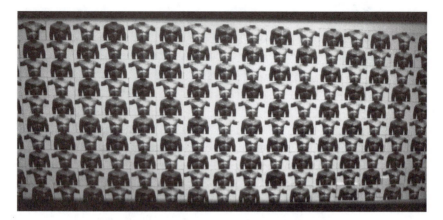

Of Mies and Men (installation detail), Mark Robbins (mixed media,
The American Academy in Rome, 1997, photo by Walter Hood)

The answer to the crucially different ethical question, *should* humans be next was, at least in early articles and interviews, a resounding, and seemingly unanimous "no." Indeed, the scientists who performed "Dolly's" cloning hastily assured us that they are not in favor of extending these technological feats to human beings. Rather, we were told, these technologies are intended to be used primarily for animal husbandry; for instance, cloning will allow us to increase the milk output on dairy farms by cloning cows that are "superproducers of milk." One "expert," Dr. Neal First, clearly oblivious to the impact of his pronouncement upon a general media audience, has gone so far as to proclaim "that if—and it's a very big if—cloning were highly efficient, then it could be a more significant revolution to the livestock industry than even artificial insemination."[3]

Although I have never been an animal rights advocate, Dr. First's sanguine pronouncement plunged me into speculation on the existence of those future female bovine "superproducers" whose lives will be technologically regulated from birth (via cloning) through maternity (artificial insemination by donor [AID] pregnancies), lactation (the milking machines which will be the only way for them to relieve their super-full udders since their calves are not allowed to nurse), and finally, in death (through the technological apparatus of the contemporary slaughterhouse which kills, packages what is edible, and efficiently disposes of all waste).

My carnivorous reflections on the cow's intimate relationship to technology led me next to those human scientists and farmers who are making it possible, and to the recognition that these cybernetic possibilities can in no way be construed as affecting only the cows; rather, they are directed toward *we* human beings who drink their milk, eat their flesh, wear their skin—in short, consume them. So, to restrict the questions raised by cloning purely to animals such as sheep, monkeys, and cows, fails to eliminate the "human" factor. Moreover, since cloning is itself a reproductive technology, the issues it raises seem to implicate some human beings more than others, namely, those females whose reproductive experiences are capable of being radically altered by these procedures and the related procedures that are likely to follow such as ectogenesis (gestation and birth outside the female body). Of course, cloning and ectogenesis will alter the reproductive experiences of males as well as females, especially since they may, via genetic engineering, allow for male-male reproduction in the absence of a female or even of her egg. Now, whether or not these technologies are ever developed for humans (and my guess is that cloning will not be, but that ectogenesis eventually will be), the question I asked earlier, *could* they be, is itself enough to cause us to interrogate anew the interface between bodies and machines, to explore the significances of an intercorporeality that defies any attempt to affirm the autonomy of the body apart from other bodies or from the disciplinary, technological practices which are continually altering and redefining them.

This is itself a vast project, and one that is being carried out on several different fronts and with several different (but largely unstated) political agendas. The barrage of statements (which themselves often appear to be clones of one another) from scientists (all of whom seem to be male) who appeal to medically "neutral" language to discuss these techno-bodily possibilities, implicitly deny the economic, metaphysical, sexual, and racial implications these new body-technologies involve, and the futuristic, hypothetical language used in their descriptions also can seduce us into believing that these technological developments and their potential consequences affect merely an impossibly distant, imaginary future, not the present, much less the past.

The specific question I would like to take up here has to do with the temporality of the techno-body, which is certainly not a future body, but is our own bodies and bodily possibilities to the extent that they are discursively represented, psychologically constructed, and physiologically re-constructed through technological processes which include the pen, the analyst's couch, the speculum, forceps, the surgeon's knife, the computer, the city and its abjected other, the "sub-urb," as well as the unassuming petrie dish, that all-important maternal substitute, which has displaced the female as the "originary" site of genetic experimentation and reproductive speculation.

In *Nomadic Subjects: Embodiment and Sexual Difference in Contemporary Feminist Theory*, Rosi Braidotti argues that our new biotechnologies, which make organs interchangeable (e.g. organ transplants), give us babies without sex (e.g. in vitro fertilization) and sex without babies (e.g. anti-contraceptive pill), reduce bodies to organisms, organisms to organs, and in the end, evacuate human (and especially female) agency by doing away with the very notion and experience of durée or becoming in time:

> Stuck between the archaic material power and the postmodern mother-
> machine, between the mystical-hysterical body and the test tube, we run the risk
> of losing our most precious ally: time. The time of process, of working through,
> of expressing transformations of the self and other and having them implement-
> ed socially. This is the time of women's own becoming. It can be taken away
> before it could ever be actualized; it could be short-circuited, aborted. (Braidotti
> 1994:55)

More particularly, Braidotti argues that these new biotechnologies "freeze" time thereby affirming not life, but death. This freezing is enacted through what she depicts as an equally frozen, masculinist figure, namely, the contemporary biotechnician, who:

> as the prototype of high-tech power, represents the modern knowing subject:
> "man-white-Western-male-adult-reasonable-heterosexual-living-in-towns-speak-
> ing a standard language."
> Under his imperious gaze the living organisms, reduced to an infinitely small

scale, lose all reference to the human shape and to the specific temporality of the human being. All reference to death disappears in the discourse about "biopower"—power over life. What seems to me at stake in the biopower situation is the progressive freezing-out of time, that is to say ultimately of death. The living material that comes under the scrutiny of the medical gaze is beyond death and time—it's "living" in the most abstract possible way. (Braidotti 1994:47)

In marked contrast to her depiction of these allegedly frozen, death-like biotechnologies (which themselves rely quite heavily on the freezer in order to promote their "timely" effects), Braidotti describes woman's excess, her "monstrosity," the monstrosity of (Deleuze's) becoming-woman, a becoming that has made her a site of fascination and horror, and which is in danger of being transubstantiated into a marketable and possibly even dispensable product. Indeed, Braidotti likens this transformation to a perennial, alchemic fantasy. Specifically, she claims that:

On the imaginary level . . . the test-tube babies of today mark the long-term triumph of the alchemists' dream of dominating nature through their self-inseminating, masturbatory practices. What is happening with the new reproductive technologies today is the final chapter in a long history of fantasy of self-generation by and for the men themselves—men of science, but men of the male kind, capable of producing new monsters and fascinated by their power. (Braidotti 1994:88)

For Braidotti, contemporary reproductive technologies such as in vitro fertilization, represent a flight from the excesses of both maternal desire and maternal imagination; they collapse the spatiality and temporality of the maternal/fetal relationship into a "homunculus, a man-made tiny man popping out of the alchemist's laboratories, fully formed and endowed with language" (Braidotti 1994:87). While clearly disparaging the fascination of these alchemic biotechnicians with their own power and with the new "monsters" they have created, Braidotti also disparages the transformation of woman as a site of excess, horror, and fascination to a reproductive instrument or machine.

Nostalgically, Braidotti asks, "Where has the Cartesian passion of wonder gone?" Paradoxically, this wonder for her turns out to be the very mixture of horror and fascination that she claims men are fleeing from *through* their fascination with the transformative possibilities offered by contemporary biotechnologies. Braidotti is seemingly oblivious to this tension in her position, a tension that appears insofar as horror and fascination are escaped through a new fascination which brings with it its own horrifying possibilities. Rather than provide justification for her implicit and extremely problematic distinction between a "legitimate" subject of horror and fascination (e.g. women before reproductive technologies existed) as opposed to an "illegitimate" one (e.g. cybernetic fetuses), Braidotti ignores these difficulties and concludes that it is impossible to see our contemporary reproductive technologies as anything other than "a form of denial of the sense of wonder, of the fantastic, of that mixture of fascination and horror that I have already mentioned" (Braidotti 1994:89).

Even if we set aside this tension, one which threatens to undermine her entire account, it would seem that Braidotti is calling for a return to an imaginary time when this horror and fascination for women's bodies accorded them dignity and respect. I think it is indeed an imaginary time because it is not clear when the combination of horror and fascination that she is valorizing has ever been advantageous to those who have been designated as "monstrous." Braidotti blames "the massive medicalization of scientific discourse" for eliminating the "marvelous, imaginary dimension of the monster," yet I would argue that this "marvelous, imaginary dimension" has never been quite so marvelous for those individuals whose monstrosities have been constructed through this phantasmatic site.

Basically, Braidotti is conflating several issues that need to be considered separately: 1) Are these new biotechnologies really "freezing time," technologies of death as opposed to life? 2) Is death adequately understood as "frozen time," fundamentally opposed to the flowing temporality of life? 3) Are contemporary reproductive technologies indeed diminishing the horror and fascination Braidotti identifies with a Cartesian passion of wonder before that which escapes our control? These questions lead, in turn, to further questions about Braidotti's own analysis: 4) Is this mixture of horror and fascination advantageous for those who are its objects, that is, is this a mixture of passions we want to privilege? 5) Does this fascination and horror and Braidotti's corresponding reification of these passions, serve to intensify, in oppressive ways, the monstrosity of the monstrous?

Before addressing these questions, I should first note that in a more recent essay, "Signs of Wonder and Traces of Doubt: On Teratology and Embodied Differences," Braidotti attempts to deconstruct the historical understanding of the monster as the radical Other; rather, she argues that:

> The peculiarity of the organic monster is that s/he is both Same and Other. The monster is neither a total stranger nor completely familiar; s/he exists in an in-between zone. I would express this as a paradox: the monstrous other is both liminal and structurally central to our perception of normal human subjectivity. The monster helps us to understand the paradox of 'difference' as a ubiquitous but perennially negative preoccupation. (Braidotti 1996:141)

The paradox, then, is that the organic monster is a liminal, phantasmatic site that refuses straightforward categorization or description and, at the same time, it is "structurally central to our perception of normal human subjectivity" insofar as it serves to establish difference by constituting an abject domain generated through the fantasies of a historically evolving, racist and sexist imaginary.

For, she tells us:

> This mechanism of 'domestic foreignness', exemplified by the monster, finds its
> closest analogy in mechanisms such as sexism and racism. The woman, the Jew,
> the black or the homosexual are certainly 'different' from the configuration of
> human subjectivity based on masculinity, whiteness, heterosexuality, and Christ-
> ian values which dominates our scientific thinking. Yet they are central to this
> thinking, linked to it by negation, and therefore structurally necessary to uphold-
> ing the dominant view of subjectivity. The real enemy is within: s/he is liminal,
> but dwells at the heart of the matter. (Braidotti 1996:141)

Ultimately, I would argue, Braidotti is profoundly ambivalent in her
response to the paradox of the monster, and this ambivalence can perhaps be
attributed to her tacit recognition that the monster's subversive potential as a
liminal entity always threatening to disrupt established (social) order can only
be maintained to the extent that, in a process well-described both by Mary
Douglas and by Julia Kristeva, we disavow our own monstrous excesses by
reincarnating them in the body of the abject Other.[4] That is, the subversive
potential of the monster is inseparable from its marginalization. In horror and
fascination, Braidotti implies, we recognize that we *are* the monster, or at least
are born of the maternal monster, and her concern about contemporary
biotechnologies is that they give us an illusory sense of control over the mon-
strous/maternal, domesticating our horror and fascination, but, in so doing, create new monsters, nonmaternal, cybernetic monsters who may end up control-
ling us. For, she concludes, the monster as the embodiment of difference:

> moves, flows, changes; because it propels discourses without ever settling into
> them; because it evades us in the very process of puzzling us, it will never be
> known what the next monster is going to look like; nor will it be possible to guess
> where it will come from. And because we *cannot* know, the monster is always
> going to get us. (Braidotti 1996:150)

Let us return, at this ominous point, to the questions I raised earlier, to see if,
in disentangling the complex and contradictory threads of Braidotti's own
analysis, her concerns about contemporary biotechnologies are indeed well-
founded. Let me first take up my initial question, and restate it as follows: Are
these new technologies "freezing" time as Braidotti suggests, by diminishing
the power of maternal imagination and maternal desire and replacing them
with a masculinist, misogynist, parthogenetic fantasy? Braidotti's own evolving
understanding of the monster as a "shifter, a vehicle that constructs a web of
interconnected and yet potentially contradictory discourses about his or her
embodied self" and, as "a process without a stable object" already calls into
question such a reductive claim (Braidotti 1996:150). For, as a moving, flowing, changing, embodiment of difference, the monster will itself subvert any
attempts that are made to "neutralize it" by "fixing" it or "freezing" it. However,

one may always respond that although these reproductive technologies will not succeed in freezing time/eliminating the monster, this does not take away from the fact that this is what they are aiming at and actively trying to achieve. Yet, I would challenge this claim as well. To support this challenge, I will turn not to an examination of the technologies themselves (though this is an important project in its own right), but to what is being presupposed but left uninterrogated in Braidotti's own discussion, namely, an understanding of temporality as lived time, embodied time, in contrast to the disembodied, "frozen" time that she claims is the goal of biotechnological practices and their scientific/medicalized discourses.

No one, I think, has offered a more profound account of this distinction between lived temporality and "objective" time than Henri Bergson, in his well-known (but all too often overlooked) essay, "An Introduction to Metaphysics."[5] Here, Bergson argues that temporality or "inner time," is irreducible to "outer" or "clock" time, and that any analysis of the latter will fail to grasp the essence of the former. To support the irreconcilability of temporality and time, Bergson appeals to the intuition each of us has of her/his own durée, that is, to the sense we possess of our own personalities flowing through time. Bergson argues that this experience of continual becoming or durée cannot be captured in discrete moments of time; our durée is itself a continuous flux or flow that is accessible to intuition but eludes analysis and its conceptual symbolizations. Durée, Bergson maintains, violates the "law" of noncontradiction; it is both a unity and a multiplicity because it "lends itself at the same time both to an indivisible apprehension and to an inexhaustible enumeration" (Bergson 1955:23). Despite its contradictory nature, Bergson argues that we can and often do grasp our durée as an absolute via a "simple act" of intuition. "By intuition" he claims:

> is meant the kind of *intellectual sympathy* by which one places oneself within an object in order to coincide with what is unique in it and consequently inexpressible. Analysis, on the contrary, is the operation which reduces the object to elements already known, that is, to elements common both to it and other objects. To analyze, therefore, is to express a thing as a function of something other than itself. All analysis is thus a translation, a development into symbols, a representation taken from successive points of view from which we note as many resemblances as possible between the new object which we are studying and others which we believe we know already. In its eternally unsatisfied desire to embrace the object around which it is compelled to turn, analysis multiplies without end the number of its points of view in order to complete its always incomplete representation, and ceaselessly varies its symbols that it may perfect the always imperfect translation. It goes on, therefore, to infinity. But intuition, if intuition is possible, is a simple act. (Bergson 1955:23–24)

One way of understanding Braidotti's claim that contemporary biotechnologies "freeze" time is to view them as attempting, through an analytic, medico-scientific process, to gain control over the durée of both maternal and fetal bodies. Moreover, one might argue that procedures such as cloning challenge the integrity of this durée, and make it impossible to grasp via a "simple act" of intuition. Although I think Bergson might well have been sympathetic to Braidotti's suspicions about contemporary biotechnologies, especially insofar as they seem inevitably to tamper with our sense of time, I also think that his account of both durée and intuition provides a means of countering Braidotti's overwhelmingly pessimistic analysis.[6]

If, as Bergson suggests above, intuition is a matter of "placing oneself within the object in order to coincide with what is unique in it and consequently inexpressible," then it would seem that intuition can always occur as long as there is a unique temporal experience there to be intuited as well as a temporal being who is capable of intuiting it. Later on in the essay, Bergson reinforces and elaborates on this point by claiming that intuition need not be restricted to our own durée since, in the very act of intuiting our own durée, we are brought "into contact with a whole continuity of durations which we must try to follow, whether downwards or upwards; in both cases we can extend ourselves indefinitely by an increasingly violent effort . . . we transcend ourselves" (Bergson 1955:48–49)

In claiming that we are able, with effort, to transcend our own durée and participate in the durations of others, Bergson is trying to show that a metaphysics based on intuition is not solipsistic. However, his claim that one duration is always in contact with a whole continuity of durations is provocative in its own right. More specifically, by invoking this "continuity of durations," Bergson seems to be arguing for the imbrication of our respective durées and, even further, for an intertemporality that need not be restricted to human experiences. Indeed, one of his most striking examples of intuition in "An Introduction to Metaphysics" is an intuition of Paris, a city with its own unique durée which, he argues, cannot be intuited "even with an infinite number of accurate sketches" if one has never seen the city oneself. Setting aside his problematic claim that one must see the city oneself in order to have an intuition of its durée, a claim that only rings true if we lose sight of the power of both art and literature to evoke the durée of a city and of its various inhabitants, I would like to turn to his suggestion that durées are never isolated but always interconnected and that, through a "violent effort" we can extend ourselves indefinitely, even transcend ourselves by intuitively grasping this continuum.

If, as Bergson argues, analysis is impotent before durée, incapable of grasping it except through "ready-made concepts" that "never actually give us more than an artificial reconstruction of the object" (Bergson 1955:29), a corresponding analysis of the durée of the techno-bodies produced by contemporary biotechnologies via an exploration of the desires and fantasies that motivate their practitioners will also fail. Ultimately, for this particular purpose, it is irrelevant what the desires and fantasies of contemporary biotechnicians turn out to be; if they indeed see themselves, as Braidotti suggests, as contemporary alchemists capable of dispensing with that horrifying/fascinating object of desire, the maternal body, once and for all, this does not mean that their productions will fulfill their "fathers'" wishes. For, as Donna Haraway notes in "A Cyborg Manifesto," "illegitimate offspring are often exceedingly unfaithful to their origins. Their fathers, after all, are inessential" (Haraway 1991:151).

The durée of the techno-body, whether this body be that of a newly cloned sheep, a "test-tube" baby, or a woman in labor hooked up to technological devices that record fetal movement, fetal heartbeat, maternal blood pressure, and labor pains, a boy with a liver transplant, or a woman with a prosthetic leg, arises out of a violent effort and requires a violent effort in order to see the interconnections that link this durée with our own. Indeed, what is most violent, I think, is the recognition that technology is part and parcel of our own durée—the monster will "get us" precisely to the extent that we view it as a threat from the "outside," incarnated in demonic biotechnologists and their allegedly masturbatory fantasies, rather than recognizing that it is not "out there" but within our own bodies, facilitating the death of solipsism by affirming the intercorporeality of time. As Haraway notes, "The machine is not an *it* to be animated, worshipped, and dominated. The machine is us, our processes, an aspect of our embodiment" (Haraway 1991:180).

One danger of emphasizing the gulf between temporality and time as I have done thus far, is that it makes us liable to forget the ways in which our own lived experience continually traverses the divide between them. For surely it is overly simplistic to say that time, as measured by calendars, watches, sundials, and the movement of planets and stars, is "out there" while our temporal experience is within us; rather, we "inhabit" time and are inhabited by it, through our own bodily rhythms and movements, and through the interconnections between our own durée and the durée of all that we encounter. Indeed, to the extent that the conventions of clock time are themselves based on the movement of the earth around the sun, clock time is not merely an external, analytical device that helps us negotiate our everyday affairs, but is based on corporeal movement, movement that is inscribed in our own bodies. "Freezing time" would lead to a corresponding freezing of temporality; it would require the severing of the continuum that unites one durée with another durée and would collapse an instant into an eternity. To turn to the second question I asked earlier on, is this frozen time, which seems so counter to the "rhythms of life," the time of death as Braidotti suggests?

"Freezing time" is itself a conundrum, because there is no way to imagine how time could be "frozen." People, rich people like Walt Disney, for instance, can be frozen, embryos can be frozen, but time itself cannot be frozen without time itself being transformed into something it is not, namely, a specific entity rather than a fluid, corporeal process. Sometimes, these liminal entities (frozen embryos and cyrogenically preserved people) are referred to as existing in "suspended animation" and I think this term is more accurate in expressing their temporal existence as opposed to saying that they are instances of "frozen time." Dead bodies that are not preserved in this way decay, a temporal process that leaves tangible effects on those bodies (and less tangible effects on other bodies) and which eventually transforms them into nonorganic matter.[7] Death is therefore not a stopping of time, though it is indeed a disruptive alteration of bodily temporality, an alteration which can be intuited through the interconnections between our own durée and the durée of others who have died. So, in a certain sense, Epicurus was wrong to proclaim that the experience of death is impossible since when death is, we are not and when we are, death is not. Death does not occur outside of time, but in time; death inhabits time as a virtuality which is continually embodied or actualized.

"Freezing time," I would argue, is not the goal or even the outcome of a death-like biotechnology, but a metaphorical strategy in the Ricoeurian sense, a strategy that is productive to the extent that it shatters and increases "our sense of reality by shattering and increasing our language" (Ricoeur 1991:85). To the extent that we acknowledge the compelling force of this contradictory metaphor, and to the extent that we view it as applicable to the contemporary biotechnologies Braidotti discusses, we must recognize its power to disrupt our understanding and experience of durée, a durée that extends, transforms, and transcends itself through these very technologies, technologies which, whether we actively make use of them, ignore them, or even avoid them, actively re-temporalize our lives.

Braidotti's use of the metaphor of "freezing time" is rendered even more complex by the ambiguity and ambivalence in her discussion of a related metaphor which I have already mentioned, namely, the metaphor of the monster. As we have already noted, she privileges (in problematic ways) the monster as a site of wonder which she identifies with fascination and horror and valorizes the power of the monster as the maternal body or even the "freakish" body of those whose corporeality resists normalization, and yet, she also appeals to the metaphor of the monster to characterize the destructive, death-inducing, time-freezing fantasies of contemporary biotechnicians who, she argues, are creating organs without bodies, that is, who are decorporealizing bodies in order to control, manipulate, and exchange them. Can she have it both ways? Do contemporary biotechnologies signify the erasure of the monster of old in favor of genetically-engineered cyborgs, which in turn take their place as the new monsters, monsters which threaten to "get us"? This leads me back to my third question, are contemporary reproductive technologies indeed diminishing the horror and fascination Braidotti identifies with a Cartesian passion of wonder before that which escapes our control?

In a strange sense, there seems to be an almost natural progression in the category of the monstrous. Once we have ceased to be horrified and fascinated by alleged pathologies of the human, the impetus to create new monsters, new sites of horror and fascination seems almost inevitable. Moreover, this follows from, rather than challenges, Braidotti's own valorization of the monster and the fascination and horror it invokes. In her essay, "Between Monsters, Goddesses and Cyborgs: Feminist Confrontations with Science," Nina Lykke extends the metaphorical domain of the monster by claiming that it:

> can perform as a representation of boundary phenomena in the interdisciplinary or hybrid grey zone between the cultural and natural sciences. In this zone, boundary subjects and boundary objects, monsters which cannot be defined as either human or non-human, challenge established borders between the sciences. This is a zone where confrontations between feminism and science take place. (Lykke 1996:14)

To make these confrontations productive, it is essential, I think, that we recognize that, as Patricia Bayer Richard notes, we cannot "put the technological genie back in the bottle" (Richard 1995:18). Nonetheless, to recognize that these technologies are here to stay does not mean that we should simply endorse them or overlook the racist, classist, and misogynistic presuppositions that may underlie and motivate them. On the other hand, I would argue that the metaphor of the monster or even the metaphor of "freezing time" won't work to capture what may be pernicious about these technologies. These technologies and the new, virtual realities that they have spawned, the virtual realities of frozen embryos, cryogenically preserved "corpses," and even their "cyborgian cousins," the virtual realities that "inhabit" cyberspace, replicate, rather than efface, the horror and fascination that have always accompanied the interpellation of the monster. To the extent that they offer themselves as a way of reconfiguring our own corporeal possibilities, they may indeed serve as sites of wonder and of passion. But, what we often find through these technologies is not an escape from the conventional, but a reinscription of convention, whether this reinscription takes the form, through reproductive technologies, of Richard's "tailor-made child" or, in the domain of virtual reality, of "cyberspace heroes" who, as Anne Balsamo notes, are "usually men, whose racial identity, although rarely described explicitly, is contextually white." Their counterparts, "cyberspace playmates," she observes, "are usually beautiful, sexualized, albeit sometimes violently powerful women." For Balsamo:

> Cyberspace offers white men an enticing retreat from the burdens of their *cultural* identities. In this sense, it is apparent that although cyberspace seems to represent a territory free from the burdens of history, it will, in effect, serve as another site for the technological and no less conventional inscription of the gendered, race-marked body. So despite the fact that VR [virtual reality] technologies offer a new stage for the construction and performance of body-based identities, it is

likely that old identities will continue to be more comfortable, and thus more frequently produced. (Balsamo 1996:130–131)

If, as Haraway argues, "communication technologies and biotechnologies are the crucial tools recrafting our bodies," then we need to think carefully about the ways in which these latter reinscribe, rather than oppose, challenge, or subvert, the patriarchal status quo (Haraway 1991:164). As Balsamo suggests in the passage just cited, cyberspace may seem to promise an escape from one's cultural identity but it may end up reinforcing that identity through the replication of the aesthetic ideals that help to constitute and solidify its normative, hegemonic structure. So, far from leaving the body behind, or of absorbing "the material into the semiotic" in a process according to which "the material is constructed as potentially changeable by semiotic, sign-producing acts, by programming and reprogramming," the cyborg may turn out to be both less and more monstrous than we have imagined; less monstrous insofar as its reprogramming may not lead to radical innovation but to fairly conventional repetition, more monstrous insofar as oppressive corporeal practices are reinscribed in a more ubiquitous, virtual register (Lykke 1996:27).

The metaphor of the monster, I would argue, has become so pervasive that it has lost its potency, more specifically, it has lost the "shattering" power which Ricoeur identifies with a metaphor's ability to create a novel reality through its redescription of reality. "The strategy of metaphor," he proclaims, "is heuristic fiction for the sake of redescribing reality" (Ricoeur 1991:85). To the extent that the metaphor of the monster has drawn much of its power from the mixture of fascination and horror that the figure of the monster has evoked, the time has come to think long and hard about the consequences of privileging responses that may stem more from bad faith than from a "genuine" sense of wonder in the face of that which refuses normalization. As Beauvoir reminds us in *The Second Sex*, it is a bourgeois luxury to view the Other as mysterious, as beyond our comprehension. And, for those all too numerous Others whose various "excesses" and/or "lacks" are constructed as mysterious, as monstrous, the price of this "heuristic fiction" may be far too high. For Beauvoir, it justifies a refusal to recognize the concrete situation of the mysterious/monstrous other by appealing to a mythical understanding that refuses to give way to any reality that conflicts with it.

So, my response to the fourth question I asked earlier, namely, is this mixture of horror and fascination advantageous for those who are its objects, that is, is this a mixture of passions we want to privilege, is a resounding "no." If contemporary biotechnologists and the techno-bodies they help to produce are indeed replacing the monsters of old with new monsters, this may be advantageous for the former, but the advantage will be relative to the disadvantageous position of the latter. Too much focus on how these technologies are instruments of control runs the danger of transforming the technologies themselves into agents rather than recognizing that, as Balsamo reminds us, "technologies have *limited* agency" (Balsamo 1996:123). It also takes our collective attention away from the ways in which women and men who fail to comply with society's corporeal ideals are themselves controlled and regulated by both technological and nontechnological practices.

If Bergson indeed teaches us, as Deleuze argues, "that my duration essentially has the power to enclose other durations, to encompass the others, and to encompass itself ad infinitum" then we can move beyond what Haraway has called "an informatics of domination" toward an understanding of technology as offering new ways of linking bodies up to one another, expanding their interconnections, and, in so doing, increasing their intercorporeal potentialities (Deleuze 1988:80). Such a view does not, as I have already stated, lead to a wholehearted endorsement of each and every new technology that is proposed or developed; rather, it displaces the focus from the technology as such to a careful examination of its corporeal effects and, in turn, to the discursive practices which situate it as desirable, inevitable, or horrifying.

If, as I believe, fascination and horror and Braidotti's corresponding reification of these passions, oppressively intensifies the monstrosity of the monstrous (in response to my fifth question), the answer will not be to condemn the passions themselves as oppressive, but rather, to recognize that passions are always passions *for* something or other, and are not capable of being analyzed in the absence of the objects (or persons) that arouse them. The passion for technology need not lead to the technologization of passion. But if it does, we should hesitate from calling this a new monster until we have interrogated its intercorporeal implications and effects. And, to the extent that we are embedded and encompassed within the techniques and practices we critique, such an interrogation can never point the finger at a monster without a mirror being present. One day, perhaps, this mirror will itself be technologically transformed so that it reveals not a frozen, alienating, monstrous image of otherness, but the lived, intercorporeal durée of our own techno-bodies.

{6}

Écart

The Space of Corporeal Difference

[U]ltimately, it is only the strange which is familiar and only difference which is repeated.

—Gilles Deleuze (1994:109)

It is not clear who makes and who is made in the relation between human and machine.

—Donna Haraway (1991:177)

Taken together, these two claims challenge clear-cut divisions between the familiar and the unfamiliar, the natural and the unnatural. Inverting the Platonic understanding of mimesis in which copies not only depend for their existence upon a prior origin(al), but derive their own (moral) value and aesthetic merit through the preciseness with which they imitate that origin(al), Deleuze argues that the new and the different can only arise through repetition; in his words: "We produce something new only on condition that we repeat" (Deleuze 1994:90). Repetition, he maintains, cannot be understood as a recurrence of the same, rather, "repetition is the power of difference and differenciation: because it condenses the singularities, or because it accelerates or decelerates time, or because it alters spaces" (Deleuze 1994:220).

Although Deleuze and Haraway have markedly different projects and methodologies, as well as different conceptions of both humans and machines, I would argue that both are indebted to the notion of reversibility articulated in the later Merleau-Ponty. While for Deleuze this connection is more obvious given that he acknowledges Merleau-Ponty as a formative influence on his thought, I would maintain that Haraway's own understanding of the cyborg as "a hybrid of machine and organism, a creature of social reality as well as a creature of fiction" (Haraway 1991:149) is itself a chiasmatic notion that foregrounds the reversible, mutually constitutive relationship between the human and the nonhuman.

The place where Merleau-Ponty most eloquently (and enigmatically) articulates what he means by reversibility is in the chapter, "The Intertwining—

Untitled, Peter W. Brooke (pen and pencil sketch, 1998)

The Chiasm" of his final, unfinished work, *The Visible and the Invisible*. Feminist theorists, in particular, have focused on this particular essay, critically examining the examples of reversibility Merleau-Ponty offers there, challenging the limitations of this "metaphysical principle," and exploring its radical possibilities. Most of the recent work feminist theorists have done on this essay has approached it through Luce Irigaray's "mimetic" reading of it, in "The Invisible of the Flesh: A Reading of Merleau-Ponty, *The Visible and the Invisible*, The Intertwining—The Chiasm."[1] In this essay, Irigaray repeats the Merleau-Pontian text, challenging its omissions and exploring its fissures, in order to produce an alternative account of reversibility that could be said, paradoxically, to precede Merleau-Ponty's prior articulation of it.

Passing in and out of Merleau-Ponty's essay, picking up certain themes only to drop them and move on to related issues, Irigaray folds her own essay into his, intertwining them to produce an account of corporeality that extends back before birth (Merleau-Ponty's starting point) and forward to an imagined future in which the reversible relations that continuously unfold within women's own bodies are recognized and appreciated sites of knowledge, pleasure, and desire. Before examining Irigaray's subversive strategy and the critique of Merleau-Ponty's understanding of reversibility that issues from it more closely, let me begin by discussing those aspects of reversibility that are crucial for both thinkers as well as for Deleuze and Haraway.

First, and foremost, it should be noted that the image of reversibility Merleau-Ponty provides in *The Visible and the Invisible* and in his earlier essay, "Eye and Mind," is extremely spatial. Reversibility, as depicted by Merleau-Ponty, might best be described as a metaphysical principle that functions on both a micro-level and a macro-level to characterize the body's interactions with itself, with others, and with the world. On a micro-level, reversibility breaks down the (conceptual) boundaries between what have traditionally been understood as discrete bodily sensations, performing what Judith Butler has called a kind of "transubstantiation" of vision into touch, movement into expression, whereby I see by "touching" and move by "speaking" with my body.[2] On a macro-level, reversibility describes an ongoing interaction between the flesh of the body, the flesh of others, and the flesh of the world, a process in which corporeal boundaries are simultaneously erected and dismantled. Bringing these two levels together, Grosz maintains that:

> Flesh is being as reversibility, being's capacity to fold in on itself, being's dual orientation inward and outward, being's openness, its reflexivity, the fundamental gap or dehiscence of being that Merleau-Ponty illustrates with a favorite example—the notion of "double sensation," the capacity of one hand to touch another that is itself touching an object. . . . (Grosz 1993:44)

If reversibility indeed is, as Merleau-Ponty implies, an operative principle that makes perception, thought, and language possible, the paradox involved in interrogating it is both temporal and spatial. The temporal dimension of the paradox can be understood as analogous to the paradox that Butler identifies in attempting to provide an account of the becoming of the subject, a becoming that constitutes the subject as such, but which can only be interrogated from a given subject position which it both anticipates and repeats:

> The temporal paradox of the subject is such that, of necessity, we must lose the perspective of a subject already formed in order to account for our own becoming. That "becoming" is no simple or continuous affair, but an uneasy practice of repetition and its risks, compelled yet incomplete, wavering on the horizon of social being. (Butler 1997:30)

To trace the process of becoming that forms the subject is itself a transformative enterprise. As Butler argues, the becoming of the subject cannot be described through a linear trajectory, but involves a disparate series of backward and forward movements in which the subject repetitively, reflexively, turns back upon itself, and moreover, this self that the subject returns to is not a fixed self but a self that is phantasmatically projected as a stable site of significance. Butler's own chiasmatic account of a subject turning back upon itself, forming itself through its subjection to this compulsive desire for repetition of an original moment which it can never reproduce, is indebted not only to Freud and Lacan, Nietzsche and Foucault, figures whose work she analyzes and critiques at length, but also to Merleau-Ponty's articulation of the phenomenon of reversibility.[3]

To foreground the spatial dimensions of the chiasm, one must recognize that the intimate interrelationships which reversibility makes possible between humans and humans, between humans and nonhumans and between nonhumans and nonhumans, are themselves grounded upon what Merleau-Ponty calls écart, a space of non-coincidence that resists articulation. More specifically, in order for human beings to "interface" with machines, in order for us to become one with our familiar, mass-produced or even "one-of-a-kind" prostheses (e.g. glasses, clothes, artificial limbs, moussed-up hair, cars, watches, etc.), there must be, as Deleuze affirms, a strange space of disincorporation that makes incorporation possible. While Merleau-Ponty never explicitly addresses the relationship between humans and machines, Deleuze argues that human beings are themselves machines, desiring-machines that "work only when they break down, and by continually breaking down" (Deleuze 1983:8).

The body's sudden rejection of a transplanted organ that hitherto had been working "just fine," reminds us that the crossover between human and machine is never seamless or untroubled. Discussing her experience of hearing renowned physicist Steven Hawking give a "talk" through a Vortrax, a computer-generated speech device, Allucquère Rosanne Stone asks:

> Who is doing the talking up there on stage? In an important sense, Hawking doesn't stop being Hawking at the edge of his visible body. There is the obvious

physical Hawking, vividly outlined by the way our social conditioning teaches us to see a person as a person. But a serious part of Hawking extends into the box in his lap. In mirror image, a serious part of that silicon and plastic assemblage in his lap extends into him as well . . . not to mention the invisible ways, displaced in time and space, in which discourses of medical technology and their physical accretions already permeate him and us. No box, no discourse; in the absence of the prosthetic, Hawking's intellect becomes a tree falling in the forest with nobody around to hear it. (Stone 1995:5)

According to Stone, Hawking is not Hawking without his prosthetic voice. His Vortrax is inextricably tied to who "he" is in a complex, boundary-defying relationship in which the machine is the person and the person is the machine. And yet, to ask "who is doing the talking up there on stage?" itself gestures toward a space of disincorporation, a virtual site that sets the terms for the reversible relationship between man and machine.

It is this site, the unrepresentable space of differentiation that makes reversibility possible which interests me.[4] The seductiveness of the chiasmatic intertwining that Merleau-Ponty invokes to describe reversibility has led many to focus on how corporeal reversibility is lived rather than on the invisible "hinge" that both makes reversibility possible and, simultaneously, prevents it from being fully achieved. For Irigaray, this invisible, yet indispensable place is what she calls the "maternal-feminine," the site of all sexual difference.[5]

While Irigaray is clearly drawing upon Merleau-Ponty's own understanding of reversibility in tracing out the chiasmatic relationship between mother and fetus as the ground for all future instances of reversibility that we experience in our lives, she uses this paradigmatic experience to illustrate that Merleau-Ponty has not taken reversibility far enough. According to Irigaray, he doesn't extend it far enough because he begins with bodies that are already sexually individuated and talks about the reversible relations that play out within those bodies (e.g. one hand touching the other), and between those bodies and other, equally individuated bodies. In doing so, she argues, Merleau-Ponty offers us a "labyrinthine solipsism"—whereby all touching, all looking, all hearing, reverberate back upon an individuated subject who experiences herself as touched, looked at, heard. By gesturing toward that originary, maternal, phantasmatic site we all once inhabited but to which we can never return, Irigaray points out that reversibility is already operative before the subject is differentiated as such, and that it involves, from the outset, a relationship between bodies that are non-discrete, one enveloped within the other.

This is a trenchant critique that I believe Merleau-Ponty, with his interest in early childhood development, may have been responsive to, but Irigaray challenges his account on other grounds as well. Specifically, she also claims that Merleau-Ponty takes reversibility too far, in that he describes a harmonious, flowing, two-way interaction between the tangible and the visible whereby, as noted earlier, we "see" through touching and "touch" through seeing, a process that involves not merely these two senses alone but all the other senses that comprise our "aesthesiological" bodies. Although, historically, vision has been accorded primacy over all the other senses, and although Merleau-Ponty himself seems to subvert this primacy by placing touch (and later on hearing) on an equal footing with vision, Irigaray maintains that Merleau-Ponty nonetheless refuses to grant the primacy of touch, a primacy which she claims can be seen once we acknowledge our previous, intrauterine experience in which we touched before seeing and were touched before being seen.

For Irigaray then, Merleau-Ponty takes reversibility too far because he does not acknowledge that certain tactile experiences (e.g. intrauterine existence, and female sexuality more generally) cannot be rendered visible nor does he recognize that the reversible relationships that are nonetheless occurring (e.g. the fetus's relationship with its mother and a woman's relationship with her own body) are ruptured through attempts to specularise them.[6] Rather than opening up the body to other bodies, to the world and to itself, Merleau-Ponty's notion of reversibility, Irigaray asserts, closes off these rich corporeal sites because it weaves them too tightly together, and, in so doing, fails to acknowledge differences that are nonreversible, such as the sexually specific differences between maternal and nonmaternal, female and male bodies.[7] Thus:

> According to Merleau-Ponty, energy plays itself out in the backward-and-forward
> motion of a loom. But weaving the visible and my look in this way, I could just as
> well say that I close them off from myself. The texture becomes increasingly
> tight, taking me into it, sheltering me there but imprisoning me as well. (Irigaray
> 1993:183)

To view Irigaray's own critique as a decisive repudiation of Merleau-Ponty is itself an act of foreclosure that refuses to take the notion of écart that is so foundational to his thought seriously. While one may argue that this is precisely what Irigaray herself is accusing Merleau-Ponty of doing, it is also possible to take Irigaray to task for offering an idealized account of intrauterine existence characterized by fluid interactions between mother and fetus, in which each resonates, aggressively as well as lovingly, to the movements and demands of the other (the same could be said of her depiction of female sexuality).

In her well-known essay, "And the One Doesn't Stir Without the Other," Irigaray articulates the reversibility between the fetus/mother relationship and the daughter/mother relationship and, in both cases, views the intervention of "third-parties" such as the father, as disruptions to the flow of their exchange. "Nourishing," she claims:

> takes place before there are any images. There's just a pause: the time for the
> one to become the other. Consuming comes before any vision of her who gives
> herself. You've disappeared, unperceived-imperceptible if not for this flow that

fills up to the edge. That enters the other in the container of her skin. That penetrates and occupies the container until it takes away all possible space from both
the one and the other, removes every interval between the one and the other.
Until there is only this liquid that flows from the one into the other, and that is
nameless. (Irigaray 1981:63)

Passages such as these leave no room for any other parties to this symbiotic relationship between the one and the other. Indeed, Irigaray portrays the (invisible)
father as someone who is turned to when the daughter seeks to escape the all-
encompassing intensity of the mother/daughter relationship, an escape that is
an illusion because rather than provide the daughter with the space needed to
develop her own identity, he disregards her needs and continues on his own
path, graciously allowing her to follow behind him. Repudiating the (imaginary) mother for attempting to fix the fluidity of their relationship by adhering
to established patterns of exchange, Irigaray's daughter threatens:

if you turn your face from me, giving yourself to me only in an already inanimate
form, abandoning me to competent men to undo my/your paralysis, I'll turn to
my father. I'll leave you for someone who seems more alive than you. For someone who doesn't prepare anything for me to eat. For someone who leaves me
empty of him, mouth gaping on his truth. I'll follow him with my eyes, I'll listen
to what he says, I'll try to walk behind him.

He leaves the house, I follow in his steps. Farewell, Mother, I shall never
become your likeness. (Irigaray 1981:62)

The mother, however, is not so easily left behind. She appears in the mirror as
the daughter's "double" and haunts the daughter's attempts to establish her
"own" identity.

What concerns me about this account, is Irigaray's failure to acknowledge
the numerous and often positive ways in which the mother/daughter and moth-
er/fetus relationships themselves are always already mediated by others, even at
the moments when they are most intense and seemingly all-encompassing.
These "third-party" interventions are not established with birth and the cutting
of the umbilical cord, rather, the interventions occur before, during, and after
the pregnancy and profoundly affect the woman's and the fetus's relationship to
one another.

A woman who becomes impregnated through rape, for instance, sustains a
reversible relationship with her fetus that is often mediated by hatred, resentment, shame, and disgust, feelings that the fetus's responsive movements may
actually enhance rather than overcome. Although Irigaray might respond that
these interventions come from the "outside," from a phallocratic society that
has historically blamed women for their rape, blamed the child for being born
"out of wedlock" and, through a calculated act of *invisibility*, absolved the man
from accountability for his violence against them both, the point is that even

when sex and pregnancy are actively chosen, the interactions that unfold between mother and fetus are never just a matter of "the one and the other." Nor, and this is the more important point, should these interventions be viewed negatively as they often seem to be in Irigaray's work, disturbing the maternal-fetal dyad with their specular intrusions.

Irigaray's position is complicated, for while she does seek a space of disidentification between mother and daughter that will allow the daughter to recognize her maternal debt without seeking to collapse her own identity into her mother's, she will only depict this space positively insofar as it emerges from *within* the mother/daughter relationship and not from the contribution that others make to it. More generally, Irigaray's intensely anti-specular approach, an approach which Martin Jay has shown is itself part of a larger, twentieth-century French critique of ocularcentrism, leaves her in a position where she seems forced to view all visible interventions into women's sexuality and procreative potentiality negatively. On her account, the reversibility of looking freezes the looker and the looked-at in a mirror-like relationship which has historically reflected, not the genuine otherness of she who is looked at, but the seer's own narcissistic desires. By contrast, Irigaray celebrates the tactile domain as a potential sphere of self-knowledge and genuine intimacy which will allow bodies to interact with one another in a manner that preserves their differences apart from the "leveling" gaze that reduces irreducible difference to sameness in difference.

Écart, for Irigaray, is tied to multiplicity: two lips that never become one, two sexes that will never be one. While affirming these differences, Irigaray also articulates a hope for a new chiasmatic relationship between them, one which is predicated on an incorporation of difference *as* difference rather than a transubstantiation of difference into sameness. Unfortunately, I would argue, her resistance to visibility, despite her own attempts to make these differences visible in her work, doesn't enhance but restricts her own understanding of difference and the potentiality for corporeal incorporation of difference.

The speculum, ultrasound, and laporoscopies, are all technologies of the visible that reveal women's bodies to others and to themselves. That these invasive technologies are often uncomfortable, embarrassing, painful, and alienating, is undeniable, but what also must be affirmed is the way in which they open up women's bodies to experiences and possibilities that would not be available otherwise. To endorse uncritically these technologies is as problematic as uncritically rejecting them: both maternal and fetal lives have been saved through their use but their easy availability (in the Western world in particular) and lack of complete accuracy has also greatly complicated the decisions women, their families, and those crucial intermediaries, the doctor and the insurance companies, have had to face regarding if, when, where, and how to have children.[8]

Merleau-Ponty's conception of flesh, flesh that is not just of bodies but a "flesh of the world," allows us to see the intercorporeal possibilities inherent in the chiasmatic relationship between humans and machines. "For if the body" he asserts,

> is a thing among things, it is so in a stronger and deeper sense than they: in the sense that, we said, it *is of them*, and this means that it detaches itself upon them, and, accordingly, detaches itself from them. (Merleau-Ponty 1964:137)

While Irigaray argues that Merleau-Ponty leaves no room for silence, because "[t]he structure of a mute world is such that all the possibilities of language are already given there" (Irigaray 1995:180), she also deliberately ignores the ways in which these possibilities are, on his account, predicated on "a presentation of a certain absence" which remains inexplicable. This inexplicable absence which in different ways makes visibility, language, and perception possible, comprises a paradox which Merleau-Ponty begins to articulate in the following passage:

> our body commands the visible for us, but it does not explain it, does not clarify it, it only concentrates the mystery of its scattered visibility; and it is indeed a paradox of Being, not a paradox of man, that we are dealing with here. (Merleau-Ponty 1964:136)

This paradox of Being arises insofar as visibility can only emerge from the ground of invisibility, language from silence, and perception from that which is imperceptible. While Irigaray objects to the image of an invisibility that awaits visibility to be recognized and a silence that attains significance through being regarded as pregnant with linguistic possibilities, it is passages such as the one above which remind us that Merleau-Ponty savored the irresolvable mysteries of visibility, language, thought and perception, mysteries that both defy and are constitutive of reversibility.

In the introduction to their edited collection, *Posthuman Bodies*, Judith Halberstam and Ira Livingston articulate the paradoxes that arise out of the interface between technology and the human body through the trope of the posthuman body. "The posthuman" they argue,

> does not necessitate the obsolescence of the human; it does not represent an evolution or devolution of the human. Rather it participates in re-distributions of difference and identity. The human functions to domesticate and hierarchize difference within the human (whether according to race, class, gender) and to absolutize difference between the human and the nonhuman. The posthuman does not reduce difference-from-others to difference-from-self, but rather emerges in the pattern of resonance and interference between the two. (Halberstam and Livingston 1995:10)

The posthuman body, they suggest, is both a present reality and a future possibility. It is a present reality insofar as any conception of the human depends upon the active positing of that which it is not, the nonhuman, of which machines are both the most paradigmatic and most contested example (e.g. artificial intelligence as well as artificial life have served as primary cases for and primary challenges to the nonhumanness of machines). It is a future possibility as well since there is a significant difference between living this complicated interface between the biological, the psychical, the cultural, and the technological, an interface which is inscribed and expressed in our body images, and recognizing the transformative potential it makes possible both within and across these interdependent dimensions of our existence. Opposed even to a *phantasmatic* ideal of coherence, wholeness, or completeness, a phallic fantasy that structures the Symbolic domain and plays such a crucial role in the construction of the psyche in Lacanian psychoanalytic theory, Halberstam and Livingston argue, in Deleuzian fashion, that the posthuman subject has no telos to cling to:

> Unlike the human subject-to-be (Lacan's "l'hommelette"), who sees his own mirror image and fixed gender identity discrete and sovereign before him in a way that will forever exceed him, the posthuman becoming-subject vibrates across and among an assemblage of semi-autonomous collectivities it knows it can never either be coextensive with nor altogether separate from. (Halberstam and Livingston 1995:14)

Reinforcing and simultaneously deconstructing the importance of the prenatal ties that link us to our mothers, Halberstam and Livingston stress that: "Posthuman bodies never/always leave the womb. The dependence or interdependence of bodies on the material and discursive networks through which they operate means that the umbilical cords that supply us (without which we would die) are always multiple" (Halberstam and Livingston 1995:17). Whether these multiple umbilical cords take the form of medical technologies such as feeding tubes, respiratory apparati, and dialysis machines or electronic and mechanical technologies such as computers, telephones, and cars, the body's chiasmatic relationship with them has resulted in their incorporation into our body images, an incorporation that is continually renegotiated through the space of disincorporation that makes new linkages possible, a space that Merleau-Ponty calls écart.

Discussing the ways in which mobile technologies such as the railway system allow relatively unmoving bodies to be moved across great distances (i.e. as passengers sit in their compartments watching the landscape unfold outside their windows), Mark Seltzer argues that "[w]hat these mobile technologies make possible, in different forms, are the thrill and panic of agency at once extended and suspended" (Seltzer 1992:18). Virtual reality devices also offer the promise of moving without being moved, and their increasing popularity testifies to an increasing desire to challenge the very terms that traditionally established what it means to be a bodily agent. This, in turn, forces a reconceptualization not only of movement and agency, but also of desire.[9]

According to Deleuze and Guattari, "[d]esire constantly couples continuous flows and partial objects that are by nature fragmentary and fragmented. Desire causes the current to flow, itself flows in turn, and breaks the flows" (Deleuze and Guattari 1983:5). Through the intensification of desire that comes from pursuing some linkages over others, they maintain, new "assemblages" are formed.[10] These assemblages are also fragmentary, contingent, and multiple, and, I would argue, their intercorporeal transformations are registered in a series of body images that are linked together through their own chiasmatic interchanges.

As a space of disincorporation, écart marks the fissures and gaps that allow us to separate bodies from what they were, what they are not now, and what they may or may not become. It is this space of differentiation, I suggest, that holds out the promise for new linkages between bodies and machines, and which therefore guarantees that our own body images will always be multiple.

To take the Merleau-Pontian notion of écart seriously is crucial as well for the Irigarayan project of coming to terms with sexual difference in its materiality and corporeality. Irigaray depicts this possibility through the image of a double desire, the desire of two who can never be reduced to one. "If," she argues,

> there is no double desire, the positive and negative poles divide themselves
> between the two sexes instead of establishing a chiasmus or a double loop in
> which each can go toward the other and come back to itself. (Irigaray 1984:9)

On Deleuze's and Guattari's model, these double desires unfold not only between bodies but also within bodies, bodies conceived as micro-machines producing a multiplicity of (often conflicting) micro-desires. While Grosz calls attention to Deleuze's and Guattari's problematic tendency to "utilize models and metaphors that have been made possible only at the expense of women's exclusion and denigration" (Grosz 1994:190), she also asserts that:

> Deleuze and Guattari's notion of the body as a discontinuous, nontotalized
> series of processes, organs, flows, energies, corporeal substances and incorporeal
> events, intensities, and durations may be of great relevance to those feminists
> attempting to reconceive bodies, especially women's bodies, outside of the binary polarizations imposed on the body by the mind/body, nature/culture, subject/obect, and interior/exterior oppositions. (Grosz 1994:193–194)

Interestingly, Deleuze and Guattari depict the body's excessive, multiple desires as functioning fairly independently on a micro-level or local level even while they are, on a macro-level, completely interconnected. Just as parts of a car such as a battery, engine, transmission, and radiator, perform their different functions in relative isolation from one another even as these performances are coordinated with other necessary operations in the running of the car, intracorporeal desires ennervate local bodily regions and these ennervations reverberate, in surprisingly consistent ways, throughout the body.[11]

Haraway, in contrast to Deleuze and Guattari, is much more concerned with the political implications of models of multiplicity as well as with the power of metaphors such as that of the cyborg. Indeed, the figure of the cyborg, Haraway suggests, expresses both the dangers as well as the possibilities of multiplicities that transgress ideologically-established boundaries. According to Haraway:

> The home, workplace, market, public arena, the body itself—all can be dispersed and interfaced in nearly infinite, polymorphous ways, with large consequences for women and others—consequences that themselves are very different for different people. . . . (Haraway 1991:163)

Without these reversible relationships, communication itself would become impossible. And yet, a predictable effect of our branching network of communication technologies (like that of our reproductive technologies) is that they have spawned new cyborgian constructions (e.g. the internet), cyborgs that exceed and disrupt the multiple discourses out of which they have emerged.

Écart, as the moment of disincorporation that makes all forms of corporeal differentiation possible, is also precisely what allows us to establish boundaries between bodies, boundaries that must be respected in order to respect the agencies that flow from them. From a Merleau-Pontian perspective, these boundaries can best be respected not by artificially viewing bodies as isolated from one another but by acknowledging the reversible relationships that are exhibited within and across them. Thus, to demonize any form of technology as an alien force "out to get us," can cause us to lose sight of technology's own fleshly existence. More specifically, I would argue, we may fail to recognize that: 1) technology is itself embodied and not simply a means of transforming bodies and 2) that to demonize technology or even certain technologies on the basis of their artificiality is to demonize the body that is continually being reconfigured through them. On the other hand, to defend these claims does not entail uncritically affirming each and every technology or each and every bodily practice that incorporates those technologies; indeed one way of assessing the promise of new technologies and the new bodies and body images produced by them should be the extent to which they promote and preserve the space of differentiation that makes our intercorporeal exchanges possible.[12] In short, as Jonathan Benthall notes, "[u]ntil we become more aware of the body's power and resourcefulness, we will not feel a sufficiently educated outrage against its manipulation and exploitation" (Benthall 1976:92).

Bodily Imperatives

Toward an Embodied Ethics

[E]verything that is empirical is, as a contribution to the principle
of morality, not only wholly unsuitable for the purpose, but is even
highly injurious to the purity of morals; for in morals the proper
worth of an absolutely good will, a worth elevated above all price,
lies precisely in this—that the principle of action is free from all
influence by contingent grounds, the only kind that experience can
supply.

—Immanuel Kant (1964:93)

The object is to explore the huge, distant, and thorougly hidden
country of morality, morality as it has actually existed and actually
been lived, with new questions in mind and with fresh eyes. Is not
this tantamount to saying that that country must be discovered
anew?

—Friedrich Nietzsche (1956:155–156)

Maman had not been in the habit of taking notice of herself. Now
her body forced itself upon her attention. Ballasted with this
weight, she no longer floated in the clouds and she no longer said
anything that shocked me.

—Simone de Beauvoir (1965:59)

No investigation of body images would be complete without a discussion of their moral dimensions. To acknowledge that body images have moral
dimensions is itself a rejection of the mind/body dualism that has led to an
exclusive identification of morality with the mind (and with reason in particular). Overcoming this rationalist bias is essential to an embodied morality, and
significant progress toward this goal has been made by several feminist moral
philosophers including Marilyn Friedman, Virginia Held, Annette Baier, and
Claudia Card.

In general, there have been two basic strategies employed by moral theorists
(both nonfeminist and feminist) who seek to challenge the notion that moral
agency is achieved solely through exercising our "cognitive" faculties to deter-

Auvergne—Toi et Moi, Muriel Hasbun (gelatin silver emulsion on linen, 1995–1998)

Pobre Mami
Retrato, Hospital de la Mujer, San Salvador 1996
Pétain, 6 Janvier 1943
Retrato III, Hospital de la Mujer, San Salvador 1996
Avec Kamomyl
Retrato II, Hospital de la Mujer, San Salvador 1996
"Château amusant . . ." (Barthel, s.v.p.)
Potrait, circa 1943
"Château amusant . . ." II

mine how we ought to act in a given situation.[1] These strategies are often not employed in isolation, but conjointly. The first strategy focuses on or offers alternatives *within* the philosophical tradition to a Kantian approach which proclaims that it is reason alone that tells us what our moral duty is and that it is reason alone which should motivate us to do our duty in a particular situation.[2] The second strategy looks *outside* of the philosophical tradition to discover and/or generate new moral frameworks, frameworks that are intended either to replace or at least achieve the same recognition and value as our dominant, reason-based moral systems.

Before discussing the work of some well-known ethical theorists who offer alternatives to a Kantian, reason-based morality, we must begin with a brief discussion of Immanuel Kant's own view. I will follow this with a rough overview of other dominant philosophical positions, positions which depart significantly from the Kantian model and which have formed the basis for many contemporary feminist ethical theories. I conclude this chapter with a discussion of the limits of several of these accounts insofar as they ultimately fail to do justice to how ethics is corporeally enacted. I argue instead for a serious philosophical (re)consideration of Simone de Beauvoir's autobiographical account of her mother's final illness and death, entitled *A Very Easy Death*. In this text, I will demonstrate, Beauvoir offers an original, albeit incipient, embodied ethics, one that does justice to what I am calling, in contrast to a Kantian categorical imperative, "bodily imperatives."

A Historical Perspective

Although Kant believes that our feelings or "sentiments" play an indispensable role in the aesthetic and perceptual domains, he is quite clear that they should be not influential in the moral domain. Feelings, for Kant, as well as the body itself, are autonomous from reason insofar as they are part of that historically unruly realm of the "inclinations," a bundle of nonrational instincts, drives, desires, and emotions which are often not inclined to obey reason's principles. To act morally, for Kant, these inclinations must be discounted altogether because they are a threat to the universality that reason alone can guarantee. Therefore, if our feelings and/or bodily inclinations should come in conflict with what reason suggests we ought to do in a given situation, there is no contest. In his words:

> an action done from duty has to set aside altogether the influence of inclination, and along with inclination every object of the will; so there is nothing left able to determine the will except objectively the *law* and subjectively *pure reverence* for this practical law, and therefore the maxim of obeying this law *even to the detriment of all my inclinations*. (Kant 1964:68–69, last part my emphasis)

One popular means of critiquing Kant's exclusion of feelings, in particular, from the domain of morality, has been to champion the emotivist ethics suggested by David Hume. For it is Hume who forcefully illustrates the "inertia" of reason and who reminds us of the crucial, motivating role played by the "sentiments," as he calls them, in our moral activity. He argues that not only are our passions, rather than reason, the source for our moral behavior, but our moral activity reciprocally affects our passions which in turn produces new actions:

> Since morals . . . have an influence on the actions and affections, it follows, that they cannot be deriv'd from reason; and that because reason alone, as we have already prov'd can never have any such influence. Morals excite passions, and produce or prevent actions. Reason of itself is utterly impotent in this particular. The rules of morality, therefore, are not conclusions of our reason. (Hume 1978:457)

In his famous essay on aesthetics, "Of the Standard of Taste," Hume implies that our sentiments are educable, that is, that they are not fixed but are capable of changing over time as we learn to attend more carefully to the "finer details" of a particular work of art. He also acknowledges in this essay, that the customs prevalent in any one community and an individual's "natural" dispositions will influence (but need not determine) her/his affective response to a given work. While these comments are made in the midst of a discussion of the aesthetic domain, it is clear that they apply equally well to the moral domain. In radical contrast to a Kantian conception of morality which does not view culture-specific experiences as a constitutive factor of moral decision making, Hume paves the way for a consideration of how different moral systems can be operative in different moral communities, and allows us to see how actions which might produce an extremely negative affective response in one culture (e.g. suicidal practices), might be more neutrally or even positively regarded in another culture. This does not mean that Hume is a moral relativist, however, for to understand how these systems differ is not the same thing as maintaining that both sentiments are on an equal moral footing.[3]

One can also go back even further than Hume, to Aristotle, as Alasdair MacIntyre does in *After Virtue*, to show how the Greek conception of the virtues (importantly plural rather than singular) encompasses one's body as well as one's mind, one's private life as well as one's public life, one's appetites and passions as well as reason. While Aristotle carefully distinguishes virtue (and vice) from the passions, his equation of virtue with moderation as presented in *Nichomachean Ethics*, emphasizes that what is moderate (the mean) for one person will not necessarily be moderate for another. What is courageous behavior for a timid person, might be restrained behavior for an individual who is prone to rashness.

Aristotle uses the example of food to illustrate that although all of us should be seeking the mean in our behavior, the mean itself is relative to the particular individual in question:

> By the intermediate in the object I mean that which is equidistant from each of
> the extremes, which is one and the same for all men; by the intermediate relativ-
> ity to us that which is neither too much nor too little—and this is not one, nor
> the same for all. For instance, if ten is many and two is few, six is the intermedi-
> ate taken in terms of the object; for it exceeds and is exceeded by an equal
> amount; this is intermediate according to arithmetical proportion. But the inter-
> mediate relatively to us is not to be taken so; if ten pounds are too much for a
> particular person to eat and two too little, it does not follow that the trainer will
> order six pounds; for this also is perhaps too much for the beginner in athletic
> exercises. . . . Thus a master of any art avoids excess and defect, but seeks the
> intermediate and chooses this—the intermediate not in the object but relatively
> to us. (Aristotle 1941:958)

This example is striking precisely because it shows that the virtues are not
restricted to a particular sphere of one's existence; providing the proper nourishment for the body is itself a moral activity for Aristotle. In turn, one who
cares properly for the body can be understood as the master of an art.

These inextricable connections between morality, the body, aesthetics, and
truth are perhaps best depicted in the following passage by Foucault who
observes that for the Greeks:

> A moral value . . . was also an aesthetic value and a truth value since it was by
> aiming at the satisfaction of real needs, by respecting the true hierarchy of the
> human being, and by never forgetting where one stood in regard to truth, that
> one would be able to give one's conduct the form that would assure one of a
> name meriting remembrance. (Foucault 1985:92)

So, for Aristotle as well as for Hume, morality can never be a matter of exercising reason in abstraction from the particular, contextual features of a given situation, but rather, as Aristotle suggests, our moral behavior must be sensitive to
the changing demands of our own bodies as well as the bodies of others. And, as
Hume emphasizes, this will especially involve being attuned to our sentiments
(feelings) regarding a given situation.

Martin Heidegger also argues that feelings are central to human being-in-
the-world, and he stresses this point through a "negative" definition of what a
feeling is not and cannot be:

> What we call a "feeling" is neither a transitory epiphenomenon of our thinking
> and willing behavior nor simply an impulse that provokes such behavior nor
> merely a present condition we have to put up with somehow or other. (Heideg-
> ger 1993:100)

Put positively, for Heidegger, feelings are an indispensable feature of our existence. This is because mood, the fundamental, existential structure that
grounds our feelings, expresses the nature of our attunement toward a given sit-

uation, guaranteeing that we are never neutral to our existence but always experience any situation through a particular affective response.

Critical Responses to the Moral Tradition

Let me turn now to another famous philosophical figure, Friedrich Nietzsche, someone who successfully, I believe, deconstructs the view that the rationalist tradition that has so dominated philosophy since the time of Plato has left us with a purely rationalist morality and no viable alternatives. Nietzsche not only discovers alternative moralities preceding a rational morality, but also calls for a "new" morality, one that would reject any and all universal, transcendentally-derived values.

In *After Virtue*, Alasdair MacIntyre claims that, "Nietzsche is *the* moral philosopher of the present age" (MacIntyre 1981:108). Specifically, MacIntyre asserts that Nietzsche's main contribution to morality lies in his rejection of "the notion of basing morality on inner moral sentiments, on conscience, on the one hand, or on the Kantian categorical imperative, on universalizability, on the other" (MacIntyre 1981:107). Although MacIntyre does not agree with Nietzsche's assertion of the "will to power" as the motivating force which replaces these "impotent moral fictions," MacIntyre applauds his dual destruction of:

> the Enlightenment project to discover rational foundations for an objective morality and . . . the confidence of the everyday moral agent in post-Enlightenment culture that his moral practice and utterance are in good order. (MacIntyre 1981:107)

I use the expression "impotent moral fictions" because it is in keeping with Nietzsche's discussion of the development of a reason-based morality as a response to feelings of impotence in the face of the historically older, aristocratic morality which equated moral strength with a social, physical, economic, and emotional superiority conferred upon one through the good fortune of birth. On Nietzsche's account, as developed in *The Genealogy of Morals*, the lower (nonaristocratic) classes could not bear that their inferior moral status was tied to the contingency of their births.[4] Nietzsche suggests that, in response, the "peasants" developed their own reactive morality, a "slave" morality which is best exemplified through Kierkegaard's recitation of the well-known cliché: "only one who works gets bread" (Kierkegaard 1983:27).

Although he agrees with Nietzsche that the "moral turn" taken by philosophers such as Kant (or even Hume) has not advanced but actually hindered a genuine understanding of morality, MacIntyre is concerned (and is not alone in his concern) about the form a Nietzschean "revaluation of values" will take. Feminist philosophers too, have found Nietzsche's historical relativization of allegedly universal moral frameworks to be a liberating point of departure for the creation of new understandings of morality, but have focused their critical response to Nietzsche on something MacIntyre does not address, namely, the misogynist, hyper-masculinity of that quixotic, Nietzschean "moral" agent, the Ubermensch. Even leaving the problematic characterization of the Ubermensch aside, Nietzsche's rejection of "slave" morality often takes the form, as Luce Irigaray has noted, of identifying it with the historically abject domain of the feminine.[5] Moreover, this latter tendency is not restricted to Nietzsche for, as Kelly Oliver observes in the preface to *Womanizing Nietzsche*:

> both Nietzsche and Derrida, even while opening philosophy onto other voices, prevent the possibility of a feminine voice. Moreover, I argue that their strategies for opening philosophy onto its other(s) are often dependent on the preclusion of a feminine other. So even their various shifts from a philosophy of the subject to a philosophy of the other are constructed through the sacrifice of the feminine other, especially the feminine mother. (Oliver 1995:x–xi)

One of the most important aspects of Nietzsche's critique of morality, that I believe can be retained even while we reject its misogyny and racism, is his recognition of the need to reexamine moral *values* themselves, rather than focusing so heavily on the actions that are meant to affirm or deny them. In section VI of the *Preface* of *The Genealogy of Morals*, Nietzsche argues that: "[t]he intrinsic worth of these values has been taken for granted as a fact of experience and put beyond question" (Nietzsche 1956:155). In a phenomenological vein, Nietzsche calls for us to become attuned to that which has been taken for granted, indeed, to go further than "mere" interrogation by embarking upon "a critique of all moral values." We must begin this process, he suggests, by calling into question the self-justificatory character of these moral values since, on his account, it is this imputation of intrinsic worth that has hitherto granted our (society's) moral values immunity from rigorous scrutiny. "To this end" as Nietzsche provocatively asserts,

> we need to know the conditions from which these values have sprung and how they have developed and changed: morality as consequence, symptom, mask, *tartufferie*, sickness, misunderstanding; but also, morality as cause, remedy, stimulant, inhibition, poison. (Nietzsche 1956:155)

Nietzsche's genealogical project has a very specific aim, namely, once we have recognized the historical, and therefore contingent foundations of the "transcendental" moral frameworks which we have inherited, we should raze them and set about building new ones. Despite the undeniable destruction that must accompany this process, Nietzsche's goal is not a rejection but a constructive "rehabilitation" of morality. And, as with any rehabilitation project, construction must be preceded by destruction. The destruction of our existing moral frameworks is itself legitimated by his genealogical discovery that they have been established not by divine right (or even by the self-evidence of reason) but by historical contingency. Since, as Bob Dylan reminds us, "the times they are a changing" while the same moral structures have stayed in place, Nietzsche maintains that we need to condemn these inflexible human constructions in order to erect new ones that are more adaptable to the changing demands of each and every situation.[6]

Nietzsche emphasizes the "moral" uniqueness of each situation in the following chastisement directed toward the Kantian deontologist:

> Anyone who still judges "in this case everybody would have to act like this" has not yet taken five steps toward self-knowledge. Otherwise he would know that there neither are nor can be actions that are the same; that every action that has ever been done was done in an altogether unique and irretrievable way, and that this will be equally true of every future action; that all regulations about actions relate only to their coarse exterior (even the most inward and subtle regulations of moralities so far); that these regulations may lead to some semblance of sameness, *but really only to some semblance*; that as one contemplates or looks back upon *any* action at all, it is and remains impenetrable; that our opinions, valuations, and tables of what is good certainly belong among the most powerful levers in the involved mechanism of our actions, but that in any particular case the law of their mechanism is indemonstrable. (Nietzsche 1974:265)

Recognizing the need to develop a moral framework that does not attempt to reduce diverse situations to a "common moral denominator" (my expression, not Nietzsche's), is still a far cry from providing one, however; while Nietzsche is most effective when it comes to the destruction of existing moral frameworks, he is much less successful at their rehabilitation, and it is largely for this reason that he has been so often mistakenly identified as a nihilist. Given the sexist and racist forms his condemnation of the "impotence" of existing morality so frequently takes as well as his equally problematic conception of how this constructive "revaluation of value" is to occur (via a hyper-masculinist will to power), Nietzsche's contribution to an embodied morality is absolutely crucial, but more limited than it could and should have been. And, given his own misogynist tendencies, it is curious to think what his response would be to the fact that it is feminist philosophers, in particular, who have led the way in offering alternative, more flexible moral frameworks that seek to affirm rather than deny the differences between one situation and another.

The Ethics of Care and the Ethics of Justice

While the first strategy I mentioned at the outset of this chapter often pits Aristotelian/Humean accounts of morality against Kantian/Utilitarian accounts and argues that the former give us a much more robust view of the moral domain than the latter, the second strategy responds to the Nietzschean challenge by offering new moral frameworks, ones which are intended either to replace the old models, or to stand beside them as viable alternatives. Carol Gilligan's landmark text, *In a Different Voice*, was a pioneer in this regard, although there has been a lot of controversy in the fifteen years that have elapsed since it first appeared over how the different voice she articulates there is to be understood. Gilligan herself has published a few responses to her critics to clarify her position, but her position itself seems to have changed over the years.[7] More recently, she argues that the two moral orientations depicted in the book, the ethic of justice and the ethic of care, should be understood as two distinct moral frameworks analogous to the ambiguous figures discussed by Gestalt psychologists such as the duck/rabbit, old woman/young woman drawings which can be perceived two different ways but only one way at a time. The Gestalt psychologists used these figures to demonstrate that we do not tolerate perceptual ambiguity but resolve it through organizational strategies which always involve the isolation of a particular figure against a background. It is impossible, they noted, to view these ambiguous figures both ways at once; rather, we continually switch back and forth from one organizational style to the other, allowing what was previously the figure to merge with the ground and a new figure to emerge from what had previously been the ground.

Gilligan's point, then, is that the ethic of care and the ethic of justice provide two distinct moral frameworks that we can and do alternate between, although her research has shown that most individuals have a preference for one or the other and that this preference can vary throughout an individual's life (Gilligan 1995). Feminist moral theorists who have followed Gilligan, almost always begin their own essays by taking a stand on the issue of whether the ethic of justice and the ethic of care are: 1) separate moral frameworks (e.g. Nel Noddings and Carol Gilligan); 2) capable of being brought together by encompassing one within the other (e.g. Marilyn Friedman, Claudia Card, and Seyla Benhabib); or 3) able to be synthesized in a manner that refuses to privilege one approach over the other (Grace Clement).

What unites all three positions is their rejection of a cognitive-developmental (Kohlbergian) account of moral reasoning as a sufficient description of moral agency. The accounts that I find most persuasive are those that refuse simply to oppose an ethic of care that stresses relationships and responsibilities to others to an ethic of justice that emphasizes autonomy and individual rights. Instead, as Grace Clement argues, what is necessary is to acknowledge that both perspectives can be utilized by the same person in the same situation. While Seyla Benhabib, in her classic essay entitled, "The Generalized and the Concrete Other: The Kohlberg-Gilligan Controversy and Moral Theory," asserts that we tend to move back and forth between viewing others from a more contextual, particularized (ethic of care) perspective to a more impersonal, generalized (ethic of justice) perspective depending on the nature of the problem confronting us, others such as Marilyn Friedman and Claudia Card, argue that a concern with fairness and rights is integral to an ethic of care rather than a separate moral perspective that alternates with it. As Card notes in "Gender and Moral Luck":

> Why contrast the search for inclusive solutions with justice or with *fairness*? Fairness is not only a matter of ranking, taking turns, or balancing claims—ways of distributing power among competing parties—but also a matter of recognizing who deserves what from whom. . . . Although inclusion is an alternative to balancing claims, it is not necessarily an alternative to justice. (Card 1995:86)

Both Card and Friedman affirm that a care orientation seeks to "do justice" to the reciprocal obligations we share with others thereby contextualizing what justice means and allowing for varying moral strategies from one situation to another. They suggest that a problem with the justice perspective as it has been traditionally conceived, is that it is theoretically possible to treat someone ethically from the justice perspective without that treatment implying or requiring any intimacy or affection for the person with whom I am interacting.[8] Friedman offers a sympathetic reading of the justice perspective that nonetheless reveals its affective deficiency in the following passage:

> Based on my analysis, the 'justice perspective' might be said to rest, at bottom, on the assumption that the best way to *care* for persons is to respect their rights, and to accord them their due, both in distribution of the burdens and benefits of social cooperation, and in the rectification of wrongs done. But to uphold these principles, it is not necessary to respond with emotion, feeling, passion, or compassion to other persons. Upholding justice does not require the full range of mutual responsiveness which is possible between persons. (Friedman 1995:70–71)

From a Kantian standpoint, for instance, my "inclinations" to treat someone well because I like them and want them to be happy, are "nonmoral" sentiments that make it more rather than less difficult to determine if my action is moral since the latter judgment must be reserved solely for actions motivated by duty alone. Recognizing that it is impossible ever to be sure if duty (which is defined exclusively by reason which "tests" a maxim against the categorical imperative), and only duty is responsible for my decision to act, Kant acknowledges that no proof can be provided to show how a purely rational morality can be practically realized or why such a noninclination-based morality should even interest us at all:

> But *how* pure reason can be practical in itself without further motives drawn from some other source; that is, how the bare *principle of the universal validity of all its maxims as laws* (which would admittedly be a form of pure practical reason) can by itself—without any matter (or object) of the will in which we could take some antecedent interest—supply a motive and create an interest which could be called purely *moral*; or, in other words, *how pure reason can be practi-*

cal—all human reason is totally incapable of explaining this, and all the effort and labour to seek such an explanation is wasted. (Kant 1964:129)

And yet, despite his acknowledgement that it is possible that no one has ever committed a truly moral act, Kant maintains that a deontic or duty-based morality can and should serve as a regulative ideal in evaluating our ethical conduct.

John Rawls shares Kant's commitment to a deontological position, and articulates the basic structure of such a morality by appealing to what he calls the "original condition," namely, a hypothetical standpoint one would occupy *in advance* of becoming a member of a particular society, in which one does not yet know one's race, gender, class, age, abilities, etc. or that society's attitudes towards these latter. Rawls postulates that if we, as rational, mutually self-interested agents, hypothetically reflect from behind this "veil of ignorance" (since none of us can ever occupy this disembodied standpoint in reality), we can generate the fundamental moral principles necessary to govern society justly and fairly.

Although John Rawls has a very original and by now quite famous account of morality, he is also known for working from within a Kantian framework. This is because his model supports Kant's demand for abstract, universal principles based on reason that are divorced from specific, contextual features of a given situation. Hence, it is not surprising that feminist critiques of Rawls' position often take a similar form to feminist critiques of Kant. Marilyn Friedman, in particular, observes that:

> While such an account promises to disclose duties of justice owed to all other parties to the social contract, it may fail to uncover *special* duties of justice which arise in close personal relationships the foundation of which is affection or kinship, rather than contract. (Friedman 1995:67)

For feminist theorists such as Friedman and Card, not only is the care perspective as originally discussed by Gilligan correct in asserting that relations of care structure moral situations for many individuals (let me leave the claims that this is a gendered phenomenon aside for the moment—I will address them later), but they go further to argue that these relations: 1) already involve concerns about just treatment of individuals, and 2) have the potential to teach us something about how and why we ought to care morally about other human beings and about our shared situation. Thus, to set aside inclinations (which includes the whole domain of feelings) as Kant does or to decontextualize justice as Rawls does, are misguided and unhelpful strategies that fail to achieve what is itself a problematic goal, namely, developing universal principles of justice.

Now, what does this discussion of feminist critiques of a traditional justice perspective from the standpoint of an ethic of care have to do with the body?

This is precisely the question I would like to address in the pages that follow. Although I am very sympathetic both to Card's arguments that our "moral luck" has an enormous amount to do with our capacity for and ability to care for others, and to Friedman's arguments that we need to get beyond caring if the latter is viewed as something that takes place apart from considerations for justice, I am concerned about a few of the directions their respective accounts might move us toward. Specifically, I am worried that the body has been left out of the picture altogether. Although Card and Friedman would definitely agree that moral agency is an embodied phenomenon and their sensitivity to the context-specificity of different moral situations lends itself to a consideration of the role that the body itself plays in our moral interactions, bodily demands, needs, and desires are not foregrounded in either of their discussions.

To emphasize the moral agency of particular bodies at once involves paying attention to how gender, race, ethnicity, age, and class status are embodied and to how these (differentially) affect the nature of the interactions between individuals as well as the obligations that arise out of those interactions. Although I am in agreement with Friedman that "we would do well to progress beyond gender stereotypes which assign distinct and different moral roles to women and men" I am disturbed by the characterization of this project which immediately follows: "Our ultimate goal should be a non-gendered, non-dichotomized moral framework in which all moral concerns could be expressed. We might, with intentional irony, call this project, 'demoralizing the genders'" (Friedman 1995:70).

Why do I find this goal disturbing? For one, it seems to me that to "demoralize" the genders, even in Friedman's ironic sense, is at the same time to disembody morality. And, if demoralizing gender and disembodying morality go hand in hand, then the moral framework we end up with is liable to "throw out the baby with the bath water," namely, to forgo specificity, historicity, and individual differences in favor of an abstract, impersonal moral framework. Let me illustrate why genders cannot and should not be "demoralized" by returning to a point Judith Butler makes which we discussed in a different context in chapter one. In the passage we cited earlier, Butler claims that "gender is a corporeal style, a way of acting the body, a way of wearing one's own flesh as a cultural sign" (Butler 1989:256). A few sentences earlier, Butler also maintains that "gender is a project, a skill, a pursuit, an enterprise, even an industry, the aim of which is to compel the body to signify one historical idea rather than another" (Butler 1989:256). Taken together, these claims imply: 1) that gender is not a state but an ongoing activity; 2) that the "project of gender" is not (merely) a matter of choice but takes place within an historical context which gives us guidelines for how our gender is to be enacted; and, most importantly for my purposes, 3) that we cannot refrain from the "project of gender" even if we do not deliberately "intend" gender as our project, insofar as we live and express our genders through our bodies.

In sum, Butler is arguing that gender is not a collection of attributes or behaviors, or even social expectations, though all of these are part of the very meaning of gender; rather, gender is a lived bodily project and hence is an integral component of human existence. To say that it is integral, though, does not mean that there is only one way to live one's gender. Since gender is not reducible to a fixed set of roles but is rather a way of "wearing one's flesh as a cultural sign," both the sign and the meaning of that sign are constantly changing as gender is differentially performed (to use Butler's own terminology) from one situation to another.

Thus, while Friedman's call for a nondichotomized moral framework seems right, her simultaneous appeal for a nongendered moral framework is a problem. It would seem, given the contiguity of these terms within the same sentence, that Friedman merely intends to reject gender as it has been traditionally understood, namely, as a binary, and undeniably regulatory system. Specifically, Friedman is concerned (and rightly so) about traditional accounts of morality including those of such venerable figures as Aristotle, Kant, and even Freud, who suggest that one's gender determines or, at the very least, profoundly influences one's capacity for moral reasoning.

What Friedman is arguing against, then, is a very popular and very powerful essentialist view, namely, that one's gender defines (and, as far as women are concerned, has traditionally been viewed as limiting) one's possibilities for moral reasoning. By failing to distinguish between this limited and quite artificial, historical conception of gender, and a nondichotomous view of gender as an embodied project such as the one presented by Butler, however, Friedman ends up disassociating morality from its source, namely, the *bodies* of moral agents, and this leaves her in an unlikely (and unintended) alliance with some of the very accounts that she is rejecting. Kant and Rawls, in particular, offer what I take to be disembodied accounts of moral reasoning, and Kohlberg might be said to offer a progressively disembodied account of moral development insofar as the morally mature (Stage 5/Stage 6 postconventional) individual regulates her/his conduct with reference to abstract moral principles in contrast to the morally immature (Stage 1/Stage 2 preconventional) individual's concerns for the types of punishment that might ensue or interests that may fail to be met if she or he acts "wrongly."[9]

Ultimately, I believe that Friedman's goal of "demoralizing" gender, while it is ostensibly intended to keep us from associating a given gender with a given moral framework, would nonetheless lead to "demoralized" bodies. One of the ways in which bodies have historically been demoralized, I would argue, is precisely through their exclusion from the "exalted" domain of morality despite the fact that it is in and through our bodies that we feel the effects of our moral judgments and practices (a point Foucault well recognizes in his genealogical account of subjection and surveillance, *Discipline and Punish*).

It is striking that not only Friedman, but other moral theorists who seek to

give us a picture of morality "as a socially embodied medium of mutual understanding and adjustment between persons in certain terms, particularly those
that define those persons' identities, relationships, and values" (Walker
1992:32), inadvertently end up moving away from the embodied aspect of
moral reasoning toward a liberal humanist conception of the moral subject that
is detached from the very contexts that give morality its "flesh and blood." In
Ethnic Ethics, Anthony Cortese persuasively argues that "gender is established
by the existential experience of ethnicity, race, culture, social class, caste and
consciousness"[10] (1990:101). Armed with this robust understanding of gender,
Cortese goes on to deliver a powerful, multi-faceted critique of Kohlberg's cognitive development model:

> The assertion that there are six and only six stages with one and only one final,
> mature mode of moral judgment preempts all other moral systems for all time.
> An alternative view is that each ethnic group constructs a sequence for moral
> development and a mode of moral judgment appropriate to its own culture
> which are morally neither superior nor inferior to the cognitive development
> model. Rather, in that diverse social ends are sought, they simply are different.
> One must consider the possibility that ethnic groups have different moral struc-
> tures, each adequate to the reproduction of the social life-world found in each
> ethnic group. One must also consider the possibility that the "scientific findings"
> on moral development are more appropriately viewed as ideology that sets the
> Western European social life-world as the model for all people in all places.
> Finally, one must consider the possibility that morality is located more in the
> structure of society than it is in the consciousness of individual human beings. If
> this possiblity is valid, then measures of moral development need to focus on
> quality of life variables found in a given society or social class or subculture with-
> in a society, rather than upon individuals' oral or written replies to hypothetical
> dilemmas. (Cortese 1990:107)

Despite the profound objections Cortese has to what Kohlberg's scale is measuring, who is doing the measuring, how it is being measured, and, most importantly, how the results of that measurement are evaluated, in the end he does
not abandon the notion that moral development can be assessed and evaluated
according to a hierarchical, *cognitive* scale. After demonstrating that Kohlberg's
ethnocentric model problematically results in well-educated, white males from
postindustrialized countries scoring higher in "moral maturity" than their
female counterparts, and higher than men and women with less education
and/or from rural areas, Cortese ends up with the far too modest conclusion
that:

> The stage definitions and scoring system [in Kohlberg's cognitive development
> moral scale] are incomplete, especially st Stage Five [postconventional morali-
> ty]. They should be expanded to include postconventional reasoning from cul-

turally and subculturally diverse world views. In short, a more culturally pluralistic stage theory of moral reasoning is needed. (Cortese 1990:113)

A central problem with Cortese's account is that he reestablishes the validity of a cognitive, stage theory of morality even after he has cast serious doubts upon the problematic assumptions that undergird such an approach to moral reasoning. In doing so, he too, moves away from the embodied dimensions of his own account of morality toward an abstract scale that will reveal the underlying moral principles that define a given community. Although he maintains, against a traditional, deontological position, that there are no universal (cross-cultural) principles, he nonetheless affirms that there are cognitive principles that guide moral reasoning which hold for all members of a community and which can be determined and hierarchically ranked in a nonethnocentric, Kohlbergian manner. This ranking, in turn, will make possible a corresponding ranking of individuals within that community in terms of their own moral development.

In short, Cortese offers a trenchant critique of the methods and results of a Kohlbergian model of moral reasoning, yet he remains within the parameters of a cognitive development model, thereby moving away from the embodied ethics he is trying to embrace. Friedman, on the other hand, rejects this type of model altogether, but ends up in an equally untenable position by moving to a nongendered moral framework. Both, I would argue, subvert their own goals by failing to do justice to the particularities of the lived body, particularities which are an indispensable feature of our moral practices and which have yet to become an equally indispensable feature of our moral theorizing.

An alternative means of addressing the varying moral challenges posed by specific bodies is provided by Seyla Benhabib, in "The Generalized and the Concrete Other: The Kohlberg-Gilligan Controversy and Moral Theory." In this essay, Benhabib seeks to reconcile the justice and care orientations by "nesting" the latter within the former. Specifically, Benhabib argues that in order to take up the (Kohlbergian) standpoint of the generalized other, a standpoint that "requires us to view each and every individual as a rational being entitled to the same rights and duties we would want to ascribe to ourselves," we must first assume the (Gilliganesque) standpoint of the concrete other, a perspective which "requires us to view each and every rational being as an individual with a concrete history, identity, and affective-emotional constitution" (Benhabib 1992:158–159). When we view others from this latter perspective, she claims, we "seek to comprehend the needs of the other, his or her motivations, what she searches for, and what s/he desires" (Benhabib 1992:159).

Benhabib, like Kant and Rawls before her, affirms the need for universalizability in our moral reasoning. Her point, however, is that in a moral theory that operates exclusively from the standpoint of the generalized other, universalizability cannot be achieved, precisely because we abstract from the concrete differences that distinguish individuals from one another and, in so doing, reduce human beings to a single, common element, namely our capacity to be rational moral agents. And, she convincingly maintains, if we are all the same then there is no way to meet the criterion of reversibility so essential to universalizability; that is, I am unable to take the standpoint of another into account in my rational deliberations because the other's standpoint would, qua rational moral agent, be the same as my own. Hence, she concludes, it is only when we recognize and affirm one another's "embodied and embedded" identities that we can truly be said to incorporate the standpoint of others into our moral reasoning and thereby achieve what she terms "interactive universalism." Benhabib defines this type of universality as follows:

> Interactive universalism acknowledges the plurality of modes of being human, and differences among humans, without endorsing all these pluralities and differences as morally and politically valid. While agreeing that normative disputes can be settled rationally, and that fairness, reciprocity and some procedure of universalizability are constituents, that is, necessary conditions of the moral standpoint, interactive universalism regards difference as a starting point for reflection and action. In this sense, "universality" is a regulative ideal that does not deny our embodied and embedded identity, but aims at developing moral attitudes and encouraging political transformations that can yield a point of view acceptable to all. (Benhabib 1992:153)

Influenced by Jürgen Habermas, Benhabib's interactive universalism is achieved via a "discourse ethics" in which, *beginning* from the standpoint of the concrete other, we enter into a dialogue with one another about how best to meet the (universal) norms that guide the standpoint of the generalized other, namely, formal equality and reciprocity whereby "each is entitled to expect and to assume from us what we can expect and assume from him or her" (Benhabib 1992:159). The corresponding norms that are operative with respect to concrete others, she claims, are equity and complementary reciprocity in which "each is entitled to expect and to assume from the other forms of behavior through which the other feels recognized and confirmed as a concrete, individual being with specific needs, talents and capacities (Benhabib 1992:159). The key question on this account becomes, how do we move from affirming our concrete and differing needs and desires to the norms of formal equality and reciprocity that govern the standpoint of the generalized other? Moreover, is discourse really the means for enabling us to transition from the differences-oriented standpoint of the concrete other to the formal equality based on shared rational capacity that distinguishes the position of the generalized other?

Benhabib shares a Habermasian confidence that discourse will "conquer all," that is, that as long as we are willing to dialogue with one another, we can work through any conflicts that arise between us as concrete others, and achieve consensus as generalized others. Although she acknowledges that: "our identities as concrete others are what distinguish us from each other according to gender, race, class, cultural differentials, as well as psychic and natural abilities," she asks whether "a moral theory restricted to the standpoint of the concrete other [would] not be a racist, sexist, cultural relativist and discriminatory one?" (Benhabib 1992:164). Leaving this question unanswered but clearly implying that the answer would be in the affirmative, Benhabib suggests that the standpoint of the generalized other is what is necessary to lift us out of these unpalatable positions and to arrive at acceptable (i.e. universalizable) resolutions of our moral conflicts.

What is noteworthy about Benhabib's own account is that despite her affirmation of the standpoint of the concrete other as a necessary starting place for moral reasoning, this standpoint itself is intended to be superseded within ethical discourse by the more encompassing standpoint of the generalized other, a standpoint which depends upon the attainment of universalizability via rationality and which is equivalent to a Kantian understanding of moral reasoning. Moreover, Benhabib implies that the transition between these two orientations will always (or at least in principle is capable of being) a smooth one. To reformulate the two questions I asked above, is it always possible, much less desirable to arrive at the standpoint of the generalized other from the standpoint of the concrete other, and is discourse the best means of doing so?

Earlier on in her essay, Benhabib tacitly relies upon a feminist psychoanalytic critique of the privileging of the notion of the autonomous self, a crucial, masculinist presupposition that undergirds Kant's, Rawl's and Kohlberg's respective accounts of morality. She makes use of this critique, which shows how women, conceived by both Freud and Kant as less autonomous than men, end up being depicted, not surprisingly, as less moral than men, to reject these traditional accounts of the generalized standpoint as a sufficient framework for moral reasoning. So, on the one hand, she rejects the possibility of developing an adequate moral framework by relying upon the standpoint of the concrete other alone and also maintains that we can't work from the standpoint of the generalized other alone either. She spends quite a bit of time in the first part of the essay demonstrating the latter point, but, aside from suggesting that we'd end up with a sexist, racist, culturally relativist moral position if we worked exclusively from the standpoint of the concrete other, she doesn't adequately consider whether the standpoint of the concrete other could be sufficient in some situations without appealing to the allegedly more encompassing perspective of the generalized other.

What worries me is that, despite the important differences between their three positions, Benhabib ends up in the same camp as Friedman and Cortese: all three move away from embodied differences toward a universal moral framework that is supposed to encompass and do justice to these differences. And, in Benhabib's and Cortese's cases especially, this framework: 1) privileges the cognitive domain; 2) implies that there is a clear, discernible path that people take to recognizing and resolving moral dilemmas; and, 3) suggests that the only way to work through moral dilemmas satisfactorily is by different individuals adopting the same moral standpoint.

Beauvoir's Embodied Ethics

To show how and why these theories fail to do justice to the embodied differences they seek to explain, let me turn to what may seem, at first glance, to be a rather unlikely source, Simone de Beauvoir's autobiographical narrative, A *Very Easy Death*. It is in this nonfictional account of the last month of her mother's life, I will argue, that Beauvoir offers us an embodied ethics, one that works from bodily as opposed to categorical imperatives and which arrives at a noncognitivist resolution that lacks formal universalizability but which can nonetheless serve as a model for how we *live*, rather than (merely) think about, morality. In addition, the evolving, relational account offered in A *Very Easy Death*, I will show, places Beauvoir not only at odds with Sartre's ethics but is also in tension with the position she offers in her own, explicitly philosophical work, *The Ethics of Ambiguity*. Through posing and grappling continuously with what in the abstract seems to be a classic moral dilemma, namely, can deceiving another ever be justified, Beauvoir definitively moves out from under Sartre's philosophical shadow, provides a hitherto unrecognized anticipation of, and contribution to, the development of an ethics of care (one that precedes Gilligan's own work by almost two decades), and expands the moral domain so that it can no longer be understood through the limiting dichotomies of intentions versus actions on the one hand, feelings versus principles on the other, but rather, as incorporating and contextualizing all of these moral dimensions in the wider, embodied realm that Virginia Held calls "moral experience" (Held 1995).

Beauvoir's ethics, even as it is explicitly formulated in *The Ethics of Ambiguity*, is virtually ignored in contempory feminist ethics.[11] This is not to say, however, that the ethics she does develop has not received a great deal of attention from both Sartre and Beauvoir scholars. One possible explanation for many feminist moral theorists' inattention to her work on ethics, may be that even though Beauvoir substantially refines Sartre's understanding of freedom in *The Ethics of Ambiguity* by distinguishing between an original freedom and a genuine, *willed* freedom (which latter is indicative of a moral commitment one makes in a particular situation), she, like Sartre, seems to view freedom as a supreme value in moral decision making.

Debra Bergoffen refers to the ethical project that results from this emphasis on freedom, as an "ethic of liberation," a term that aligns Sartre and Beauvoir with a larger, liberal humanist tradition.[12] Although this ethic of liberation affirms the need for oppressed peoples to assert themselves as equals to their oppressors, it also, as Bergoffen notes, ends up giving us a morality based on conflict among individuals, since the affirmation of a given individual's free-dom (as depicted by Sartre in *Being and Nothingness* and Beauvoir in *The Ethics of Ambiguity* and *The Second Sex*) seems almost inevitably to jeopardize in some way the freedom of other members of the moral community. As Beau-voir tersely notes in *The Second Sex*, "every human relationship implies con-flict, all love brings jealousy" (Beauvoir 1989:347). As a result of this (presum-ably) inevitable conflict, the moral challenge presented by an ethic of liberation ends up being a rather individualistic one, namely, how do I respon-sibly enact my own freedom in a manner that affirms rather than denies the freedom (and responsibility) of others?

For many contemporary feminist ethical theorists, this conflictual model of human relationships is problematic because it seems to be posited as an ontolo-gicial condition of human existence rather than a reflection of life within a patriarchal system that generates conflict through its privileging of some gen-ders, races, and classes over others. Moreover, as Beauvoir herself acknowl-edges again and again in *The Second Sex*, women have historically found their "choices" to reflect not an affirmation of their freedom, but rather, a limited set of "options" which they are not free not to choose. Beauvoir reinforces this point in her discussion of the pressure adolescent girls face regarding marriage: "[t]he girl's choice is usually quite limited; and it could not be really free unless she felt free also not to marry" (Beauvoir 1989:433).

If men have indeed had more freedom to choose the course their existence will take than have women, to place such a high value on freedom may end up leading to a paradoxical situation in which those best able to realize their free-dom are seen as higher on the moral scale than those individuals who feel so overwhelmed by the societal constraints placed upon their actions, that they succumb to these latter without great resistance. From a Sartrian perspective, such people would almost certainly be understood as existing in bad faith, both for their failure to recognize the alternatives available to them (even if these reduce to no more than silently rebelling, in Camus' Sisyphean fashion, against that situation) and for their failure to act on them. Beauvoir recognizes this danger and responds to it by acknowledging that some people may be so oppressed that it becomes impossible for them to imagine an alternative to their situation. For, she notes:

> There are cases where the slave does not know his servitude and where it is nec-essary to bring the seed of his liberation to him from the outside: his submission is not enough to justify the tyranny which is imposed upon him. The slave is submissive when one has succeeded in mystifying him in such a way that his sit-uation does not seem to him to be imposed by men, but to be immediately given by nature, by the gods, by the powers against whom revolt has no meaning; *thus, he does not accept his condition through a resignation of his freedom since he can not even dream of any other; and in his relationships with his friends, for example,*

*he can live as a free and moral man within this world where his ignorance has
enclosed him.* (Beauvoir 1976:85, my emphasis)

Here, Beauvoir contextualizes freedom in a radical manner. Even for the slave
who does not know the meaning of freedom, and for whom revolt is unthink-
able, a "free and moral" existence is still possible within the confines of that
slavery. Such an individual cannot be morally judged with reference to an
abstract standard of freedom and found wanting on the basis of that judgement.

In this passage and elsewhere in *The Ethics of Ambiguity*, Beauvoir amply
demonstrates that affirming one's freedom is meaningless unless one is able to
will that freedom, and that willing one's freedom is not always possible if the
nature of one's oppression has been concealed through a pervasive mystification. Yet, rather than reject the notion of freedom altogether, Beauvoir maintains that the slave can still live as a "free and moral man." What can this
mean? Clearly, for Beauvoir, freedom and morality go hand in hand. But here,
in the case of the slave, freedom is not synonymous with freedom from the
oppressor, that is, with liberation. Instead, as I will show in what follows, freedom and the corresponding possibility of living morally have to do with meet-
ing the ambiguous demands of a particular situation with a nonambiguous
response.

Through her distinction between an "original," but existentially meaningless freedom (one that is basically equivalent to the metaphysical freedom
established in *Being and Nothingness*), and a concretely situated, "genuine"
freedom, Beauvoir indirectly (but quite powerfully) dissolves the lucidity
demanded by a Sartrian ethics, a lucidity that is itself deceptive insofar as it presupposes what Bergoffen calls, using Irigaray's language, the desire of the same
whereby, "each desires the same thing, to be recognized as the source of the
meaning of the world, to have power over others/all; and each lives this desire
in the same way" (Bergoffen 1997:27). On this specular model, conflicts are
inevitable since others constantly bring me face to face with the impossibility
of fulfilling my desires; this is because my desires can only be met at the
expense of their desires, desires that they will not and cannot relinquish without relinquishing their own freedom and subjectivity.[13]

Despite Beauvoir's own refinement of Sartre's ethics in both *The Ethics of
Ambiguity* and *The Second Sex*, I do not think she herself recognizes fully the
limitations of his account until she has to contend with the bodily imperatives
that are suddenly generated through her mother's "accident" and subsequent
hospitalization, events which are depicted in great detail in *A Very Easy Death*.
As we shall see, these bodily imperatives are themselves constructed not only
out of her mother's deteriorating physical condition which necessitates immediate, "life-and-death" decisions, but also out of her mother's, her sister's, the
doctors' and Beauvoir's own ambiguous desires and demands, desires and
demands that are dramatically enacted upon and through the ravaged body of

Françoise de Beauvoir. In this retrospective narrative, we do not have one subjectivity pitted against another, but rather, one dying woman whose progressively worsening cancer sets the terms for the relationships the other parties all come to sustain with her and with one another. Though the question of how best to meet these bodily imperatives leads to conflict between the parties involved, the imperatives themselves arise out of the unique moral demands *relationships* place upon us, demands that are too complex to be understood through the confines of a master/slave battle in which each seeks the death of the other subjectivity.

It is perhaps because Beauvoir has for so long been understood as unproblematically aligned with a phallocentric model in which human relationships are inherently conflictual, that feminist moral theorists have tended not to look closely at Beauvoir's own, evolving reflections on morality much less to focus on the ethical implications of a "nonphilosophical" piece such as *A Very Easy Death*. Instead, what seems to have happened is that while most feminists acknowledge Beauvoir's landmark contributions to feminism, these contributions tend to be confined to her success in revealing the seemingly universal (but by no means justifiable) subordinate status of women in contemporary society. Moreover, these contributions are often seen as issuing primarily from *The Second Sex*. This tendency is visible even in sensitive readings of Beauvoir, such as the one offered in Tina Chanter's recent book, *Ethics of Eros: Irigaray's Rewriting of the Philosophers*. In a chapter entitled, "The Legacy of Simone de Beauvoir," Chanter tracks Beauvoir's significant influence on Irigaray and readily acknowledges that, "Beauvoir's inquiries into women's condition helped to decisively shape feminism" (Chanter 1995:77). Two pages later, however, she radically circumscribes Beauvoir's contribution by claiming that feminists must "recognize the limitations of discourses which may once have been feminist in a revolutionary way, but which might have become reactionary, and even complicitous (Chanter 1995:79).

Feminist philosophers who have engaged in a sustained inquiry into Beauvoir's specific (and evolving) understanding of ethical ambiguity have disregarded this warning and have been amply rewarded.[14] Debra Bergoffen, in particular, argues that Beauvoir offers not one but two ethics in her work: an ethic of liberation that is grounded in the Hegelian master-slave dialectic, and a much less visible, but no less important, ethic of generosity which is grounded in the erotic. In what follows, I will argue for a third Beauvoirian ethic, an ethic of embodiment, which, I believe, undergirds both the well-known ethic of liberation (or, as Bergoffen often refers to it, the ethic of the project) and the more subtle, but no less insistent, ethic of erotic generosity identified by Bergoffen.[15] This embodied ethics, as I will show, is developed in a very thorough, but also very unthematized way in *A Very Easy Death*.

The narrative of *A Very Easy Death* is tied together by the cancerous body of Françoise de Beauvoir. In this essay, Beauvoir never loses sight of her mother's body, since it is that body which is Beauvoir's own raison d'être, both as the agency that made her existence possible (by giving birth to her) as well as the urgent imperative that calls Beauvoir to her mother's bedside and which keeps her there until the body itself becomes a corpse. Beauvoir depicts her response to this imperative as follows:

> The transition from my mother to a living corpse had been definitively established. The world had shrunk to the size of her room: when I crossed Paris in a taxi I saw nothing more than a stage with extras walking about on it. My real life took place at her side, and it had only one aim — protecting her. (Beauvoir 1965:73)

Beauvoir's powerful narrative foregrounds a particular, gendered, maternal body and the imperatives that issue from that body in a way that belies any attempt to ground morality on abstract cognitive principles or even a nongendered moral framework. What I find especially striking about this account, is that Beauvoir herself is compelled to grant the moral legitimacy of these bodily imperatives, despite the fact that her mother's interests, needs, and desires are so very much in conflict with her own.

My guess is that one of the reasons Beauvoir feels compelled to write about her mother's death is precisely because she wants to come to terms with her own participation in a deception that she herself would never have consented to have practiced. By acquiescing in her mother's tacit, but none the less forceful demand to pretend that she is not in fact dying, Beauvoir acts against her own, very Sartrian "moral principles" and, in so doing, reveals the limits of moral principles themselves when one acknowledges what Eva Feder Kittay calls "the network of interdependencies that form the central bonds of human social life"[16] (Kittay 1995:12).

Through her daily confrontation with the moral dilemmas generated by her mother's sickness and imminent death, Beauvoir simultaneously belies the title of her narrative, A Very Easy Death, and the Sartrian model which seems to equate deception of any form with bad faith. For Beauvoir, her sister, and even their mother, Françoise de Beauvoir's death was anything but easy (douce). Moreover, in an important sense, the central philosophical issue raised by this autobiographical text — can deception ever be ethically justified — remains unanswered. In accordance with her refusal to pit the interests of the individual against the interests of other individuals (and of a larger community) in The Ethics of Ambiguity, Beauvoir retraces and reinscribes the complex emotional ties that link her, her mother, and her sister to one another as well as to the doctors and nurses involved in caring for her mother. While for Sartre, bad faith and deception seem to be inextricably linked, the honesty (and simultaneous lack of sincerity) of Beauvoir's "deception," undermines facile attempts to identify her behavior (and that of her sister, the doctors and the nurses) as bad faith.

Although the concept of "a very easy (douce) death" itself seems to be exposed as a myth in the course of this painful narrative of bodily suffering, there is also a paradoxical truth to the title of the text that Beauvoir is forced and forces us to acknowledge. To give her mother a "sweet" (*douce*) death, is to give her mother what she both desires and disavows. The bittersweet experience of Françoise de Beauvoir's pain and suffering, a pain and suffering enhanced by the additional exhaustion of believing against the evidence of her own body that she is indeed getting better, is "douce," I would argue, precisely because it produces her own bodily subjectivation. More specifically, her illness is what gives Françoise de Beauvoir the "courage" to demand recognition as an individual with specific needs and desires.

To give their mother a sense of being in control in the midst of a cancer that is irrevocably removing that control once and for all, Beauvoir and her sister force themselves to participate in a deception that is maintained throughout the final days of their mother's life. I believe Sartre would view this decision as one made in "bad faith" for several reasons, reasons which will best emerge through examining how the deception unfolds.

Following an intestinal x-ray which reveals a tumor, Beauvoir and her sister go along with the doctors' decision not to mention the cancer to Madame de Beauvoir even though the size and placement of the tumor indicates the need for an immediate operation and even though their mother is conscious (though weak) and clearly capable of understanding this news. The doctors' motivations for the deception, as depicted by Beauvoir, are hardly altruistic. Their main goal, it seems, is to keep the patient in a tractable, trusting state so that she will be easier to deal with both before and after the procedure. In fact, one of the difficulties Beauvoir has with being an accomplice to this deception is her distaste for the doctors themselves, who clearly have no interest in her mother except as a "case" and for whom her mother's tragedy poses no moral dilemmas at all. Their attitude towards her mother and the situation as a whole are succinctly summed up in "Dr. N's" words, "I am doing what has to be done" (Beauvoir 1995:27).

The doctors' goal appears unambiguously straightforward: to prolong Madame de Beauvoir's life with all of the technological means available, and, in so doing, to solidify their own reputations within the medical community. If deceiving the patient enables them to get their job done more efficiently, then so be it. Indeed, the doctors treat Beauvoir's and her sister's concerns about their mother and the deception itself with clear irritation, not because the sisters' questions complicate their own understanding of what "needs to be done" but because these women are taking up their valuable time with their "pointless" questions and are challenging the authority of the doctors who view themselves as unequivocally knowing what is best for the patient. Beauvoir's description of "Dr. N's" response to his successful completion of the life-prolonging procedure (which involved removing no less than four pints of pus from her mother's abdomen), is telling:

> Maman had just been taken up to her room, N told us. He was triumphant: she
> had been half-dead that morning and yet she had withstood a long and serious
> operation excellently. Thanks to the very latest methods of anaesthesia her heart,
> lungs, the whole organism had continued to function normally. There was no
> sort of doubt that he entirely washed his hands of the consequences of that feat.
> (Beauvoir 1965:30)

Despite Dr. N's "triumph," Beauvoir is haunted by a very different response
that inadvertently spills out of the mouth of one of the nurses, Mme. Gontrand,
prior to the operation: "Don't let her be operated on!" Mme. Gontrand, horrified by the unprofessionalism of her own outburst, quickly covers her mouth:
"'If Dr N knew I had said that to you! I was speaking as if it were my own mother'" (Beauvoir 1965:28). This personalized response is precisely what Beauvoir
is seeking, but Mme. Gontrand, afraid she has already said too much and perhaps fearing that her impulsive declaration might cost her her job, refuses to
respond to Beauvoir's subsequent questions about why she would not have the
operation performed on her own mother.

The repeated refrain "Don't let them operate on her" echoes in Beauvoir's
head in the days that follow, and indeed serves as a constant reminder long after
Françoise de Beauvoir's death that an alternative could have been chosen, not
only to the operation which prolonged her mother's life for a few more days,
but also to the deception that accompanied it.

Not surprisingly, Sartre plays no role in the drama that leads up to Beauvoir's
mother's death. The moral absolutism which haunts his own conception of bad
faith makes it impossible for him to comprehend a deception that enables subjectivity, even while it compounds the pain and suffering of those who choose
to participate in it. Strikingly, there is really only one place within this narrative
that Sartre's own voice appears and this is in response to Beauvoir's description
of her mother's mouth:

> I talked to Sartre about my mother's mouth as I had seen it that morning and
> about everything I had interpreted in it—greediness refused, an almost servile
> humility, hope, distress, loneliness—the loneliness of her death and of her life—
> that did not want to admit its existence. And he told me that my own mouth was
> not obeying me any more: I had put Maman's mouth on my own face and in
> spite of myself, I copied its movements. Her whole person, her whole being, was
> concentrated there, and compassion wrung my heart. (Beauvoir 1965:31)

This is an extraordinary passage, for Beauvoir's reaction to Sartre's telling her
that her mouth has become her mother's, is not one we might expect her to
have. Rather than bristle with indignation (and indeed one wonders if Sartre,
between whom and Françoise de Beauvoir no love was lost, deliberately made
such a provocative comment to get Beauvoir to "snap out of it" and come back
to herself), she affirms this bodily identification with her mother's suffering and

distress, an identification in which her mother's "whole person, her whole being" is concentrated.

Beauvoir is unable to sustain this mimetic identification, however, when she returns to her mother's side. Indeed, before she even continues her narrative of her mother's final days, she pauses at this point to describe briefly her mother's own life, a life which was in such marked contrast to Beauvoir's own. Although Beauvoir is sympathetic to the nagging unhappiness that dogged her mother's childhood, she very callously (and sexistly) dismisses the pain her father's numerous infidelities caused her mother: "I do not blame my father. It is tolerably well known that in men habit kills desire. Maman had lost her first freshness and he his ardour" (Beauvoir 1976:36). In dramatic contrast to the more sophisticated explanations Beauvoir provides in *The Second Sex* for how and why "habit kills desire" in *both* men and women, explanations which tend to focus upon the clash between lived desires and the more static demands placed upon individuals by the institution of marriage, here we have a onesided picture that reflects the perspective of a daughter whose early idolization of her father (an idolization that Beauvoir, in *Memoirs of a Dutiful Daughter*, acknowledges, and one that she also admits led to all sorts of unrealistic idealizations), can only be preserved through a dissociation with her mother who is indirectly blamed for his indiscretions.

In *Memoirs of a Dutiful Daughter*, Beauvoir describes in great detail her mother's response to her husband's infidelities. Basically, Françoise de Beauvoir's conduct (as described by her daughter) was quite predictable for a woman of her class: having lost her husband's love and attention, she turned her own love and attention to her two daughters and made excessive demands for their love and attention in return. Beauvoir, by her own account, strongly resented her mother's attempts to "colonize" her subjectivity, and made her escape through an active, intellectual life, which gave her her mother's respect and at the same time provided her with a domain her mother could not participate in. Due to having taken this path, Beauvoir observes,

> I had a confidence in myself that my mother did not possess in the least: the road of argument, disputation—my road—was closed to her. On the contrary, she had made up her mind to share the general opinion: the last person who spoke to her was right. Exact knowledge, a decided view, would have made the sudden reversals that circumstances might force upon her impossible. (Beauvoir 1965:42)

Before resuming her description of her mother's final days, Beauvoir concludes this retrospective account of her mother's earlier life with a haunting set of images:

> In her childhood her body, her heart and her mind had been squeezed into an armour of principles and prohibitions. She had been taught to pull the laces

hard and tight herself. A full-blooded, spirited woman lived on inside her, but a stranger to herself, deformed and mutilated. (Beauvoir 1965:43)

As unwilling to acknowledge her daughters' resentment of her excessive interest in their lives as she was to acknowledge her husband's infidelities, Françoise de Beauvoir is depicted in *Memoirs of a Dutiful Daughter* as a bitter, unhappy woman who is intent upon making her daughters "pay" for her disappointments in life. The paradox is that while Beauvoir unscrupulously takes her mother to task for the weaknesses that led to her strong need for self-deception regarding her marriage and children, Beauvoir also portrays her mother as developing a sense of agency in the final month of her life that is made possible not in spite of, but *through* her own self-deception (and the deception of others) regarding her impending death. For it is clear in A *Very Easy Death*, that Françoise de Beauvoir "knows" that this is not just a serious illness but a fatal one and that she prefers not to have this "knowledge" confirmed in any way.[17]

How does she "know" this? Her knowledge does not come from conversations with her doctors, her daughters or the nursing staff—it comes from her own, cancer-ridden body, which has become a force to be reckoned with in its own right and which has generated a bodily imperative that has brought her two adult children and her grandnieces running to her bedside. The force of this imperative is the force of death—that "indefinite certainty" that, as Heidegger observes, marks the impossibility of the possibilities that characterize human being-in-the-world (Heidegger 1962).

Françoise de Beauvoir zealously protects her fragile self-deception by choosing not to see those friends who would confront her with the need to "plan" for her death and, most importantly, by refusing to see a priest whose job it is to provide spiritual solace and who is entrusted with the moral duty of delivering the "last rites." Since their mother had always been a devout Catholic, Beauvoir and her sister are surprised that she has rejected this option, yet they risk the strong disapproval of her mother's friends and the priest to honor her wishes, even though they are well aware that they themselves (and not their mother) will be blamed for the decision. After their mother's death, Beauvoir states:

> We were blamed. To be sure we did not prevent Maman from receiving the last sacraments; but we did not oblige her to take them. We ought to have told her, 'You have cancer. You are going to die.' Some devout women would have done so, I am sure, if we had left them alone with her. . . . Maman did not want these intimate conversations. What she wanted to see round her bed was young smiling faces. . . . She mistrusted the others and she spoke of some of them with a certain amount of ill-feeling—it was as though a surprising instinct enabled her to detect those people whose presence might disturb her peace of mind. (Beauvoir 1965:90)

A key to understanding this rejection of those whose way of grappling with this bodily knowledge would be to transform its "indefinite certainty" into the clear "light" of religious truth, is provided by Beauvoir in the following passage:

> Her illness had quite broken the shell of her prejudices and her pretensions: perhaps because she no longer needed these defences. No question of renunciation or sacrifice any more: her first duty was to get better and so to look after herself; giving herself up to her own wishes and her own pleasures with no holding back, she was at last freed from resentment. Her restored beauty and her recovered smile expressed her inner harmony and, on this death-bed, a kind of happiness. (Beauvoir 1965:60)

As long as Mme. de Beauvoir "believes" that she is going to get better, Beauvoir suggests, she can make taking care of herself her "first duty"; without the "excuse" provided by her illness, she cannot justify such "self-indulgence." Beauvoir has already noted that her mother cannot take her daughter's path, a path that calls for self-examination, demands confidence in oneself, and decries self-deception. Moreover, her failure to take this path should not, in and of itself, count against her since, as Heidegger so poignantly observes in *Being and Time*, "Dying is something that every Dasein itself must take upon itself at the time. By its very essence, death is in every case mine, in so far as it 'is' at all" (Heidegger 1962:284). No one can offer anyone else a "guide" for how to die; being-toward-death is something that each individual must come to terms with from the idiosyncratic standpoint of her/his own life-situation.[18]

Although Françoise de Beauvoir's denial of the inchoate knowledge provided by her body is indeed a form of self-deception, I would argue that it cannot be equated with or reduced to the failed lie to oneself that constitutes Sartrian bad faith. This is because bad faith is itself a result of the dual ontological structure of consciousness (i.e. nonthetic consciousness and thetic consciousness) and is predicated on the transcendence of consciousness rather than the immanence of one's own bodily experience. For Mme. de Beauvoir to make herself her first duty means that she herself must count as an *embodied* moral agent and it is this recognition both that she counts and that it is "ok" to count, that contributes to her "easy death." As someone whose desires and whose body count, Françoise de Beauvoir in turn counts on her daughters to "protect" her from those who would demolish her emerging agency, by tearing away what they would regard as her "veil of ignorance." Unlike Tolstoy's Ivan Ilych who cannot look to his family for compassion but who must depend on his loyal servant Gerasim to be responsive to his needs and desires, Françoise de Beauvoir has two daughters who love her enough to give her the death she demands, even though this death comes at a very high price.

Whereas Sartre would undoubtedly view Mme. de Beauvoir's self-deception as an act of bad faith and might analyze it in terms of a "clash" between a pre-reflective awareness of her impending death and a reflective attempt to distance herself from this awareness, Heidegger would undoubtedly characterize the corresponding deception practiced by her daughters, the doctors, and the nurses as archetypical manifestations of the dissembling conduct of "the they" whose:

> evasive concealment in the face of death dominates everydayness so stubbornly that, in Being with one another, the 'neighbours' often still keep talking the 'dying person' into the belief that he will escape death and soon return to the tranquillized everydayness of the world of his concern. Such 'solicitude' is meant to 'console' him. . . . In this manner the "they" provides [besorgt] a *constant tranquillization about death*. At bottom, however, this is a tranquillization not only for him who is 'dying' but just as much for those who 'console' him. (Heidegger 1962:297–298)

From a Heideggerian perspective, it is clear that the only "authentic" response to death (whether one's own or that of another) is to meet this "possibility of the impossibility of Dasein" head-on; the problem with the "tranquillization" provided by the they is that it "does not permit us the courage for anxiety in the face of death" (Heidegger 1962:298). Though Beauvoir and her sister urgently demand medical tranquillization for their mother to stop her physical suffering, I do not believe that their motivation for participating in this deception is merely to tranquillize her (and their) anxiety about her death. Moreover, I would argue that there is a tension in Heidegger's own account of being-towards-death insofar as he recognizes that death has to become, for each of us, our "ownmost possibility not to be outstripped" which necessitates an individual and individualizing response, and yet he also privileges a particular manner of comporting oneself towards one's death across all situations, namely, with resolute acceptance of it. In the end, for Heidegger, this resolute acceptance is quite abstract and, like Sartre's bad faith, it is depicted more as a conscious rather than a bodily affirmation.

Rather than attempt to come to terms with a death that refuses all terms, Françoise de Beauvoir focuses instead on her *living* body, a body that has not "counted," morally speaking, until these final days. Her daughters, doctors, and nurses aid her in this endeavor, for varying reasons, some self-serving and some not. Against the danger of self-sacrifice that seems to dog the ethic of care and which is most salient in the cared-for/one-caring duality presented by Nel Noddings, Beauvoir and her sister Hélène, care for their mother in such a way that she is in turn able to care for them, no longer by seeing to their daily needs as had the Maman of their youth, but by allowing them actively to diminish their burden of remorse, a remorse that, as Beauvoir notes, is inescapable regardless of how, when, where, or why a loved one's death has occurred:

> When someone you love dies you pay for the sin of outliving her with a thousand piercing regrets. Her death brings to light her unique quality; she grows as vast as

the world that her absence annihilates for her and whose whole existence was
caused by her being there; you feel that she should have had more room in your
life—all the room, if need be. (Beauvoir 1965:94)

It could be argued that Mme. de Beauvoir cares for her daughters by allowing
them to care for her *as daughters*, and, in doing so, the bonds that tie all three
together are strengthened, rather than weakened, in her dying days. While Heidegger portrays death as undoing one's relationships to everyone and everything else, Beauvoir offers us a picture of death that is "sweetened" by human
compassion. In this picture, the "blemish" of deception is indeed present, but it
enables a life at the same time that it denies an impending death. So, while the
need to practice the deception may reflect a "character flaw" in Françoise de
Beauvoir, to affirm the desire that gives rise to it is to affirm the person from
whom it issues as a *living being* who, in the act of dying, silently demands to be
heard.

What Beauvoir offers us in this text, is indeed an ambiguous ethics in which
the relationship between bad faith and deception is interrogated and ultimately
torn asunder. Her searing depiction of the almost unbearable tension between
feelings of guilt, love, and admiration for her mother on the one hand, and her
equally strong feelings of revulsion for her mother's naïvete, ravaged body, and
false humility on the other, parallels Beauvoir's own desire to remain loyal to
the Sartrian notion of bad faith to which she is existentially committed even
while she challenges it at every step of her narrative. Through her indirect,
deceptively "nonphilosophical" depiction of the inherent inadequacies of the
notion of bad faith, Beauvoir ultimately reveals the limits of philosophical "systems" when human relationships are at stake.

In particular, Beauvoir definitively parts company with her own philosophical peers, Heidegger and Sartre, whose respective visions of appropriate conduct in the face of death are of individuals who stand alone, neither passively
acquiescing to their death nor actively resisting it. By portraying how her mother's death reinforces rather than undoes her ties to her (m)other and to a shared
past, Beauvoir offers an incipient ethic of care that refuses to allow those who
do the caring to dominate and determine the needs and desires of the one who
is cared for. As the one who always ends up writing the memoirs of the final
days of those she loves (her best friend Zaza in *Memoirs of a Dutiful Daughter*,
her mother in *A Very Easy Death*, and Sartre in *Adieux: A Farewell to Sartre*,
and of whose final days we have no corresponding account, Beauvoir indeed
confronts the pain and anguish of death head-on, and shows us that the unresolved questions that remain at the death of a loved one are the price I pay for
binding myself to another whose interests, needs, and desires will never be the
same as my own.

Bodily Imperatives

The ground for this ethics is not a categorical imperative, nor is it the transcendence of consciousness as a nihilating activity that refuses too close an identification with any given action, relationship, or situation; rather, it is an embodied ethics grounded in the dynamic, bodily imperatives that emerge out of our intercorporeal exchanges and which in turn transform our own body images, investing them and reinvesting them with moral significance. This moral significance, which is itself continually changing, depends not on detachment from others but can only arise in and through our relations with others, relations which, as Grace Clement and others have insisted, do not preclude autonomy, but provide the necessary conditions for genuine autonomy to emerge. To act as a daughter, a mother, a sister, is not to deny my individuality or to diminish my moral agency; it is to affirm my own embodiment as well as the embodiment of others. To be moral does not require, as the Platonic model holds, separating my conscious "self" from my body and its desires; it involves developing a moral agency that can only be experienced and enacted through bodily practices, practices that both implicate and transform the bodies of others.

An embodied ethics cannot view as neutral the sexual, racial, and class differences that, along with differences in age, ability, ethnicity, and gender so often divide bodies into imaginary, incommunicable domains with disastrously *real* implications. These differences are all too often described merely as differences *among* bodies rather than active ways of living our bodies which generate bodily memories, demands, and expectations that are in turn expressed through our body images. In contrast to a Kantian position which posits that I should treat others with respect (as ends-in-themselves) purely because they are rational beings, which, for Kant, means that my respect should never be based on "contingent" corporeal features such as their sex, race, age, abilities, interests, and relationships, an embodied ethics views these bodily experiences as a source of respect both for the moral wisdom they can provide as well as for the way that they contextualize our intracorporeal and intercorporeal relations.

Rather than ignoring the particularities of our respective bodies, as Kant or Rawls would have us do in order to attain the status of impartial moral agents, the particularities of my own body and the bodies of others need to be taken into account in our moral decision making for the very reason that these decisions are not reducible to abstract, rational deliberations that take place between one mind and another mind in a phantasmatic intellectual space, but because, as Foucault has amply shown, our moral decisions themselves emerge out of specific, disciplinary practices and have material effects on the bodies of those who initiate them as well as those who are subjected to them. Moreover, as Linda Alcoff argues, there will inevitably be situations in which I am compelled to speak for others and not just for myself, and to do so effectively and appropriately, it is important, morally important, that I am attuned to the specificity of their situation and how it *differs* from my own, rather than (merely) to what we share in common.

In addition, Alcoff claims that the very act of speaking for myself, as well as for others, is an act of discursive self-creation with specific (and often unpredictable) consequences for the self being created as well as the self doing the creating:

> In speaking for myself, I (momentarily) create my self—just as much as when I speak for others I create their selves—in the sense that I create a public, discursive self, which will in most cases have an effect on the self experienced as interiority. Even if someone never hears the discursive self I present of them they may be affected by the decisions others make after hearing it. (Alcoff 1991:10)

Alcoff's point is that although one may be tempted to restrict the influence of the discursive self that is created to the discursive context in which it is evoked, the discursive self I create (whether it represents my own self or another self) can exceed its context and produce both discursive and nondiscursive effects.[19]

Appealing to Alcoff's insightful account of both the necessity and the danger of speaking for others, we should recognize that Beauvoir's own embodied ethics is generated through Beauvoir's "speaking for" her mother when explaining why her mother resisted "knowing" that she was dying of cancer. As readers, we are trained to accept the description Beauvoir provides of her mother's personality and motives, even though we know that these descriptions would not be the same if Françoise de Beauvoir was describing herself in her own voice (or even if someone else was describing her). Beauvoir herself reminds us that she and her mother are quite different individuals throughout this narrative, and she attempts to portray her mother in a dispassionate, judicious manner that neither vilifies nor glorifies her. She alerts us to the dangers of claiming to speak for another by noting the ways in which her relationship with her mother has bred an irritation that springs to the surface much more readily than it would with anyone else:

> since she was my mother, her unpleasant phrases irked me more than if they had come from any other mouth. And I was as rigid as I had been at twenty when she tried (with her usual clumsiness) to move on to an intimate plane. 'I know you don't think me intelligent; but still, you get your vitality from me. The idea makes me happy.' I should have been delighted to agree that my vitality came from her; but the beginning of her remark utterly chilled me. So we each paralysed the other. It was all that that she meant, when she looked firmly at me and said, 'You frighten me, you do.' (Beauvoir 1965:69)

Beauvoir contextualizes this lack of rapprochement between mother and daughter in a manner that neither ignores nor overly dramatizes its bodily/discursive effects. I say bodily/discursive here because the two cannot be separated into different domains: the paralysis she describes is visceral and this viscerality is discursively expressed. Its discursive expression in turn creates (or at least is capable of creating) visceral effects in the bodies of the readers who may also have experienced the *frisson* of intimacy gone awry.

In speaking for Beauvoir who speaks for her mother, I am resituating their own mother-daughter dynamic within the framework of an embodied ethics that is grounded upon the bodily imperatives that are all too often disembodied when they are removed from the specific relationships that give rise to them in the first place. These bodily imperatives vary from one situation to another and from one relationship to another, yet certain continuities can be discovered insofar as our bodily demands are rarely whimsical or capricious but are themselves responsive to the situations in which we find ourselves.

Responding to the bodily imperatives of others even when they are at odds with our own responses to a given situation need not involve acquiescing to the demands of those others. While in Beauvoir's case, her unwilling participation in a deception regarding her mother's impending death affected Beauvoir, her mother, and her sister more than it affected anyone else, there are situations that can arise where one's participation in a particular practice that one finds morally abhorrent will have more deleterious effects, not only for oneself and those others with whom one is directly engaged, but for the larger community as well. Indeed, as I have argued elsewhere, there are certain cultural practices such as sex-selective abortion for the purpose of eliminating unwanted girls in a society that values males over females, which demand resistance both from members within and outside the community. The question is, how can we guarantee that that resistance ends up acknowledging and respecting the bodily imperatives that have led to widespread acceptance of the process to begin with?

In "Sex-Selective Abortion: A Relational Approach," I argue that Sara Ruddick's relational model of maternal thinking is best-suited to dealing with the difficulties of showing how a given cultural practice (in this case sex-selective abortion) can be viewed as morally wrong even while we recognize the specific conditions that make this practice socially acceptable for a given community.[20] Ruddick outlines three "maternal interests," preservation, growth, and social acceptability, and shows in her work how all three generate bodily imperatives that cannot be ignored, and yet which are often difficult to sustain in a harmonious fashion.[21] In seeking to preserve the life of a helpless infant, there are certain things I *must* do, at the most minimal level, or the other will die. In seeking to foster the intellectual, emotional, and physical growth of a young child, there is more room for negotiation, but here, too, there are definite points at which a lack of concern or attention can lead to a failure to thrive (on the part of the mother, I would add, as well as the child). Lastly, to raise a child whom both others and I can appreciate and accept as a social peer, is not a matter of "shaping a mind" but rather, arises out of an embodied exchange and cannot be separated from the other two interests even though it may, at times, come in conflict with them.

What I find especially appealing about Ruddick's model is its emphasis on the context in which relationships unfold and develop (or fail to develop). This sensitivity to context allows her to foreground the specific and often invisible role that race, class, gender, age, religiosity, and shared cultural beliefs play in our moral decision making, in a manner that does not simply endorse or reject their influence. Instead, they become opened up as sites of interrogation, in a process that often reveals their instabilities and which thereby challenges us to reevaluate the bodily imperatives that arise from them. However, it is clear that all too often the urgency of the demands made by others' bodies upon our bodies and the urgency of the corresponding interests arising out of these demands preclude this type of radical interrogation. Hence, an embodied ethics will need to focus on how best to promote an examination not merely of bodily imperatives themselves (which is itself a challenge), but also, of the varying corporeal registers in which bodily imperatives present themselves, a process that requires closely attending to the specificities of lived bodies.

Although I find Ruddick's maternal model to be useful in allowing us to see how a focus on relations need not require an endorsement of moral relativism (since there are certain nonrelative demands that arise out of our relations with others, even if there are always a number of ways in which those demands may be met), one limitation of Ruddick's maternal model is that it best captures the specific needs emerging out of the relationship between a parent and child in which the former seeks to realize interests for the latter; this model is not, I think, as effective in describing relations between nations (which is the direction in which Ruddick wants to extend it in order to argue for a politics of peace), or in describing relations between adults where one person cannot, without being subject to the charge of paternalism, seek to define and meet the interests of another. I have similar objections to Julia Kristeva's provocative herethics and to Irigaray's ethics of sexual difference. All three models take as their point of departure the mother-child relationship (although Ruddick makes it quite clear that *anyone*, male or female, biologically or nonbiologically related to the child can be a mother), and while this is surely a neglected domain in ethics more generally, I do not think that this admittedly foundational relationship can serve as a framework for all of our moral relations with others.

To privilege the maternal, or even sexual difference, as a source of moral significance, runs the danger of effacing those corporeal realities that do not "fit" neatly into that framework. Throughout the process of writing this book, I have thought long and hard about where I "stand" on the question of sexual difference, since, in the wake of Irigaray's famous pronouncement that the question of sexual difference is "the question of our age" is seems impossible not to take a stand on its primacy or lack thereof. For a long time, I have felt that my own conflicted intuitions about this issue were a sign of some sort of failure, certainly conceptual and possibly even moral, on my part. Why, I have asked myself, am I finding it so difficult to be persuaded that sexual difference is the "bedrock" of corporeality (and therefore, of morality), and why am I also finding it equally difficult to reject the compelling arguments Irigaray, Grosz, and so many others have offered to establish its primacy? The Wittigian rejection of sexual difference (and, ultimately, all difference) as a social construction, does not appear to me to be a viable alternative either; this is because the materiality of sexual difference, on Wittig's account, has no inherent meaning apart from its social expression.

The answer I have come to, and one which is in keeping with the embodied ethics I am trying to sketch out here, is that the primacy of sexual difference and the bodily imperatives generated on the basis of that difference, is a reality in many (perhaps even most), but not all contexts in which human beings engage with one another. To "take a stand" on the question of sexual difference is an impossible task if one is asked to do this without reference to the contexts in which this question arises or fails to arise. For, to say that sexual difference is *the* question of our age is as much a commentary on "our age" as it is on sexual difference and a focus on the latter should never deflect our attention from questioning what it is about our age (and other ages) that makes sexual difference itself a bodily imperative.

To raise these questions in turn leads us to other, equally pressing questions, questions about racial difference, cultural difference and to how these and other "defining differences" are always entwined with sexual difference, an entwinement that is expressed corporeally through our bodies and body image intercourse. Moreover, any discussion of these defining differences cannot take place in the absence of a corresponding discussion of the differential exclusions, to use David Theo Goldberg's term, that are grounded upon them.[22] These differential exclusions, whether they are based on racial difference, sexual difference, age difference, religious difference, or any other corporeally enacted difference, oppress our bodies as well as our body images, and, as a result, they call for embodied responses.

Just as I have argued in earlier chapters that the body image cannot be reduced to a physiological, psychological or purely social phenomenon, since it is the site where all three interact in a complex and dynamic fashion, so too, I would argue that sexual difference is never "read off" the body in isolation from its gender, race, age, class, and sexual orientation (and this is by no means an exhaustive list), except through an artificial, decontextualizing and therefore decorporealizing process that fails to do justice to what it means to be an embodied subject. To be embodied is to be capable of being affected by the bodies of others and, therefore, to be embodied is both a necessary and a sufficient condition for the generation of a bodily imperative. This is why we must attend morally to the needs of bodies who are unable to articulate those needs for themselves; this includes those who are too young as well as those who are enfeebled by age or illness. This also includes bodies that are not human such as animal bodies, bodies of literature, and technological bodies.

While I do not think, as some care theorists do, that we must heed the call of all those human (or even nonhuman) bodies who need and/or demand our assistance, I do think that developing a sensitivity to the bodily imperatives that issue from different bodies is a necessary starting place for our moral practices. Which bodily imperatives we attend to will depend not upon some abstract teleological framework which places a higher value on some bodies as opposed to others (e.g. human over nonhuman, those I know best over those I know least, my own body versus other people's bodies), but rather, must always be a function of the bodily context that situates our relations with others. And, as I have repeatedly argued, this bodily context is not reducible to any one of its constitutive features, and so it cannot, from the outset, privilege any one of them at the expense of the others.

There is no "place" to begin to examine a relationship except from within that relationship—this Beauvoir shows us very well. To "end" a relationship through death or distance is always a matter of redefining the terms of that relationship and this "ending" itself generates new bodily imperatives and new relationships rather than taking us outside of a relational context. In writing about her mother's "easy" death, Beauvoir redefines the terms of her relationship with her mother and with her readers; she accomplishes this *through* her re-creation of her mother's body and the bodily imperatives which issue from it, imperatives that implicate her daughter's body, and which, through the body of the text, implicate the bodies of Beauvoir's readers. Finally, as readers, the text calls upon us to interrogate our own bodily imperatives, a process that involves examining how, when, where, and why they have emerged, as well as how best to meet them.

Portrait of a Teen, Michelle Marion (Nappy Production still,
Peazy Head Productions, 1997)

{conclusion}

In the essay "Style and Its Image" from *The Rustle of Language*, Roland Barthes claims that the image is an "impure notion, one which is at once a metaphoric form and a theoretical concept" (Barthes 1989:90). In this book I have attempted to show that our body images are much more than metaphoric constructs or useful theoretical tools though they can certainly serve in both capacities. The very notion of a body image is certainly "impure" if purity is intended to signify singularity, coherence, and stability. But, just as Barthes himself does not find the impurity of the notion of an image to be at all objectionable, but rather due to a positive ambiguity that is characteristic of the image itself, so too, I would maintain that the multiple, ambiguous dimensions of our body images, and, in particular, their lack of definitive borders or boundaries, should not be conceived as limitations but as rich and virtually unlimited sources of value and significance.

Shortly after completing the preceding chapters, I attended a philosophy conference and had dinner with friends who taught philosophy at other universities around the country. In response to their queries about this project, I gave a short synopsis of my main argument, namely, that human beings tend to have multiple body images and that these body images overlap with one another and are themselves constructed, reconstructed, and deconstructed through a series of ongoing, intercorporeal exchanges.[1] When I had finished my description, one of my dinner companions and a well-known continental philosopher, asked me if I was willing to hear an objection that, in his mind, threatened my entire argument. Feeling confident in my position given the many years I had spent working it out, I encouraged him to go ahead—figuring I may as well hear a "devastating" critique before rather than after the book was published (especially since there was still time left to do something about it!). To my surprise, and to the surprise, I believe, of most of our dinner companions, his objection was not about some aspect of my position regarding body images themselves, but rather, an objection to the very notion of the body image as such. More specifically, he argued that all this "talk" of body images was relevant only to women since men don't have body images at all, not even one, much less several of them.

To support his position, he elaborated on his own experience as an adolescent in which he claimed to have no real awareness (even prereflective) of his body. Basically, he argued that as a boy and later on as a man, he was never encouraged to be aware of his body and so he never could be said to have had a body image. When I and the other women philosophers present offered him a Merleau-Pontian description of the body image as that without which effective bodily movement would be impossible, and therefore a phenomenon that he surely "possessed," he was willing to grant that while men may indeed have this type of "corporeal schema," this was much different than the description of body images that I had just provided. Fair enough. I didn't have the time or the inclination to explain in detail why I think it is impossible to distinguish a "pure" sense of proprioception or a postural schema from the racialized, gendered, religious, ethnic, and able-bodied body images I have argued for here. Instead, I was more interested in the ways in which his unabashed proclamation that he did not have a body image (or at least didn't have one until feminism itself gave one to him as a white, male, heterosexual philosopher who appears to embody the patriarchal status quo), actually supported some of my own arguments about race, class, and gender. More specifically, the invisibility of his own body image (or of his multiple body images if my position is accurate), is itself, as the women at the table tried to argue (I found it interesting that the only other man there stayed silent throughout this whole discussion so it was impossible to judge his position), a function of his own privileged position vis-a-vis other men whose race, ethnicity, class, nationality, and sexuality corporeally marked them as the Other.

Ultimately, the reason why I did not find his objection to be tenable, is because our body images, as I have suggested throughout this book, are not dependent upon our recognition of them as such. That is, just because one may feel that one doesn't have a body image, doesn't mean that body images are not present and operative in one's experience. Our body images may indeed lack the stability of concrete phenomena that are visible before our eyes, but neither are they willful creations of our minds that only arise when we consciously reflect on them. My response to my colleague's objection, then, is that while his body images as an adolescent might very well have been un(re)marked (and I am doubtful that they even were so invisible thirty years ago when he actually was an adolescent experiencing numerous bodily changes), this does not mean that they did not exist or play a constitutive role in the formation of his own identity.[2]

To the extent that he was willing to grant that women have body images (though this was itself presented as a negative not a positive since it was tied to his perception that women were much more focused on their bodies than men, even if, when pressed, he granted that this was largely due to societal pressures on women to be concerned about their appearance), his belief that their body images had no bearing on his perceived lack of one was also significant. For, as we have seen, Schilder's notion of body image intercourse implies that it is impossible to distinguish sharply between "my" body images and "your" body images as if they were completely independent of one another. Rather, Schilder maintains that our own body images are constructed through constant communication with the body images of others. Accordingly, I would argue that to experience oneself as bodiless, as a "pure intellect," for example, is itself a reflection of a cultural body image ideal, one that explicitly denies or, at the very least, minimizes the lived dimensions of bodily experience, through a phantasmatic reconstruction of that experience as a disembodied agency.

Throughout this book, I have maintained that body images are themselves complex constructions that cannot be traced to a single source, whether that source be physiological, social or cultural, or psychical. This means that while our sex, race, gender, social class, age, family, religion, ethnicity, and day-to-day experiences all contribute significantly to the formation of our body images, no one of them alone plays a determinative role in their construction.[3] Indeed, it is the lack of clear boundaries between these different components of our experience that ensures that our body images can never be restricted to any one of them.

On the other hand, if we consider early childhood experiences as an example, many if not all of us undoubtedly experienced situations in which our age was considered (by ourselves and/or others) to be more salient in a given situation than our race or our sex or our class or our religion. And, situations may arise in the present that suddenly bring back a rush of corporeal memories of that childlike body image that was once so prevalent in our daily lives. So, while I am claiming that it is impossible to separate out these different strands of our experience, this does not mean that all are on an equal footing from one moment to the next. Instead, it is our projects themselves and the concrete interactions we sustain with others, that provide the ongoing context in which a particular body image becomes more significant than another.

Another point that I would like to emphasize, is that the multiplicity of body images that we possess, rather than signifying a fragmented or dispersed identity, is, paradoxically, precisely what helps us to develop a coherent sense of self. More specifically, insofar as these multiple body images are themselves generated out of the variety of situations in which we find ourselves, they enable us to develop fluid and flexible responses to them. Moreover, I would add, it is the ongoing exchange that occurs between body images, an exchange that unfolds at the very moment that one body image imperceptibly gives way to another, which provides us with a sense of intercorporeal continuity, a continuity that is reinforced through our concrete relations with others.

These concrete relations in turn generate new bodily imperatives, imperatives that demand an intercorporeal response. Unlike the singularity of a Kantian categorical imperative, there is not one but many bodily imperatives that demand our attention in any given situation, and these bodily imperatives stem from our own bodies as well as the bodies of others. To make an even stronger claim based upon chapters three, five, and six, I would say that through the different body images and body image ideals called forth by these bodily imperatives, our imaginations, our fantasies, and our very experience of space and time are continually reconfigured.

The forces of abjection or exclusion that are operative in the formation of our body images which were discussed in chapter four, also guarantee that no one body image will ever be adequate to any and all situations. Technology not only facilitates the development of new body images, by demonstrating that intercorporeality includes inanimate and even virtual objects and experiences, but it also creates new bodily imperatives and new cultural body image ideals in the process.[4] Moreover, the incorporation of these nonhuman dimensions of existence into our own body images helps to reveal the limits of the traditional transcendence/immanence distinction as a way of making sense of our lives.

While the multiple bodily imperatives that issue from our own and other bodies cannot all be explicitly acknowledged and attended to at any one point in time, I would argue that many of them are nonetheless capable of being registered and responded to corporeally. This may involve incorporating these bodily demands into our existing body images (and thereby transforming these latter in the process), establishing new connections between body images, or creating new body images and body image ideals altogether. It is especially urgent, I believe, given the rampant sexism, racism, homophobia, ageism, ethnocentrism, and religious intolerance that exists all over the world, that we develop new body image ideals, viable alternatives to those provided by what Max Horkheimer and Theodor Adorno so presciently referred to in the 1940s as the "culture industry."[5] These new body image ideals must themselves be grounded upon our own intercorporeality, rather than taking the form of singular ideals that individual, autonomous bodies are supposed to judge and be judged by.

Central to the agenda of many contemporary feminist ethicists (beginning with Carol Gilligan), is a concern to expose the limits of the notion of an autonomous individual which grounds standard liberal theories of justice. Quite a few have done this by stressing, in accordance with an ethics of care, the interdependencies that exist in our interpersonal relationships, in particular, the ways in which an individual is socially constructed, and therefore dependent on others for her/his own sense of self. While these efforts have been crucial in turning our attention to the importance of social interactions in the construction of our respective identities, there has been a surprising lack of acknowledgement of what I have been calling the intercorporeal dimensions of these relationships. More specifically, the role that our bodies (and our body images) play in this process has not been adequately developed, except perhaps in reference to the maternal/fetal dyad where the intercorporeal exchanges between mother and fetus are too striking to be ignored. Unfortunately, this failure to recognize that social interactions always have bodily implications (and vice versa), runs the danger of leaving the corporeal domain itself untouched as a distinctive, autonomous realm that, when attended to at all, tends to be described (with the exception once again of the maternal/fetal dyad) in terms of relatively discrete bodies interacting with other discrete bodies.

In short, I am arguing that the critique of the autonomous individual mounted by contemporary feminist ethicists, has often been too narrowly focused upon social autonomy and has not addressed the corresponding corporeal autonomy that is also presupposed in traditional liberal theories of justice. To remedy this, I propose that we turn our attention to the intercorporeality that already exists *within* and not just *between* our bodies, an intercorporeality that gives depth to our body images and which, I have argued, enhances rather than diminishes, our sense of bodily integrity.

An uncritical reliance upon a traditional division between the cultural and the corporeal haunts much contemporary feminist theory and is implicit in the very notion of "cultural feminism." As Elizabeth Grosz urges in *Volatile Bodies*, it is imperative not only that we situate the cultural within the corporeal rather than viewing the former as something enacted upon the latter, but that we recognize the corporeal within the cultural, not as a site of immanence or resistance to cultural transformation, or even as a stubborn remainder that refuses theorization, but as the materiality of culture itself, a fluid materiality that is characterized not by self-sameness but by alterity. For, as Grosz persuasively argues:

> Alterity is the very possibility and process of embodiment: it conditions but is also a product of the pliability or plasticity of bodies which makes them other than themselves, other than their "nature," their functions and identities. (Grosz 1994:209)

In his essay, "The Function of Fiction in Shaping Reality," Paul Ricoeur argues that we must break away from the ordinary language definition of an image "as the intuitive representation of some[thing] existing *in absentia*." On this view, "[t]o have an image of something is to 'see' it in our mind's eye, without the presence of the actual thing" (Ricoeur 1991:118). Instead, Ricoeur advocates that we recognize images as tied to language and not just to perception. If we do this, he argues, we will see that the productive aspects of the imagination long recognized as crucial to the formation of images, have a counterpart in the productive aspects of language whereby "the emergence of new meanings in the sphere of language generates an emergence of new images" (Ricoeur 1991:122). One of my goals has been to show how perceptually-based images and language-based images are themselves incorporated into and expressed through our body images (and vice-versa). Accordingly, we must also recognize that the productivity associated by Ricoeur and others with the imagination, with language, and more generally, with the "life of the mind," is a constitutive feature of embodiment.

By affirming the productivity that characterizes our body images, a productivity that leads to multiple body images that do not represent, symbolize, or substitute for something that is absent, but are themselves experienced as an ongoing intercorporeal presence, we can best see why:

In the measure to which image gives a body, a contour, a shape to meaning, it is not confined to a role of accompaniment, of illustration, but participates in the *invention* of meaning. (Ricoeur 1991:123)

Becoming more aware of the creative as well as the destructive potential of our body images, is a first and extremely necessary (but often overlooked) step in the arduous process of inventing new meanings, (re)significations which are required to enact lasting social and political change. These new meanings can only take hold if we realize that changing our relations to others and to society as a whole is always an embodied process.

{notes}

Introduction

1 See Shaun Gallagher, "Body Image and Body Schema: A Conceptual Clarification," *The Journal of Mind and Behavior* 7 (4):541–554.

2 See Judith Butler, "Gendering the Body: Beauvoir's Philosophical Contribution," *Women, Knowledge, and Reality: Explorations in Feminist Philosophy*, eds. Ann Garry and Marilyn Pearsall (New York: Routledge Press, 1989a).

3 See Sherry Ortner, "Is Female to Male as Nature is to Culture?" *Women, Culture and Society*, eds. Michelle Zimbalist Rosaldo and Louise Lamphere (Stanford: Stanford University Press, 1974). This well-known essay explicitly takes up this issue and argues that women have been viewed as closer to nature (understood as that which is immanent or given) than men because of bodily functions specific to women alone, including most notably, their procreative abilities. Ortner, like Beauvoir, argues that despite this perception and the corresponding devaluation of women that has followed from it, women and men partake equally of aspects of transcendence and aspects of immanence. However, despite the effectiveness of Ortner's analysis of how "women's work" in the domestic sphere is just as much of a contribution to the advancement of culture as is "men's work" done outside the home, the presumption that nature and the body are more immanent than culture and the mind is never sufficiently challenged. Ortner does acknowledge that "[t]he culture/nature distinction is itself a product of culture, culture being minimally defined as the transcendence, by means of systems of thought and technology, of the natural givens of existence" (84), but she concludes the essay by defending the view that creativity and transcendence are cultural/intellectual rather than natural/bodily accomplishments. This conclusion is quite disappointing for it actually reinforces the problematic association between culture and the mind on the one hand and their alleged superiority to nature and the body on the other hand. Ortner's uncritical acceptance of this hierarchical, dichotomous model even while she argues for women (and men) as borderline cases between culture/transcendence and nature/immanence is poignantly illustrated in the final sentence of the essay where she argues that "[u]ltimately, both men and women can and must be equally involved in projects of creativity and transcendence. Only then will women be seen as aligned with culture, in culture's ongoing dialectic with nature" (87).

Chapter One

1 Schilder's view of the body image as a complex social, psychical, and physiological construction is especially noteworthy because it avoids the pitfalls of an exclusively foundationalist or anti-foundationalist ontology. See Bryan S. Turner, *Regulating Bodies: Essays in Medical Sociology* (New York: Routledge Press, 1994):61, who articulates the opposition between these two positions by asking "is the fundamental nature of the body produced by social processes, in which case the body is not a unitary or universal phenomenon, or is the body an organic reality which exists independently of its social representation?" As Turner himself notes, these need not be viewed as mutually exclusive alternatives, but rather should be understood as demarcating two different approaches to the body that complement and complete one another.

2 It is noteworthy that references to Schilder's work on the body image can be found throughout Merleau-Ponty's texts, including *The Structure of Behavior*, trans. Alden L. Fisher (Boston: Beacon Press, 1967), *Phenomenology of Perception*, trans. Colin Smith (London: Routledge and Kegan Paul Press, 1962), and even in a November, 1959 Work-

ing Note from *The Visible and the Invisible*, ed. Claude Lefort, trans. Alphonso Lingis (Evanston: Northwestern University Press, 1968):220.

3 A comprehensive history of the use of the terms body image and body schema can be found in Douwe Tiemersma's *Body Schema and Body Image* (Amsterdam: Swets and Zeitlinger, 1989). Elizabeth Grosz also provides a brief historical account of interest in and use of the term body image in *Volatile Bodies: Toward a Corporeal Feminism* (Bloomington: Indiana University Press, 1994a):62–67.

4 Compelling critiques of Merleau-Ponty's "masculinism," in particular, have been offered by Irigaray (1984), Young (1990), Butler (1989,1990), and Grosz (1994). In *Volatile Bodies* (Bloomington: Indiana University Press, 1994):111, Elizabeth Grosz concludes her chapter on Merleau-Ponty with a skeptical comment regarding phenomenological methodology: "Feminists need to seriously question whether phenomenological descriptions are appropriate for women's experience and, if they are not, whether it is desirable that they should be or whether, instead, altogether new and different theoretical terms are necessary—and how such terms may be developed."

Grosz has also expressed a similar skepticism with regard to psychoanalytic theory. See Elizabeth Grosz, "The Labors of Love. Analyzing Perverse Desire: An Interrogation of Teresa de Lauretis's *The Practice of Love*" *differences: A Journal of Feminist Cultural Studies* 6, no. 2+3 (Summer-Fall 1994):276–277. While she grants that "psychoanalysis has been so useful for feminist theory and its particular concerns," she also recognizes that "[t]he relationship between psychoanalysis and feminism has always been fraught with complications, qualifications, hesitancies" and she argues that psychoanalysis cannot provide an adequate account of lesbian desire, much less lesbian—or hetero-sexuality. Although it is Freud and Lacan in particular who are the target of Grosz's critical remarks, Schilder does operate from a traditional psychoanalytic framework in his analysis of the body image and hence his work is also subject to these same difficulties. Grosz is the only feminist philosopher I know of who discusses Schilder's account of the body image, and, despite her critique of his exhibiting a typical psychoanalytic "lack" of understanding of sexual difference, she affirms his "otherwise enormously useful rethinking of mind/body relations" (Grosz 1994a:82).

5 This is precisely the type of claim that gets Merleau-Ponty into trouble from a feminist standpoint since the sexual neutrality of the body which Merleau-Ponty endeavors to maintain is completely undermined by this masculinist project of possessing without being possessed in turn. Moreover, it is interesting to note the way in which the world suddenly takes on the "feminine" characteristics of the seductress, from whose "clutches" the body successfully manages to preserve its distance. The body becomes a male protagonist engaged in a perpetual "flirtation" with a female, "worldly" antagonist, and not surprisingly, it is the male who wins the round.

6 Merleau-Ponty is quite clear about the nonequivalence between the visual image and the child's awareness of her/his body. To demonstrate the impossibility of reducing the latter to the former, he makes the strong claim that: "The child's visual experience of his own body is altogether insignificant in relation to the kinesthetic, cenesthetic, or tactile feeling he can have of it. There are numerous regions of his body that he does not see and some that he will never see or know except by means of the mirror. There is no point-for-point correspondence between the two images of the body. . . . If he comes to identify as bodies, and as animated ones, the bodies of himself and the other, this can only be because he globally identifies them and not because he constructs a point-for-point correspondence between the visual image of the other and the introceptive image of his own body" (Merleau-Ponty 1964a):116.

The point Merleau-Ponty is at pains to bring home is that the body image cannot be understood as a specular construction that somehow arises through the comparison/subordination of bodily sensations with/to the specular image; this does not mean, however, that the specular image fails to play a significant role in facilitating the development of the body image as a coherent construction.

7 In his essay, "Cézanne's Mirror Stage," *The Merleau-Ponty Aesthetics Reader*, ed. Galen A. Johnson (Evanston: Northwestern University Press, 1993), Hugh Silverman describes the process the child must go through as follows: "Identification with the specular image only occurs after the child has treated the image as an image of another and after that assumption of alterity breaks down and a radical distancing from the image as other takes place. Thus when the child sees the image as an image of him or herself, it is not so much that it is the self as that it is *not other*. The "I" ("*je*") is formed out of a dialectic in which the image is postulated as other, denied, and then affirmed as the self. One could say that it is a process of incorporation of otherness into the self" (Silverman 1993):272.

While Silverman's account provides a lucid description of the "progress" the child makes in the mirror stage, he goes on to claim that "naturally this occurs only in the case of the recognition of self in the mirror. Objects and other people remain other" (Silverman 1993):272. It is these latter claims that I take to be problematic because I do not think that Merleau-Ponty wants to make such a strong distinction between the otherness of the self and the otherness of others in his own discussion of the mirror stage. In fact, as I will go on to argue, Merleau-Ponty supports his claim that "the specular image seems to be the threshold onto the visible world," precisely by viewing the otherness revealed in the specular image as an otherness of the self that is made possible by others. Moreover, it is precisely through our intimate identification with and internalization of the otherness revealed in the mirror that others no longer remain simply "other."

8 The "outside-in perspective" has been used in a much different context by both bell hooks and Patricia Hill Collins to describe the specific, marginalized perspective of black women in a white-dominated society, a perspective that can be both oppressive and empowering. In her essay, "Marginalization as Site of Resistance," *Out There: Marginalization and Contemporary Cultures*, eds. Russell Ferguson et al. (Cambridge: MIT Press, 1990), bell hooks explains the "inside-out" perspective of black domestic workers who see their own homes "across the tracks" through their white employer's eyes. She discusses the unique position these women find themselves in since they occupy both the "outside-in" and "inside-out" perspectives. This dual perspective, on hooks' account, leads to an intimate knowledge of racism and classism as it functions on both sides of the tracks and can (but often does not) lead to a sense of empowerment. The relationship between the perspectives on oneself and the other offered by the specular image and the perspectives on oneself and the other offered by co-inhabiting the "outside-in" and "inside-out" perspectives as a black domestic worker needs to be explored in more depth in order to see how the alienation that accompanies the incorporation of the specular image can serve to reinforce and consolidate oppressive attitudes and actions.

9 What distinguishes Merleau-Ponty's account of the mirror stage from Lacan's is clearly not the former's understanding of the specular image as a source of identification since this identification is a central aspect of Lacan's account. Rather, Lacan views the mirror stage primarily in terms of the child's deceptive (yet necessary) identification with her/himself as a totality via the "complete" picture offered by the specular image, and he goes on to focus on the ramifications of this deceptive understanding of the "I" throughout an individual's psychic life. Merleau-Ponty, on the other hand, while agreeing with Lacan that "when the child looks at himself in the mirror and recognizes his own image there, it is a matter of *identification* (in the psychoanalytic sense of the word)" and while acknowledging that "the passage from the introceptive *me* to the visual *me*, from the introceptive *me* to the "specular I" (as Lacan still says), is the passage from one form or state of personality to another," (Merleau-Ponty 1964a):135–136 stresses the child's new

understanding of what it means to be *visible*, to oneself and to others, and the child's corresponding recognition of an ideal space which "can occur only in passing to a higher level of spatiality that is no longer the intuitive space in which the images [introceptive and specular] occupy their own place (Merleau-Ponty 1964a):130.

10 In *Powers of Horror: An Essay on Abjection*, trans. Leon S. Roudiez (New York: Columbia University Press, 1982):62–63, Julia Kristeva emphasizes that the "edenic image of primary narcissism" is one that can be maintained only by the neurotic subject (and, therefore, at great expense) since there is a real threat to the ego-in-formation that is invoked in and through primary narcissism, which perpetually "shatters" its mirror of perfection. This threat, as Kristeva describes it, is none other than the possibility of the dissolution of the ego into its excluded other or "non-object," the abject. Hence, for Kristeva, not only is the body image fragmented in primary narcissism but the ego of primary narcissism is equally precarious. According to Kristeva, it is: "uncertain, fragile, threatened, subjected just as much as its non-object to spatial ambivalence (inside/outside uncertainty) and to ambiguity of perception (pleasure/pain)" (62). Moreover, Kristeva maintains that the fragility of the ego of primary narcissism and the threat of its undifferentiation from all that is not-ego, does not disappear once and for all as the individual moves on to a later developmental stage: "for the subject will always be marked by the uncertainty of his borders and of his affective valency as well" (63).

As we shall see in chapter four, it is precisely how the subject responds to this ever-present threat of undifferentiation and the loss of equilibrium that it involves, that helps to determine what comes to constitute the abject for that individual. And, it is through the incorporation or refusal to incorporate the abject into the psyche that the (lack of) boundaries of the body image come to be constituted as well.

11 It is precisely this lack of equilibrium, in fact, that marks the cases of "distorted" body images which we will discuss in chapter four. In anorexia, for instance, the excessive libidinal energy concentrated upon the mouth, disgestive tract, and anus, constantly belies the anorexic's efforts to separate herself from her body, an impossible dilemma which leads directly to the unbearable angst that "Ellen West" so poignantly describes in Ludwig Binswanger's case study. See Ludwig Binswanger, "The Case of Ellen West," *Existence: A New Dimension in Psychiatry and Psychology*, eds. Rollo May et al., trans. Werner M. Mendel and Joseph Lyons (New York: Basic Books, 1958).

12 It would be interesting, but beyond the scope of this project, to compare the similarities and differences between the Derridean notion of deconstruction as it is applied to texts with this process of corporeal construction, destruction, and reconstruction that applies to the body image.

13 We will discuss the way in which the body image "shrinks," thereby restricting our bodily possibilities and "expands" to incorporate objects and other body images in chapters two and three.

14 Both Merleau-Ponty and Schilder associate a vertical posture with equilibrium and so this is why Merleau-Ponty claims that the effort at equilibrium does not occur when we are lying down. However, I do think that an effort at equilibrium is still occurring in this position, but that what constitutes this equilibrium varies widely from one person to another and, for the same person, from one period of time to another. For some, it may be lying down on the left or right side in a fetal position, for others, equilibrium can be achieved on one's back in a horizontal position. Even while one is not lying down, it does not seem to be the case that everyone (cross-culturally speaking) experiences a sense of equilibrium through an upright posture; in some African cultures, for instance, squatting may be a position of choice for all sorts of social and commercial activities that Westerners would pursue sitting or standing. While squatting, the center of bodily gravity shifts to the pelvic region, and this inevitably alters the type of equilibrium one experi-

ences. Despite their acknowledgement that the body image is not merely a physiological phenomenon, both Merleau-Ponty and Schilder seem to view equilibrium in exclusively physiological terms, that is, in terms of skeletal structure in particular.

15 It would be interesting to speculate on what would count as mutilating oneself for Schilder. My guess is that he would view body-piercings and cosmetic surgery as prime examples.

16 We will explore the relations between norms, normativity, and normalization in the next chapter, relations characterized by particular power/knowledge regimes whose significance is discussed at length by Foucault especially in *Discipline and Punish: The Birth of the Prison*, trans. Alan Sheridan (New York: Random House, 1979), *The History of Sexuality: An Introduction*, Volume 1, trans. Robert Hurley (New York: Vintage Books, 1990), and his Introduction to *Herculine Barbin: Being the Recently Discovered Memoirs of a Nineteenth Century French Hermaphrodite*, trans. Richard McDougall (New York: Pantheon Books, 1980).

17 It is precisely this problem, in fact, that Judith Butler explores in depth in both *Gender Trouble: Feminism and the Subversion of Identity* (New York: Routledge Press, 1990), and *Bodies that Matter: On the Discursive Limits of "Sex"* (New York: Routledge Press, 1993). In a 1994 interview in *Radical Philosophy* 67 (Summer 1994):32, Butler describes her central preoccupation in *Bodies that Matter* as follows: "I wanted to work out how a norm actually materialises a body, how we might understand the materiality of the body to be not only invested with a norm, but in some sense animated by a norm, or contoured by a norm."

18 Although Freud would perhaps disagree with this interpretation of primary narcissism as founded upon an illusion, Schilder's understanding of primary narcissism does support such a position.

19 The relationship between the body image and the body image ideal is both complicated and fascinating. See chapter four for a more detailed discussion of it.

20 Correspondingly, the primary narcissism that gains a new impetus in the mirror stage arises out of the child's pre-oedipal relationship with the mother. Both Kristeva and Irigaray have explored extensively the significance of Freud's (and Lacan's) association of primary narcissism with the mother and the ego-ideal with the father in their respective work.

21 I am using the terms "above" and "below" as Fanon does, to describe figuratively how both the ego-ideal and body image ideal may be viewed as "above" the ego and body image insofar as they come later developmentally, and insofar as they perform a normative (ought) function with regard to these latter. In claiming that there is another schema "below" the corporeal schema, Fanon is claiming that the body image is not the first schematic morphological construction but that there is another one which precedes it and which is imposed from the outside; an earlier schema which constructs the very "elements" that in turn form the basis for the construction of the corporeal schema. Moreover, this schema, like the ego-ideal or body image ideal, also serves as a strong normative force in the development of the body image, but unlike these latter, its "censoring" activity is in place (internalized) and operative even before the body image is fully functional.

22 Fanon does devote a chapter of this text to the erotic dynamic between the woman of color and the white man, but aside from this chapter he almost completely ignores the ways in which this historico-racial schema is also coded according to sex and gender since he takes the corporeal experiences of black men as the norm for the race as a whole. Later on in the book, Fanon does seem to acknowledge sexual difference in his discussion of the response of whites to black men; in particular, Fanon describes how the black male becomes a phobogenic object for white men (and women) through being

reduced to his penis, an identification that reinforces the white male's own castration anxiety and, in turn, enhances his own sense of (corporeal) inferiority. See Franz Fanon, *Black Skin White Masks*, trans. Charles Lam Markman (New York: Grove Press, Inc., 1967).

23 Fanon also points out that whereas the Jew poses an *intellectual* threat for the anti-Semite (due to her/his putative acquisitiveness and business acumen), the black man poses a *biological* threat as a "penis symbol." Thus, while the Jew is a threat because s/he is too smart, the black man (and, Fanon acknowledges, the black woman as well) is a threat because he (she) is too sexual. This sexuality is not only separated from intellectuality but is even viewed as opposed to it, which reinforces all the more the morphological differences that characterize what David Theo Goldberg has aptly termed "the anatomy of racism." See David Theo Goldberg, *The Anatomy of Racism* (Minneapolis: University of Minnesota Press, 1990).

24 In *Discipline and Punish: The Birth of the Prison*, trans. Alan Sheridan (New York: Random House, Inc., 1979), Foucault provides an in-depth analysis of how techniques of diligent "self-surveillance" both parallel and reinforce an ongoing societal surveillance that categorizes, individualizes, and differentiates simultaneously.

25 In *Volatile Bodies: Toward a Corporeal Feminism* (Bloomington: Indiana University Press):224, Elizabeth Grosz suggests that the cultural significance of body building is not the same for men and for women, arguing that although, "body building can be seen as an attempt to render the whole of the male body into the phallus, creating the male body as hard, impenetrable, pure muscle," female body building can and should be understood in different ways. Rodriguez's autobiographical description certainly seems to reinforce the cultural significance of body building as Grosz describes it for men.

26 Although Judith Butler discusses the radical subversive potential of parodic practices in *Gender Trouble: Feminism and the Subversion of Identity* (New York: Routledge Press, 1990), she also acknowledges in both *Gender Trouble* and *Bodies that Matter* (New York: Routledge Press, 1993), that parody can as easily (perhaps even more easily) reinforce gender norms as resist them. Rodriguez's own reduplication, in his thirties, of the youthful, physically fit body he never had in his early twenties, may indeed be a subversive parody of ageist assumptions (thought it would be more powerful if he was older), but only confirms those based on gender. The inescapability of the "regulatory mechanisms by which social ideals are psychically sustained," regulatory mechanisms which seem to be reinforced rather than dismantled in Rodriguez's account, are understood by Butler as "the juncture of racial and gendered prohibitions and regulations and their forced psychic appropriations" (Butler 1993):181.

27 There are some people who do not possess multiple body images and I will take up one particular example, that of the anorexic, in chapter four. My argument there is that it is precisely the singularity, rigidity, and overdetermination of the anorexic's body image and its corresponding body image ideal that enables her body image to be characterized as distorted.

28 See Sandra Blakeslee, "How Do You Stop Agonizing Pain In An Arm That No Longer Exists? A Scientist Does It With Mirrors," *The New York Times* (March 28, 1995):C3.

Chapter Two

1 Indeed, for Husserl, the natural sciences can not achieve more than this since all human inquiries share the same basic structure as "consciousness of 'x'." For some helpful commentary on Husserl's notion of objective validity see translator Quentin Lauer's footnote 21 on page 87 of Husserl's essay, "Philosophy as Rigorous Science," in *Phenomenology and the Crisis of Philosophy* (New York: Harper and Row Publishers, Inc., 1965).

2 While it is beyond the scope of this particular project to develop this Husserlian influ-

ence on contemporary feminist theorizing, I would argue that the significant contributions recent feminist theorists have made both to phenomenological and psychoanalytic descriptions of the body image cannot be adequately understood without recognizing the importance of his methodological legacy.

3 Cixous, Irigaray, Kristeva, and Oliver all have made claims along these lines in their respective works. Given psychoanalysis' own difficulties in adequately characterizing the influence of sex, gender, class, and race upon psychic development, the irony of such an "explanation" should not go unnoticed.

4 See "Ambiguity, Absurdity, and Reversibility: Responses to Indeterminacy" in *Journal of the British Society for Phenomenology* 26, no. 1 (January 1995):43–52.

5 Descartes had his own answer to this problem, which was to hold out for clarity and distinctness, which involved resisting indeterminacy at all costs, since this latter, for him, could only serve to undermine rather than to make clarity and distinctness possible. Husserl's affirmation of the zone of indeterminacy as an indispensable and extremely rich feature of human experience which offers a necessary background against which determinate phenomena can manifest themselves, is a welcome corrective to this Cartesian dismissal.

6 Whereas for Husserl the noesis helps to constitute the significance of the noema, the noema does not seem to have a similar influence on the noesis. Husserl does stress that there can be no noesis without a corresponding noema since consciousness is always consciousness of something or other, but particular intentional objects do not seem to affect, for Husserl, the mode of intentionality through which they are grasped.

7 Marilyn Frye makes a similar point in her provocative essay entitled "The Possibility of Feminist Theory," in *Theoretical Perspectives on Sexual Difference*, ed. Deborah Rhode (New Haven: Yale University Press, 1990):180, through her discussion of the need to develop what she calls "pattern perception," a type of perception which involves "discovering patterns and articulating them effectively, judging the strength and scope of patterns, properly locating the particulars of experience with reference to patterns, understanding the variance of experience from what we take to be a pattern."

Frye suggests in this essay that recognizing certain oppressive patterns such as racism or sexism is the necessary first step to changing those patterns, and she cautions the reader against trying to force anomalous or discrepant data to fit the pattern. Although Frye never identifies it as such, I would argue that pattern perception is itself a phenomenological enterprise with a significant feminist component, namely, a strong political commitment to overcoming oppression that motivates and guides its methodological inquiry.

8 See Iris Young, *Throwing Like a Girl and Other Essays in Feminist Philosophy and Social Theory* (Bloomington: Indiana University Press, 1990). Young notes that these "exceptional" girls are quite often athletes who have learned how to make the most effective use of their bodies while engaging in sports activities. It is less clear how a boy would come to throw "like a girl" since there are few, if any, advantages that come from this latter, more constricted, throwing style. My hope is that the implementation of Title IX in the United States, the law that guarantees equal access to sports training and facilities for boys and girls, will either eliminate the denigrating ascription, "throwing like a girl" altogether or lead to its radical revaluation as a way of maximizing, as opposed to minimizing, one's bodily potential.

9 In the discussion that follows I will use the terms "masculine" and "feminine" as gender markers for two distinct styles of bodily comportment. The use of these terms is not intended to be exhaustive in the sense of identifying all of the relevant features that constitute what is commonly referred to as "masculinity" and "femininity" respectively. Thus, there may be "feminine" girls who nonetheless throw "like boys" and, although this seems less likely, there may well be "masculine" boys who throw "like girls." Young

uses the terms "masculine" and "feminine" to highlight distinctive gender differences in bodily comportment which are exhibited by a majority of boys and men, and girls and women respectively.

10 Even for parents who are proud to have a "tomboy," there may still be occasions when the tomboy is expected to start behaving more like the "girl she really is" especially on formal occasions (e.g. weddings, funerals, holiday celebrations) when exhibiting appropriate gender roles is (tacitly) seen as reinforcing the solemnity and dignity of the occasion.

11 When I was in fifth grade, those of us who self-identified as tomboys refused to walk in either the girls' or the boys' line to march out to recess. Instead, wearing shorts under our skirts, we walked defiantly between the two columns in a veritable "no-man's" land that made the boys snicker in amusement and the other girls either scowl or regard us with awe and envy. Presumably recognizing this as a passing "fad" which indeed ended as soon as enough girls moved over into "our space" to turn our middle line into a "girls line" once again, our teacher permitted us this gesture of symbolic defiance, we who were too young to recognize the significance of this early (failed) refusal of our gendered role.

In the twenty-five years that have elapsed since I marched in that transitional space, I have come to exhibit all of the contradictory modalities that Young describes in her essay. I do, indeed, throw "like a girl," and I shy away from balls I am intended to catch, rather than moving forward to meet them, often dropping them or failing to make contact altogether in the process. Much to my partner's dismay, I bend at the waist not at the knees when trying to lift heavy things or do yardwork and often end up with a sore back a day or two later as a result. I clutch my books to my chest when I am walking rather than allowing them to swing at my side in synchronization with my stride, and I worry often about hurting myself when contemplating a physically challenging task.

Despite my increased awareness concerning the self-limitations of my own bodily comportment, motility and spatiality, I find that the old bodily habits tend to "take over" when I am in action and that it is extremely difficult to change my bodily style to one that is less restricted. And, when I think about my own daughter's future, I know that I do not want her to exhibit these same contradictory bodily modalities. I do not want her to throw, carry, bend and lift "like a girl" and yet I do not want her to pay the price of peer and social rejection or amusement (which is itself a form of rejection) for refusing "her" gender. Moreover, I realize that I will have very little to do with whether or not she ends up throwing "like a girl" and with the formation of her own body images. Instead, her body images and bodily capabilities will be affected much more by the prevailing gender norms operative at her play-group, preschool and elementary school, and with the gendered expectations of her caretaker who takes such pride in her "being a girl," a status that differentiates her from her rambunctious older and younger brothers and brings with it special attention.

12 Young defines these three contradictory modalities of bodily comportment as follows. Ambiguous transcendence refers to the way in which while seeking to perform a given task, a woman often simultaneously "lives her body as a burden which must be dragged and prodded along and at the same time protected." Inhibited intentionality "simultaneously reaches toward a projected end with an 'I can' and withholds its full bodily commitment to that end in a self-imposed 'I cannot.' Discontinuous unity is identified by Young as a "subset" of inhibited intentionality whereby "the part of the body that is transcending toward an aim is in relative disunity from those that remain immobile." See Iris Young, *Throwing Like a Girl* (Bloomington: Indiana University Press, 1990):148, 150.

13 Both Sartre and Beauvoir claim that existing is a distinctive human activity whereas living is something that human beings share with other animate creatures. The former

refers to actively assuming freedom and responsibility for one's existence and the latter to the continued physiological functioning of the living organism. It should also be noted that for both Sartre and Beauvoir there are many sources of transcendence as well as immanence in our lives; that is, although they identify these terms quite strongly with being-for-itself and being-for-others, they are not equivalent expressions. See Jean-Paul Sartre, *Being and Nothingness*, trans. Hazel E. Barnes (New York: Washington Square Press, 1956) and Simone de Beauvoir, *The Second Sex*, trans. H.M. Parshley (New York: Vintage Books, 1989).

14 This latter threat arises because of Young's claim that excessively focusing upon and questioning my body's ability to undertake a given task, transforms the body into an object (for myself as well as for others) "that must be coaxed and manipulated into performing it." See Iris Young, *Throwing Like a Girl* (Bloomington: Indiana University Press, 1990):150.

15 Examples of such activities include learning to play a new sport such as tennis, golf, and swimming where careful focus on the body's motility, comportment and spatiality is required. Of course, the goal of such activity is to transform the acquired skills into bodily habits so that such close attention to the body is no longer needed. Nonetheless, it would seem strange to identify the bodily self-reference required for learning a new sport with the contradictory bodily modalities described by Young and/or to claim that the process of learning a new sport is more immanent because of this self-reference than the activity of playing that sport once the requisite skills have been acquired.

16 It is precisely because they are taken-for-granted that these beliefs, attitudes, and values serve as a foundation for our experiences within the life-world.

17 See Foucault, *Discipline and Punish*, trans. Alan Sheridan (New York: Random House, Inc., 1979):195–228 for a description of the historical significance of the panopticon for individuals' ways of relating to each other and to their own bodies. Although Foucault fails to acknowledge or even consider how this particular disciplinary apparatus differentially impacts men and women, his account does open up the possibility for precisely this type of investigation, an investigation which is undertaken not only by Iris Young but also by Sandra Bartky in her collection of essays, *Femininity and Domination: Studies in the Phenomenology of Oppression* (New York: Routledge Press, 1990).

18 Kim Chernin's classic 1981 book, *The Obsession: The Tyranny of Slenderness* (New York: HarperCollins Books), provides wonderful examples of the seductiveness of the media images of women that bombard us on a daily basis. Chernin also discusses the self-hatred that often arises in response to one's awareness that one "falls short" of the cultural beauty standard.

19 See Iris Young, *Throwing Like a Girl* (Bloomington: Indiana University Press, 1990):161. Young notes early on that she is only speaking to the situation of those women who have chosen their pregnancy "either as an explicit decision to become pregnant or at least as choosing to be identified with and positively accepting of it." Hence, the description of pregnant existence offered in this essay makes no claims to universality; in fact, Young claims that this description currently can apply only to a minority rather than the majority of pregnant women in contemporary society. In an important sense, then, the positive description of the "split" subject offered in this essay presents a utopian vision of what pregnancy can and should embody.

20 There are many pregnant women whose fingers and feet swell to such an extent during their pregnancies that they can no longer wear rings or fit into their shoes. Talking together, pregnant women often lament the discomfort caused by the swelling and self-consciously joke about these and other unpleasant side-effects of water-retention during pregnancy. A constant concern that inevitably crops up in conversations among married women is how to "remedy" the absence of the wedding ring which can no longer fit on

its accustomed finger. Some women go out and buy inexpensive gold bands to replace the missing ring, others end up borrowing a replacement or decide to "go without" but, in any case, a degree of anxiety often remains that is brought to the surface with each encounter the pregnant woman has with the gaze of strangers. This anxiety among married women for the missing ring as a signifier of their social legitimacy is itself socially-produced, and a phenomenon worthy of further study in its own right. For the unmarried pregnant woman who may very well be in a serious, committed lesbian or heterosexual relationship, this anxiety is often intensified, and the option of purchasing a "fake" wedding ring may still be exercised, simply to terminate the prying gaze and snide observations of others. In the absence of the ring, moreover, sexual objectification can quickly return on the part of others, who may now speculate on the promiscuous sexuality that got this particular woman into "trouble" in the first place. Strikingly, in my experience, it is usually women who arouse this anxiety in other women, for not only do most men not tend to focus on whether a pregnant woman is wearing a wedding ring or not, they often fail to notice that she is even pregnant unless she is in the final months of her pregnancy!

21 The two senses of immateriality that I am thinking about here are: 1) nonmaterial and, 2) insignificant and both have been associated with the (all too mysterious) domain of the imaginary. An exploration of the significance of these dual ascriptions is taken up in chapter three.

22 Not the least of them is Young's unmarked move from gendered experience to a "sexed" imagination. Are only females capable of exhibiting this female imagination? Do all females exhibit it? There seems no reason why the narcissistic pleasure women take in clothes and fantasies about clothes are not also experienced by many men, if not through clothes, then perhaps through other cultural commodities such as cars and televisions, or even through strong identifications with athletic teams, individual athletes, and particular sports.

23 Mike Featherstone focuses on how strategies of body maintenance help to solidify the view of the body itself as a commodity in his 1991 essay, "The Body in Consumer Culture," *The Body: Social Process and Cultural Theory*, eds. Mike Featherstone et al. (London: Sage 1991). Today, one can find almost as many advertisements for the improvement of men's bodies as women's bodies. The difference in the advertising strategies, however, is striking. For women, bodily transformation is most often presented as a successful strategy in "catching" or "retaining" a man. For men, bodily transformation is much more frequently depicted as a means of achieving health, wealth, and general well-being.

24 Lingerie sections in large department stores offer frequent reminders to women with undersized, oversized, or prosthetic breasts how "unnatural" their breasts really are since it is hard to find bras that stray outside the range of the culturally established breast ideal. Often, employees of these stores are not sensitive to the embarrassment many women feel asking for a size that doesn't appear throughout the hundreds of bras on display. Once, I remember being at the cash register when a woman behind me whispered an inquiry to the saleswoman about where to find a "prosthetic bra." The saleswoman made her repeat her request several times, asking her to raise her voice each time so that she could hear her better. As I was concluding the purchase, the saleperson finally heard what she was saying but didn't seem to understand what the word prosthesis meant since she asked the woman behind me to repeat it several times. Still mystified, she yelled out to another salesperson about fifteen feet away, "hey, this woman here (pointing to her) wants to know where she can find a bra for her prosthesis." The other salesperson yelled back, "tell her we don't have anything like that here."

I walked away from the counter, ashamed for this woman whom I did not know, look at or speak to. My own shame was so intense that I found myself unwilling to look back to acknowledge her in order to avoid embarrassing her further. Even today, I think about this incident and hope that the unknown woman behind me was bold enough to pursue her request elsewhere, rather than cowed into submission by societally perpetuated insensitivity.

25 It is interesting that Freud never focused very much on female breasts in his discussion of psychosexual development (except as the primary source of oral stimulation and satisfaction for the infant), but instead concentrated on female genitalia. The clitoris was negatively associated by him with a diminished and inferior penis, and the vagina itself was a pure lack or absence of the desired organ altogether, indeed, the very sign and threat of its castration. The abundant plenitude of the mother's breasts and their eroticism for both infant and mother itself challenges any psychoanalytic interpretation of female sexuality as founded upon lack, and thereby challenges the hegemony of a phallic construction of female sexuality in psychoanalytic theory. Rather than develop the positive significance of the intense sexual gratification provided by the mother's breasts, Freud instead chose to focus on the negative psychical consequences of the mother's withdrawal of the breast from the infant during weaning.

26 The names used in Chapkis' text are pseudonyms. See Wendy Chapkis, *Beauty Secrets: Women and the Politics of Appearance* (Boston: South End Press, 1986).

Chapter Three

1 See Susan Bordo, *Unbearable Weight: Feminism, Western Culture, and the Body* (Berkeley: University of California Press, 1993). Susan Bordo's work, in particular, explicitly takes up the issue of how these phenomena interact to produce pathologies that she claims are the "crystallization" of culture rather than its negation or repudiation.

2 Early on in "Dream, Imagination and Existence," in *Dreams and Existence: Michel Foucault and Ludwig Binswanger*, ed. Keith Hoeller (New Jersey: Humanities Press, 1993;1954):41, Michel Foucault notes the "coincidence of dates" of publication of Husserl's *Logical Investigations* in 1899 and Freud's *Interpretation of Dreams* in 1900. It is not at all surprising, therefore, to find Foucault working these texts against one another, discovering a more adequate account of the expressive meaning of the image in Husserl than in Freud but at the same time arguing that "a philosophy of expression is no doubt possible only by going beyond phenomenology."

3 It is interesting to compare the parallels between Foucault's critique of the view that the image refers to reality with Judith Butler's critique, in *Bodies that Matter* (New York: Routledge Press, 1993):67–69 of the view that materiality is the (nonlinguistic) referent of language.

4 Foucault's depiction of the creative/destructive power of the poetic imagination also hearkens back to Nietzsche's discussion, in *The Birth of Tragedy*, trans. Francis Golffing (New York: Doubleday & Company, Inc., 1956) of the Dionysian forces which are capable of shattering the ideal images that characterize the Apollonian vision. By arguing that these Apollonian images are themselves dream-like, Nietzsche reveals their constructed character, specifically, he demonstrates that some dreams are dreamed in order to give a univocal order and significance to a reality that defies logic. Whereas Foucault appears to have a much more naive, even utopian understanding of the liberatory potential of the dream in "Dream, Imagination and Existence" in *Dreams and Existence: Michel Foucault and Ludwig Binswanger*, ed. Keith Hoeller (New Jersey: Humanities Press, 1993;1954), Nietzsche, in *The Birth of Tragedy*, is much more astute regarding what we might call "the politics of the dream" insofar as he explicitly attends not only to the ways in which dreams structure and produce reality but also focuses on how certain conceptions of reality are productive of our dreams.

5 This claim resonates with Bergson's arguments in *An Introduction to Metaphysics*, trans.

T.E. Hulme (New York: Macmillan Publishing Co., 1955), against too strong a reliance upon any given image of our own temporal reality, since, on Bergson's account, the flowing temporal rhythms (durée) of existence, cannot be captured in any one image. Bergson advocates our generating a multiplicity of images to communicate our experience of durée, images which can and will be in tension with one another, a productive tension that itself reveals the complexity of the phenomenon in question. Analogously, I am claiming that our body images must themselves preserve a certain fluidity in order to register and express the varying spatio-temporal dimensions of our respective existences. For, as I will argue in the next chapter, it is when a body image becomes fixed, and when the multiplicity of body images are thereby reduced, with one replacing all others, that both our imagination and our own corporeal agency are radically diminished.

6 Indeed, a central distinction between this very early Foucault and his later work can be made precisely on this issue. For, it is the later Foucault who is best known for his archaeological and genealogical investigations into madness, sexuality, disciplinary techniques, and technologies of the self; investigations which foreground the cultural forces that combine in unpredictable ways to construct selves, families, communities, and societies. Nonetheless, as numerous feminist scholars have pointed out, even in these later studies Foucault fails to acknowledge how sexual difference, gender, race, and ethnicity are themselves cultural forces actively inscribed upon individual and societal bodies, an ongoing process through which these forces become naturalized and corporeally stylized.

7 Pocahontas' impossibly high, pointed, and firm breasts, her ever so tiny waist, shapely hips, and long, long legs make her a "dead ringer" for Barbie despite her racial difference from the classically white doll. Since much was made in the media of Disney Corporation's attempts to avoid derogatory racial stereotypes in the depiction of Pocahontas and the other Native American characters in the movie, it is fascinating to see how they resolved the issue as far as Pocahontas was concerned. The solution was simple and effective: make it clear that Native Americans can embody white aesthetic ideals of feminine beauty as well as (if not better than) white girls can. And the tactic has worked. Now there are millions of white girls as well as girls of color who want to grow up to look just like Pocahontas. Every woman I know who saw the movie, found Pocahontas' valorization of phallocentric femininity revolting; most young girls found (and continue to find) it worthy of admiration and emulation. Small wonder that eating disorders are especially increasing in the preteenage female population!

8 See Jean Baudrillard, *Simulations*, trans. Paul Foss et al. (New York: Semiotext(e) Inc., 1983). In "The Precession of Simulacra," Baudrillard distinguishes simulation from dissimulation as follows: "To dissimulate is to feign not to have what one has. To simulate is to feign to have what one hasn't. One implies a presence, the other an absence. But the matter is more complicated, since to simulate is not simply to feign: 'Someone who feigns an illness can simply go to bed and make believe he is ill. Someone who simulates an illness produces in himself some of the symptoms' (Littre). Thus, feigning or dissimulating leaves the reality principle intact: the difference is always clear, it is only masked; whereas simulation threatens the difference between 'true' and 'false,' between 'real' and 'imaginary.'" (5)

On my reading, a dissimulating simulation would be one which seeks to mask its simulated constructions through specific dissimulating strategies, strategies that simultaneously invoke and undermine the reality principle. The result, for Baudrillard, is the creation of a hyperreal domain, where events compete with one another to achieve the status of "more real than real" (think of CNN's media coverage of the Gulf War in 1991 which was far more "real" than the war itself ever was or could be), thereby demanding to be measured against an equally fatuous truth standard, the "truer than true."

9 The bodily transformations that occur during pregnancy are, I think, the most common and most visible examples of morphological change. However, the gradual nature of these changes over the course of the nine months of pregnancy makes them appear far less dramatic then the Power Rangers' instantaneous morphing. Perhaps the only parallel to the Power Rangers that can be drawn is in reference not to pregnancy, but to the first thirty-six hours or so after giving birth, when the body radically reorganizes its own spatiality (the uterus alone shrinks from its two-pound weight and watermelon size to the size of a grapefruit within a few hours or even minutes after delivery), develops new temporal rhythms (established by the breasts' lactation patterns which are in turn developed in response to the infant's needs), and establishes new hormonal cycles.

Interestingly enough, very little is written in the popular pregnancy handbooks about these remarkable bodily changes following birth. The emphasis is overwhelmingly on the pregnancy and birth itself, and those books that focus on postpartum experience at all, tend to concentrate on relating to your new baby and coping with unexpected postpartum depression. The absence of specific information about these radical bodily changes often makes them needlessly alarming for the mothers who experience them. Although I can only speculate on why pregnancy books choose not to focus on this experience and why some women also choose not to learn anything about it, my guess is that severe bodily transformation is indeed threatening to many members of our society who are concerned with maintaining what they take to be their bodily integrity.

By contrast, if, as I have argued in the previous chapter, bodily integrity consists not in an unchanging body and body image, but in developing a greater awareness of, and attunement to ongoing bodily changes, then the dramatic corporeal upheavals that take place after birth should not pose a threat at all. On the contrary, this relatively brief period when the body demands more attention and recognition than it usually receives, provides a fascinating opportunity to question the normative parameters that constitute "ordinary" bodily experience.

10 For an earlier, and more complete account of how the ego's melancholic incorporation of homosexuality is constitutive of its gender identification, see chapter two of Judith Butler's *Gender Trouble: Feminism and the Subversion of Identity* (New York: Routledge Press, 1990).

11 According to Butler, the child's pre-oedipal desire is always homosexual regardless of the sex of the child. This is because, in the case of the young boy, the phallic mother is viewed as possessing the penis, hence, his love for her is, in an important sense, an incestuous love of the same. For the young girl who has not yet recognized that both she and her mother lack the penis, the identification with and desire for the mother is also incestuously homosexual.

12 Indeed, even for an identification to be an "identification with the same" already involves an awareness of difference, an awareness that is not available to the pre-oedipal child. In this sense, it is only from within an already established heterosexual matrix that the child's pre-oedipal desire for the mother can be viewed as homosexual. To say that this sexed morphology is grounded upon difference rather than sameness also invokes at least two, less obvious kinds of difference: 1) the child's recognition of her/his difference from the phallic mother (the latter of whom, as a result of this recognition, ceases to exist as such); 2) the child's difference from her/his own, prior, sexually undifferentiated, narcissistic state.

13 See Judith Butler, *Gender Trouble* (New York: Routledge Press, 1990), and *Bodies that Matter* (New York: Routledge Press, 1993). By no means, however, should the persistence of the imaginary be equated with invariance, for the imaginary has its own historicity and cannot be understood as an ahistorical phenomenon. Moreover, recent feminist and queer theorists have argued that there is more than one imaginary operative within

any given society at any given time. Not only Butler but others such as Trevor Hope suggest that rather than pre-exist the symbolic, the imaginary is itself one of the symbolic domain's most productive (and potentially subversive) effects.

In his essay, "Sexual Indifference and the Homosexual Male Imaginary," *Diacritics* 24 (2–3):161–163, Hope discusses Freud's projection of an archaic homosexuality, encrypted in a contemporary homosocial (heterosexist) imaginary and argues that the positing of a male homosexual imaginary at the origin of the social contract fails to acknowledge its own retroactive installment of homosexuality as prior to the symbolic realm. Ultimately, Hope is calling for a reassessment not only of the putative originary, prehistoric status of the homosexual imaginary, but also of any theoretical position which declares the imaginary to be beyond the reach of (and hence untouched by) phallocentric law.

14 Joan Copjec is one of the most notable of these critics. See "Sex and the Euthanasia of Reason," in *Supposing the Subject*, ed. Joan Copjec (London: Verso, 1994) and Copjec's book, *Read My Desire: Lacan against the Historicists* (Cambridge: The MIT Press, 1994).

15 The difference between these two terms is itself instructive. While "creation" has largely retained its biblical connotation of a momentous event that occurs *ex nihilo* as in God's creation of the universe, the term "acquisition" suggests an ongoing temporal process in which something that lies beyond an individual subject or agency is somehow appropriated, and ultimately, incorporated over time by that individual. In addition, while the classic postulation of a lapsed temporality between cause and effect guarantees that the creation will always be distinguishable from its creator, no such separation (whether conceptual or material) need exist between what is acquired and who or what does the acquiring.

16 Although neither Butler nor Hope believes that it is possible to reject these prohibited projections outright since the rejection, in effect, reinstalls the prohibition as the ground of its emergence.

17 In the Introduction to the Summer/Fall 1994 issue of *Diacritics* 24 (203):3, entitled "Critical Crossings," its guest editors, Judith Butler and Biddy Martin, state the following: "The notion of 'cross-identification' may seem paradoxical, for every identification presumes a crossing of sorts, a movement towards some other site with which or by which an identification is said to take place. But it is because this 'crossing' is not well understood that we underscore it through redundancy here. 'Crossing' may be conceived, on the one hand, as an appropriation, assimilation, or even a territorialization of another site or position, or it can be understood as a movement beyond the stasis attributed to 'positions' located on a closed map of social power."

Here, Butler and Martin further refine the notion of cross-identifications discussed by Butler in *Bodies that Matter* (New York: Routledge Press, 1993). Not only is it the case that an individual assumes more than one identification at any given time (which can and often do "cross" one another through reinforcement as well as contradiction), but it is also the case that each of these identifications involves what Husserl has called an "interior horizon" which consists of numerous crossings characterized by the reciprocal interplay between projections and what Schilder terms introjections. A productive line of inquiry could, I think, be opened up by exploring Butler's and Martin's notion of "cross-identification" through Merleau-Ponty's understanding of the noncoincident, reversible crossing of the chiasm, as it is discussed in *The Visible and the Invisible*, ed. Claude Lefort, trans. Alphonso Lingis (Evanston: Northwestern University Press, 1968).

Butler herself invokes the Merleau-Pontian figure of the chiasm to express the limitations that discursive cross-identifications reveal in the very notion of the subject: "The temporal structure of such a subject is chiasmic in this sense: in the place of a substantial or self-determining 'subject,' this juncture of discursive demands is something like a 'crossroads,' to use Gloria Anzaldúa's phrase, a crossroads of cultural and political discursive forces, which she herself claims cannot be understood through the notion of the 'subject.' There is no subject prior to its constructions, and neither is the subject determined by those constructions; it is always the nexus, the non-space of cultural collision, in which the demand to resignify or repeat the very terms which constitute the 'we' cannot be summarily refused, but neither can they be followed in strict obedience. It is the space of this ambivalence which opens up the possibility of a reworking of the very terms by which subjectivation proceeds—and fails to proceed." See Judith Butler, *Bodies that Matter* (New York: Routledge Press, 1993):124.

18 It is clear that Butler is referring to (and challenging) at least two senses of "before" in this passage, a body that is posited as temporally preceding its mirroring, and a body that stands "before" the mirror as a self-contained entity.

19 See Anne Sexton, *Transformations* (Boston: Houghton Mifflin Company, 1971). Although Sexton's "Snow White" is undoubtedly grimmer than that of the Brothers Grimm, both versions depict the wicked Queen's gruesome dance of death at Snow White's wedding. The popular Disney version of Snow White, on the other hand, makes the Queen's death her own doing; she falls while being chased by the dwarves who seek revenge for the "death" of Snow White. Moreover, she dies (while disguised as) an ugly old hag, reinforcing the equation of ugliness with evil and death and beauty with goodness and life. In this reworking of the original fairy tale, Disney seeks to reinforce this absolute opposition between good and evil. The stepmother's forced dance of death, presumably ordered by Snow White and her prince, on the other hand, disrupts the boundary between good and evil, one which Sexton challenges further in the "reincarnation" of the dead Queen as the newly married (and no longer quite so) Snow White.

20 Beauvoir also makes this point in her discussion of the doll as representing both the whole body and a passive object in the "Childhood" chapter of *The Second Sex* (New York: Vintage Books, 1989):278.

21 Even in homosexual relationships, on an Irigarayan account, sexual difference still plays a crucial role, since we are all socialized to view what Wittig calls "the category of sex" as a primary marker of an individual's difference from (and sameness to) others. See Monique Wittig, "The Category of Sex" in *The Straight Mind and Other Essays* (Boston: Beacon Press, 1992). For instance, two gay lovers may regard each other as men, but, as Beauvoir showed us so long ago, this is already a relational term. A man is never simply a man. Rather the lover as a man is, first and foremost, *not* a woman. Within a society that is racist as well as sexist, this picture becomes more complicated: for a black lesbian, for instance, her white partner is both "a woman (and not a man)" and "white (rather than black like me)."

While Wittig and Irigaray agree that sexual difference is always privileged over other differences and that the effects of this privileging are extremely deleterious for women, they disagree on the solutions. Wittig argues that it is the recognition of difference itself that leads to oppression and she offers a utopian vision of a post-revolutionary society in which we are all just viewed as human beings, without having our differences identified and thereby hierarchicalized. Irigaray, on the other hand, proposes a celebration of sexual difference, rather than its annihilation. Her main concern is to stake a place for women not only outside of, but squarely within the Symbolic order, a place they have not had designated for them, but one which they have created for themselves. This in turn, will require a reworking of the Symbolic order so that women are no longer inscribed within its register through their patrilineal heritage, that is, through the "name-of-the-father."

Chapter Four

1 It is important to note, however, that Butler and Kristeva differ markedly in their characterization of this abject domain; indeed, Butler explicitly critiques Kristeva's view of the abject/semiotic as inextricably associated with the maternal body and as pre-Symbolic. See Judith Butler, *Gender Trouble: Feminism and the Subversion of Identity* (New York: Routledge Press, 1990:79–93).

2 There are numerous examples of individuals with distorted body images that fall into each of these categories in the clinical, philosophical, and popular literature on the body image. Maurice Merleau-Ponty focuses on the case of Schneider, a World War I veteran who suffered a shrapnel wound to his head and whose peculiar physiological and psychological deficiencies created intense interest among the neurologists who treated him, as well as the Gestalt psychologists who provided their own diagnosis of his unique case. In *Volatile Bodies: Toward a Corporeal Feminism* (Bloomington: Indiana University Press, 1994):190, Elizabeth Grosz discusses the phenomenon of multiple personality syndrome, "in which one of the many personalities inhabiting an individual body has different abilities and defects than another. One personality may require glasses to correct faults in the optical apparatus while another personality has perfect vision; one personality is left-handed, the other right, one personality has certain allergies or disorders missing in the other." Grosz goes on to note that "[t]hese are not simply transformations at the level of our ideas of or representations of the body. Our ideas and attitudes seep into the functioning of the body itself, making up the realm of its possibilities or impossibilities."

   In *Beauty Secrets: Women and the Politics of Appearance* (Boston: South End Press, 1986):20, Wendy Chapkis includes the autobiographical perspective of "Ann," a woman with diastrophic dwarfism who reflects retrospectively on her own distorted body image as an adolescent and young adult. "Ann" traces the cause of this distortion to an inability to "integrate what I really look like with who I am." The difficulty of doing this is encapsulated in her next statement: "You don't want to be confronted with your physical difference all the time. But the shock is enough to kill you if you keep hiding from it."

   All of these examples reveal the complexity of the phenomenon of distortion and also belie the notion that there may be a single cause of the distortion or a single solution to the process of developing a nondistorted body image. As Susan Bordo argues in relation to anorexia and the body image distortions it produces, the phenomenon is overdetermined and therefore multidimensional; this means that it must be approached on a variety of levels (e.g. cultural, familial, physiological, etc.) and from a variety of disciplines in order to be adequately understood, much less treated. See Susan Bordo, *Unbearable Weight: Feminism, Western Culture, and the Body* (Berkeley: University of California Press, 1993).

3 For present purposes, I am distinguishing abjection from the abject as follows: abjection refers to a process of expulsion, whereby that which has been designated as abject (this can include other people, food, vermin, body fluids, rodents and an infinite number of phenomena) is rejected and, at the same time, the rejection itself is disavowed. The generic term, "the abject object," is used to cover all of the possible sites of abjection.

4 And yet, Kristeva seems to be advocating that we embrace the abject precisely because of its subversive potential to disrupt the hegemony of the Symbolic order. See Julia Kristeva, *Powers of Horror: An Essay on Abjection*, trans. Leon S. Roudiez (New York: Columbia University Press, 1982). This perverse utopian vision, however, is questioned by Butler, who argues in *Bodies that Matter* (New York: Routledge Press, 1993) that the process of identity formation will always involve moments of exclusion, which in turn lead to the designation of an abject domain which consists of all that I-am-not. Butler, unlike Kristeva, sees no way out of this untenable, uninhabitable position that is *our* position as mem-

bers of the Symbolic order. Her own political strategy involves becoming aware of the exclusions we are performing in order to be sure that we know what is at stake in basing our identity upon them.

5 See Morag MacSween, *Anorexic Bodies: A Feminist and Sociological Perspective on Anorexia Nervosa* (London: Routledge Press, 1993). I wholeheartedly agree with Mac-Sween that "in anorexia women transform the social meanings and practices through which the feminine body is constructed" (8), a process that makes anorexia and anorexic symptoms meaningful in their own right, rather than, as the predominant medical models suggest, meaningful only insofar as they point to more fundamental conflicts in the anorexic's psychic development (e.g. resulting from early childhood, familial experiences). I also agree with her subsequent claim that "'scientific' psychiatric analyses contain an unquestioned and unanalysed set of 'common-sense' assumptions about 'normality'—that, in short, being 'normal' or 'sane' means being able to function appropriately in a bourgeois patriarchal culture" (25), a task, as MacSween goes on to show, that is much more difficult for women than for men to do successfully, especially since the criteria that mark success are quite different for each gender. However, I am less convinced by her argument that anorexia is above all a way of contending with the conflicting demands placed upon contemporary middle-class women to simultaneously assert their individuality and their femininity. For, if this was indeed so, it seems that many more women would be anorexics than currently are. Ultimately, my reservations regarding both MacSween's and Bordo's analyses of anorexia have to do with their adhering too strictly to a social constructionist perspective since I think that the latter position fails to do justice to aspects of embodied experience that fail to achieve cultural expression, as well as those that exceed or even resist cultural analysis.

6 One difficulty with this latter claim is that it sets up a problematic distinction between the "body itself" and "how that body is socially constructed" as if these were two separable phenomena. Since, from a social constructionist perspective, one cannot "get at" the body itself, all one is left with is its social construction. Although the body is undeniably socially constructed, I do not think that this is the only way in which the body is constructed. As Judith Butler observes in the Introduction to *Bodies that Matter* (New York: Routledge Press, 1993):10, "To claim that discourse is formative is not to claim that it originates, causes, or exhaustively composes that which it concedes. . . . "

7 Bordo cites studies which show that most women think they are overweight even when many are not only not overweight, but actually underweight. See Susan Bordo, *Unbearable Weight* (Berkeley: University of California Press, 1993). While this is itself a very disturbing phenomenon, it should also be pointed out that others often see women as being overweight when they are not. Men, in particular, often urge their female partners to lose a few more pounds so that they can more closely embody this homogeneous, culturally-established bodily aesthetic.

8 The cultural bias towards tallness is rarely articulated explicitly but almost always goes hand-in-hand with thinness. "Tall and thin" is a body ideal not only for women but also for men. It is a well-known fact that female models need to be close to six feet tall to have successful modeling careers. While it is seen as a liability for a woman to be "too" tall, and while short, thin women can still be viewed as "cute" or "petite" (expressions which are themselves infantilizing and demeaning), the appellation "beautiful" tends to be reserved for the regal, svelte figure, epitomized by the late Princess Diana.

Popular expressions such as the "short man complex," aptly express both the negative stigma to being a shorter than average male, as well as the cultural assumption that short men mind being short, that is, that they view their height as a defect that they must compensate for by being overly competitive and aggressive.

Chapter Five

1 Interestingly, when I went back to confirm this reference in our library archives, I found that this sensationalist heading did not appear in the local version of the *New York Times*; instead it only appeared in the out-of-town version of the paper.

2 The issues raised by animal cloning have far from died down in the year that has elapsed since "Dolly" the cloned sheep, was born. On January 21, 1998, the *New York Times* reported that American scientists successfully cloned two calves from fetal cells using a more efficient procedure than the one Scottish scientists had used to produce Dolly. Not only was the cloning procedure itself different (showing that successful cloning can occur through more than one method), but the American scientists also inserted a "dummy" gene into the twin calves' makeup which will pave the way for further genetic manipulation of the dairy livestock population in the future. This "accomplishment," aptly termed "pharming," holds out the promise of producing cows who can be neural cell donors for human beings suffering from hemophilia, Parkinson's disease, and diabetes. Some scientists are also working with pharmaceutical companies to generate proposals for genetically engineered cattle that will produce human serum albumin, a protein currently given to people who have suffered severe blood loss. See Gina Kolata, "Scientist Reports First Cloning Ever of Adult Mammal" *New York Times* (February 23, 1997):A1,A22; Carey Goldberg and Gina Kolata, "Scientists Announce Births of Cows Cloned in New Way" *New York Times* (January 21, 1998):A14.

   The January 21, 1998 article discussing the successful cloning of the twin calves, "George" and "Charlie," in contrast to the February 23, 1997 article announcing the birth of "Dolly" the sheep, did not even merit the front page (with the exception, in the out-of-town paper, of a color photo of the two calves huddled together with a subtitle that informed the reader where the story was to be found). This reveals the extent to which the media (and perhaps the public) no longer views animal cloning as such a worrisome issue. Nonetheless, concerns about human cloning remain and these concerns were amplified a few weeks before the birth of "George" and "Charlie" by one midwestern doctor's media announcement that he was planning to open up a "cloning clinic" for infertile couples (his name is Dr. Richard Seed). Now the issue seems to be one of determining which governmental agency, if any, has the authority to regulate and prohibit the use of cloning technology on a human population. The fact that the issue has changed in one year from horrified denials that humans could ever be next to whether the U.S. Food and Drug Administration has the authority to prohibit their being next, makes it seem quite plausible that the move to prohibit human cloning will itself be transformed in time to the development of policies designed to regulate how, where, when, and to/for whom it will happen.

   Indeed, it is striking that the *New York Times* article published less than a year after the miracle of "Dolly's" birth to announce the birth of "George" and "Charlie," doesn't even focus on the ethical ramifications of the cloning and genetic alteration procedures undertaken to produce them. Instead, the article emphasizes the possibilities for improving human health through genetic alteration of future herds of cattle and seems to assume that such genetic manipulation of the livestock population is ethically permissible. Indeed, there are already several cows pregnant with similar "offspring" all over the country.

3 See Gina Kolata, "Scientist Reports First Cloning Ever of Adult Mammal" *New York Times* (February 23, 1997):22.

4 Braidotti's invocation of the "monster within" who is projected onto the other as the "true" monster, can best be understood as a particular instantiation of Douglas' and Kristeva's descriptions of how certain bodily zones and fluids are designated as abject, detached from our own corporeal experience, and incarnated in others' bodies to render

them "disgusting." This complex psychic affirmation and corporeal repudiation was discussed extensively in chapter four.

5 See Henri Bergson, *An Introduction to Metaphysics*, trans. T.E. Hulme (New York: Macmillan Publishing Company, 1955). Bergson also discusses this distinction extensively elsewhere in his works. What is striking about *An Introduction to Metaphysics*, in particular, is Bergson's claim that essentially different philosophical methodologies (i.e. analytical vs. intuitive approaches) are necessary to study time and temporality respectively. While I am not completely in agreement with him on this issue, insofar as I do not view time and temporality to be as separable as he considers them to be, I do find his insight that different phenomena have their own forms of temporalization and therefore require different methodological approaches to be helpful and illuminating with regard to new (and as yet unimagined) biotechnologies.

6 How contemporary biotechnologies alter our sense of time both in its "inner" and "outer" dimensions, is an issue that does need to be taken up, but this project is not only beyond the scope of the present study but also beyond the scope of traditional philosophical inquiry. This does not mean that this issue cannot be interrogated, but that to do so requires multiple, interdisciplinary approaches and requires an enormous amount of experimental data not usually available to or made use of by philosophers. It is crucial that philosophers make themselves better acquainted with such data, however, if they are to speculate, as Braidotti does, on how our new biotechnologies will alter our experience of time.

7 Although whether there is any matter that is truly devoid of organic properties is itself a debatable question for some contemporary scientists.

Chapter Six

1 Examples of prominent feminist theorists who have offered readings of Irigaray's reading of Merleau-Ponty include Elizabeth Grosz, "Merleau-Ponty and Irigaray in the Flesh" *Thesis Eleven* (36):37–59, Tina Chanter, "Wild Meaning: Luce Irigaray's Reading of Merleau-Ponty" (paper presented at the 1995 *Merleau-Ponty Circle* at Duquesne University), and Judith Butler (two lectures given at the 1994 National Endowment for the Humanities Institute on *Embodiment: The Intersection between Nature and Culture* at the University of California, Santa Cruz).

2 Butler used this expression in a lecture she gave on Merleau-Ponty and Irigaray at the 1994 National Endowment for the Humanities Institute on *Embodiment: The Intersection of Nature and Culture* at the University of California, Santa Cruz directed by Hubert Dreyfus and David Hoy.

3 What surprises me is not this indebtedness, but how rarely it is acknowledged in contemporary readings by and of Butler.

4 This unrepresentable space of differentiation is a central focus of several recent French theorists, including Deleuze and Derrida as well as Merleau-Ponty and Irigaray. I would argue that this undifferentiated space which makes differentiation possible is yet another manifestation of several twentieth-century French philosophers' preoccupation with what Husserl has called the "zone of indeterminacy." See Gail Weiss, "Ambiguity, Absurdity, and Reversibility: Responses to Indeterminacy," *Journal of the British Society for Phenomenology* (26) 1:43–51.

5 Irigaray's linking of the maternal with the feminine mimetically reproduces Western societies' own identification of the one with the other, but, as Chanter and others have argued, Irigaray also subversively deploys this term to expose the ordinarily invisible ways in which the undifferentiated maternal-feminine makes the individuation of specific subjects possible. See Tina Chanter, *Ethics of Eros: Irigaray's Rewriting of the Philosophers* (New York: Routledge Press, 1995).

6 These include the cutting of the umbilical cord that connects mother to fetus, and the specular gaze of the traditionally male medical establishment that mediates women's understandings of their own bodies and bodily potentialities, a gaze that is increasingly facilitated and amplified through the utilization of machinic imagery such as the sonogram.

7 A serious and presumably deliberate omission in Irigaray's own account is an explanation of the differences between what she calls the "maternal-feminine" and the culturally oxymoronic but nonetheless experienciable "non-maternal-feminine." Her strategic coupling of the maternal and the feminine, while perhaps successful in offering a more positive, powerful image of woman as mother, also assumes the risk of leaving women who are not and will not be mothers out of account altogether, except as daughters to their own mothers.

8 I know of at least two fairly recent cases where families were told that a fetus had serious abnormalities as a result of ultrasonography. In one case, numerous ultrasounds revealed that the developing fetus had seriously large kidneys and the family worried throughout the remaining months of the pregnancy until the birth when the baby's kidneys turned out to be normal size. The grandmother (a well-known contemporary feminist philosopher) reflected that if her daughter had had this pregnancy prior to the existence of this technology, an incredible amount of stress and anguish would have been eliminated. In the other case, the family was told first that the fetus had a serious heart condition that would require open-heart surgery immediately after birth. Later, after subsequent testing and ultrasounds, they were told that the baby would die within a few hours after birth. Miraculously, the baby survived birth and had the open-heart surgery. The family, however, already had purchased a casket and a plot for the baby and had even scheduled the funeral service. Tragically, the baby did die four months after birth but the family was extremely grateful for the short life their child did have and the four months in which Leah "beat the odds" offered a bittersweet reminder that predictions based on prenatal technology can be proved wrong.

9 Several feminist theorists, in particular, have focused on this latter project including Teresa de Lauretis who reconfigures lesbian desire from within a psychoanalytic framework in *The Practice of Love: Lesbian Sexuality and Perverse Desire* (Bloomington: Indiana University Press, 1994) and Elizabeth Grosz who, in her collection of essays, *Space, Time, and Perversion: Essays on the Politics of Bodies* (New York: Routledge Press, 1995), rejects the psychoanalytic model of desire based on lack and instead works from a Deleuzian perspective, emphasizing the multiplicity of desires, subjects of desire, and objects of desire.

10 It is crucial to note, however, that pursuing some linkages over others is not a matter of choice for Deleuze and Guattari because that would transform desire into an intentional agency, a position they explicitly reject. Instead, the "desiring-machines" they describe are "formative machines, whose very misfirings are functional, and whose functioning is indiscernible from their formation." See Gilles Deleuze and Félix Guattari, *Anti-Oedipus: Capitalism and Schizophrenia*, trans. Robert Hurley et al. (Minneapolis: University of Minnesota Press, 1983):286.

11 In "The Body in Consumer Culture" *The Body: Social Process and Cultural Theory*, eds. Mike Featherstone et al. (London: Sage, 1991):182, Mike Featherstone argues that this analogy between bodies and cars is rendered explicit through the contemporary call for increased "body maintenance," a term that "indicates the popularity of the machine metaphor for the body."

12 One of the best descriptions Merleau-Ponty offers of the productive/seductive promise of the chiasm, a promise grounded in difference, noncoincidence, and contingent, intercorporeal connections, occurs in *The Visible and the Invisible*, ed. Claude Lefort, trans.

Alphonso Lingis (Evanston: Northwestern University Press, 1968):135, where Merleau-Ponty writes: "The thickness of the body, far from rivaling that of the world, is on the contrary the sole means I have to go unto the heart of the things, by making myself a world and by making them flesh."

Chapter Seven

1 I'm putting "cognitive" in parentheses here because I want to emphasize how distinctive (i.e. most notably as disembodied) our mental faculties are for most rationalists.

2 Although even for Kant, it should be noted, it is necessary to take note of the particulars of the situation in order to frame the maxim that will be tested (rationally) against the universal law provided by the categorical imperative. Hence, context is important for a Kantian morality but feelings (which Kant refers to as "inclinations") are not considered to be a genuine component of that context. See Immanuel Kant, *Groundwork of the Metaphysic of Morals*, trans. H.J. Paton (New York: Harper and Row, Publishers, 1964).

3 And, just as Hume is confident that an aesthetic standard of taste *can* be arrived at in the aesthetic domain, against those who would argue for the "natural equality" of tastes, so too, he would like to see subjective universality, or what we might call consensus of moral sentiments, hold sway in the moral domain. See David Hume, *A Treatise of Human Nature*, ed. L.A. Selby-Bigge (Oxford: Oxford University Press, 1978).

4 Thomas Nagel and others have called this "moral luck." See Thomas Nagel, *Mortal Questions* (Cambridge: Cambridge University Press, 1979). In the case of the aristocratic, "ruling class" morality, moral luck favored the landed gentry and worked against the peasants since the former were viewed as more moral *by nature* than the latter were or ever could be.

5 This is an issue that Irigaray explicitly takes up in *Marine Lover of Friedrich Nietzsche*, trans. Gillian Gill (New York: Columbia University Press, 1991). The title of this book alone indicates that rather than reject Nietzsche wholeheartedly, Irigaray uses her profound ambivalence towards his work to generate a productive feminist response that refuses the equation of the feminine with the abject.

6 I am deliberately using architectural imagery here since it is used not only by Nietzsche, but also, and to great effect, by both Descartes in his *Meditations* and by Kant in his discussion of morality. See René Descartes, *Meditations on First Philosophy*, trans. Donald A. Cress (Indianapolis: Hackett Publishing Company, 1979) and Immanuel Kant, *Groundwork of the Metaphysic of Morals*, trans. H.J. Paton (New York: Harper and Row, Publishers, 1964).

7 For an insightful discussion of the shifts in Gilligan's views see Claudia Card's "Gender and Moral Luck," *Justice and Care: Essential Readings in Feminist Ethics*, ed. Virginia Held (Boulder: Westview Press, 1995).

8 Indeed for Kant, my affection for others is precisely what dilutes the purity of my moral duty towards them. On his account, paradoxically, the less affection I feel for another makes it *more* likely that my good actions towards them are truly moral. See Immanuel Kant, *Groundwork of the Metaphysic of Morals*, trans. H.J. Paton (New York: Harper and Row, Publishers, 1964).

9 It should be noted that it is the *embodied* effects of the projected punishment that makes it so dreadful whether that punishment be physical (e.g. spanking), social (e.g. ostracism, ridicule), and/or legal (e.g. incarceration). For the postconventional individual, by contrast, to act against one's moral principles will result in a lack of moral integrity, but the very notion of moral integrity is defined, in this context, in an exclusively cognitive (deontological) sense.

10 What Cortese is ultimately suggesting, I believe, is that ethnicity, race, culture, social class, caste and consciousness as well as gender are mutually constitutive of the moral

agent and that none of them occupy a privileged or exclusive point of reference either for moral theorizing or moral practices. See Anthony Joseph Paul Cortese, *Ethnic Ethics: The Restructuring of Moral Theory* (New York: SUNY Press, 1990).

11 This is a point taken up explicitly by Linda Singer in *Erotic Welfare: Sexual Theory and Politics in the Age of Epidemic*, eds. Judith Butler and Maureen MacGrogan (New York: Routledge Press, 1993):139. Singer is herself a notable exception in this regard. Specifically, in the essay, "Interpretation and Retrieval: Rereading Beauvoir," she convincingly demonstrates that Beauvoir's ethics is grounded upon relations to others, and that Gilligan's later focus on caring for and feeling connected to others is already present in Beauvoir's work. In contradistinction to Sartre, Singer argues, Beauvoir offers us a "conception of moral agency marked by a privileging of affinity and care in a way which contributes to, rather than compromises, the integrity of moral agents or the world they constitute in common."

12 See Debra Bergoffen, *The Philosophy of Simone de Beauvoir: Gendered Phenomenologies, Erotic Generosities* (Albany: SUNY Press, 1997).

13 Perhaps Sartre comes closest to affirming the challenges to freedom placed upon us by a particular situation in his play, "Dirty Hands," *No Exit and Three Other Plays* (New York: Vintage Books, 1955), but here we are left with a "damned because I did and damned because I didn't" situation that overwhelmingly remains a negative moment. Also, Bergoffen observes that in Sartre's later work on Genet and Flaubert, "the subject subjected to the power of the situation is not accused of bad faith. The situation, now seen as setting the conditions of our (free) choices, is never, however, given the power to divest the subject of its freedom." See Debra Bergoffen, *The Philosophy of Simone de Beauvoir* (Albany: SUNY Press, 1997):26.

14 This is not to say that they have uncritically accepted or ignored Beauvoir's masculinist presuppositions, but that they have carefully examined and brought to light the complexity of her thought in ways that are useful for contemporary feminist theorizing and practice.

15 This ethic of embodiment, which I will refer to from here on in as an embodied ethics, does not preclude the formation of other ethics. Indeed, I would argue that the traditional ethical frameworks I discuss at the outset of this chapter are themselves developed by focusing on one aspect of embodiment and generating moral guidelines in reference to it. A Kantian approach, for instance, isolates reason as the key factor in our moral decision-making and the problems it gives rise to stem, in large part, from its viewing the motivational roles played by the body as well as other, non-rational human faculties as threats to the "purity" of the moral domain. A utilitarian account makes consideration of the possible consequences of an action the motivating moral factor, but fails to acknowledge that this is only part of the context that must be considered in determining how one should act.

For Bergoffen, the ethic of the project emerges from an essentially conflictual (very Sartrian) picture of human relationships in which each subjectivity seeks to dominate every other subjectivity. The ethic of generosity, by contrast, is not based on a conflictual model of intersubjectivity, but it applies to erotic relationships with others and so cannot, without problematically reducing all relationships to an erotic dimension, be extended to all relationships. I would maintain, for instance, that the relationship between Beauvoir and her dying mother, as depicted in *A Very Easy Death*, trans. Patrick O'Brian (New York: Pantheon Books, 1965), cannot be encompassed within this model. This does not mean that these two ethics are not operative for many of us in the course of our existence, but rather, that neither of them (whether considered separately or together) can serve as a foundation for the other or for an embodied ethics.

16 See Eva Feder Kittay, "Taking Dependency Seriously: The Family and the Medical

Leave Act considered in Light of the Social Organization of Dependency Work and Gender Equality," *Hypatia* 10 (1):8–29. Toward the end of this essay, Kittay substitutes the expression "nested dependencies" for "network of interdependencies," yet I think the two are quite different from one another and prefer the latter expression to the former one. This is because her claim that "society is constituted by the nested dependencies that require a concept of justice between persons who are equal in their connectedness but unequal in their vulnerability" (24) seems to privilege relations of dependency in ways that both Anita Silvers and Alison Jaggar have shown to be problematic. Silvers attacks such a conception by challenging the ways in which the status of dependent is projected upon certain individuals such as the disabled who then end up in the unpalatable position of clinging to that status in order to receive certain societal benefits that should have been available to them without their having to be construed as dependent in the first place. See Anita Silvers, "Reconciling Equality to Difference: Caring (F)or Justice for People with Disabilities," *Hypatia* 10 (1):30–55.

Jaggar, in criticizing prevailing ethics of care for focusing on particularities at the expense of the general, societal structures that may be responsible for those particularities, forces us to address the issue of *why* certain people are viewed as dependent, and thereby challenges an account such as Kittay's which does not look beneath the *fact* of dependency to see whether it is due to essential (and therefore unchangeable) or contingent (alterable) circumstances. See Alison M. Jaggar, "Caring as a Feminist Practice of Moral Reason," *Justice and Care: Essential Readings in Feminist Ethics*, ed. Virginia Held (Boulder: Westview Press, 1995). For instance, while the dependency of infancy does indeed seem to be essential, the dependency of the elderly and the disabled need not fall into the same category though it often seems to; this is largely due to the latter's lack of financial resources, resources that both define and enable independence in our society.

In light of these trenchant critiques regarding how we can and should view dependency, I find the expression, "network of interdependencies," to be a less problematic and more accurate description of social relations because it points to the ways in which individuals can and do depend upon one another without implying a hierarchy of dependency as an essential or even desirable social framework.

17 An "objective" confirmation of this knowledge occurs after her mother has died when Beauvoir discovers, while picking up her mother's personal papers from the clinic, Françoise's handwritten instructions for her burial: "'I should like a very simple funeral. No flowers or wreaths. But a great many prayers.'" See Simone de Beauvoir, *A Very Easy Death*, trans. Patrick O'Brian (New York: Pantheon Books, 1965):101.

18 There is no question, however, that Heidegger would decry Françoise de Beauvoir's way of dealing with her death insofar as she refuses to face her impending death with the steadfast resoluteness he associates with authenticity.

19 However, I would not claim, nor do I think Alcoff would claim, that nondiscursive effects can be isolated from discursive effects. The following point made by Butler in reference to the relationship between language and materiality applies equally well, I would argue, to the relationship between discursive and nondiscursive effects: "every effort to refer to materiality takes place through a signifying process which, in its phenomenality, is always already material. In this sense, then, language and materiality are not opposed, for language both is and refers to that which is material, and what is material never fully escapes from the process by which it is signified." See Judith Butler, *Bodies that Matter: On the Discursive Limits of "Sex"* (New York: Routledge Press, 1993):68.

20 See Gail Weiss, "Sex-Selective Abortion: A Relational Approach," *Hypatia* 10 (1):202–217.

21 Ruddick does not use the term "bodily imperatives" but I think it is in keeping with her

emphasis on the embodied demands that emerge out of the mother-child relationship.

22 See David Theo Goldberg, "The Social Formation of Racist Discourse," *The Anatomy of Racism*, ed. David Theo Goldberg (Minneapolis: University of Minnesota Press, 1990). According to Goldberg, once racial differentiation is established in a given community to demarcate its members, individuals within that community internalize these racial identities and identify with them. And, once identification takes place, Goldberg suggests that exclusionary practices follow, practices which entail providing (or withholding) certain benefits for some races rather than others, practices which further legitimate and consolidate the hegemony of those races that have become sites of privilege.

Conclusion

1 An exception, which I have noted in chapter four, is the case of individuals such as anorexics whose illness may take the form of a reduction of their body images to a singular, overdetermined body image that has come to dominate their own self-perceptions.

2 In *Racism, Sexism, Power and Ideology* (London: Routledge Press, 1995), and especially in the chapter entitled, "Race and Nature: the System of Marks," Colette Guillaumin offers an excellent discussion of how allegedly natural categories such as race and sex, mark those who are designated as other (e.g. women of color) while leaving those who occupy the socially dominant position with the illusory belief that they don't have a race or even a sex (e.g. there is no alternative designation for a white women; we would never say of a white woman that she is "without color" because this is clearly inaccurate, and moreover, such an expression exposes the artificiality of the racial designation "of color"). According to Guillaumin, the ascription of a particular race or sex, "inscribes the system of domination on the body of the individual, assigning to the individual his/her place as a dominated person: but it does not assign any place to the dominator. Membership in the dominant group, on the contrary, is legally marked by a convenient lack of interdiction, by unlimited possibilities." (149)

Whiteness, as Guillaumin, Ruth Frankenberg, and others have suggested, is itself an ethnicity even if this ethnicity is itself invisible to those who identify themselves or are identified as white. Similarly, to be male is to be sexed even if, as Monique Wittig has argued, women are the only ones who cannot be conceived outside of their sex. See Monique Wittig, *The Straight Mind and Other Essays* (Boston: Beacon Press, 1992):8. This, in turn, means that men have body images just as women do. It does not mean that their body images are the same for they are not, but this is irrelevant since it is impossible for any two individuals to have the exact same body images despite similarities in race, class, gender, sexuality, age and religion, given the anatomical distinctness of their respective bodies as well as the inevitable differences that arise in their experiences as embodied subjects.

3 Indeed, as I have shown in chapter four, it is precisely when one aspect of our existence comes to dominate all others (e.g. a fear of getting fat for Ellen West) that this multiplicity tends to be reduced to a single body image that can be extremely unhealthy and even self-destructive.

4 Donna Haraway's discussion of the remarkable power and promise of the figure of the cyborg provides a perfect example of this. See Donna Haraway, *Simians, Cyborgs, and Women: The Reinvention of Nature* (New York: Routledge Press, 1991).

5 See, in particular, the chapter: "The Culture Industry: Enlightenment as Mass Deception" in Horkheimer and Adorno, *Dialectic of Englightenment*, trans. John Cumming (New York: The Continuum Publishing Company, 1993).

{bibliography}

Adams, Parveen. 1994. "The Bald Truth." *diacritics* 24 (52): 184–189.

Alcoff, Linda. 1991. "The Problem of Speaking for Others." *Cultural Critique* 20 (Winter): 5–32.

Aristotle. 1941. "Nicomachean Ethics, Books I and II." In *The Basic Works of Aristotle*. Edited by Richard McKeon. New York: Random House.

Balsamo, Anne. 1996. *Technologies of the Gendered Body: Reading Cyborg Women*. Durham: Duke University Press.

Barthes, Roland. 1986. *The Rustle of Language*. Translated by Richard Howard. Berkeley: University of California Press. Originally published as *Le bruissement de la langue* (Paris: Editions de Seuil, 1984).

Bartky, Sandra. 1990. *Femininity and Domination: Studies in the Phenomenology of Oppression*. New York: Routledge Press.

Baudrillard, Jean. 1983. *Simulations*. Translated by Paul Foss, P. Patton, and P. Beitchman. New York: Semiotext(e) Inc.

Beauvoir, Simone de. 1959. *Memoirs of a Dutiful Daughter*. Translated by James Kirkup. Cleveland: World Publishing Company. Originally published as *Memoires d'une jeune fille rangée* (Paris: Editions Gallimard, 1958).

___. 1965. *A Very Easy Death*. Translated by Patrick O'Brian. New York: Pantheon Books. Originally published as *Une mort très douce* (Paris: Editions Gallimard, 1964).

___. 1976. *The Ethics of Ambiguity*. Translated by Bernard Frechtman. New York: Citadel Books. Originally published as *Pour une Morale de l'ambiguité* (Paris: Editions Gallimard, 1947).

___. 1984. *Adieux: A Farewell to Sartre*. Translated by Patrick O'Brian. New York: Pantheon Books. Originally published as *La Cérémonie des adieux* (Paris: Editions Gallimard, 1981).

___. 1989. *The Second Sex*. Translated by H.M. Parshley. New York: Vintage Books. Originally published as *Le Deuxième Sexe*, 2 Vols. (Paris: Editions Gallimard, 1949).

Benhabib, Seyla. 1992. "The Generalized and the Concrete Other: The Kohlberg-Gilligan Controversy and Moral Theory." In *Situating the Self: Gender, Community and Postmodernism in Contemporary Ethics*. New York: Routledge.

Benthall, Jonathan. 1976. *The Body Electric: Patterns of Western Industrial Culture*. London: Thames and Hudson.

Bergoffen, Debra. 1997. *The Philosophy of Simone de Beauvoir: Gendered Phenomenologies, Erotic Generosities*. Albany: SUNY Press.

Bergson, Henri. 1955. *An Introduction to Metaphysics*. Translated by T.E. Hulme. New York: Macmillan Publishing Company. First Published in *Revue de métaphysique et de morale* (January, 1903).

___. 1975. *Mind-Energy: Lectures and Essays*. Translated by H. Wildon Carr. Westport: Greenwood Press. Originally published as *L'Énergie spirituelle* (Paris: Presses Universitaires de France, 1919).

___. [1896] 1991. *Matter and Memory*. Translated by Nancy Margaret Paul and W. Scott Palmer. New York: Zone Books.

Biddick, Kathleen. 1993. "Genders, Bodies, Borders: Technologies of the Visible." *Speculum* 68: 389–418.

Bigwood, Carol. 1991. "Renaturalizing the Body (With the Help of Merleau-Ponty)." *Hypatia* 6 (3) (fall): 54–73.

Binswanger, Ludwig. 1958. "The Case of Ellen West." In *Existence: A New Dimension in Psy-*

chiatry and Psychology. Edited by Rollo May, E. Angel, and H. F. Ellenberger. Translated by Werner M. Mendel and Joseph Lyons. New York: Basic Books. Originally published as "Der Fall Ellen West." *Schweizer Archiv für Neurologie und Psychiatrie*, vol. 53 (1944): 255–277; vol. 54 (1944): 69–117, 330–360; vol. 55 (1945): 16–40.

___. [1930] 1993. "Dream and Existence." In *Dream and Existence: Michel Foucault and Ludwig Binswanger*. Translated by Jacob Needleman. Edited by Keith Hoeller. New Jersey: Humanities Press.

Bordo, Susan. 1993. *Unbearable Weight: Feminism, Western Culture, and the Body*. Berkeley: University of California Press.

Bourdieu, Pierre. 1980. *The Logic of Practice*. Translated by Richard Nice. Stanford: Stanford University Press. Originally published as *Le Sens practique* (Paris: Les Editions de Minuit, 1980).

Braidotti, Rosi. 1994. *Nomadic Subjects: Embodiment and Sexual Difference in Contemporary Feminist Theory*. New York: Columbia University Press.

___. 1996. "Signs of Wonder and Traces of Doubt: On Teratology and Embodied Differences." In *Between Monsters, Goddesses, and Cyborgs: Feminist Confrontations with Science, Medicine and Cyberspace*. Edited by Nina Lykke and Rosi Braidotti. London: Zed Books.

Bruch, Hilde. 1978. *The Golden Cage: The Enigma of Anorexia Nervosa*. Cambridge: Harvard University Press.

Burgin, Victor. 1990. "Geometry and Abjection." In *Abjection, Melancholia and Love: The Work of Julia Kristeva*. Edited by John Fletcher and Andrew Benjamin. New York: Routledge Press.

Butler, Judith. 1989a. "Gendering the Body: Beauvoir's Philosophical Contribution." In *Women, Knowledge, and Reality: Explorations in Feminist Philosophy*. Edited by Ann Garry and Marilyn Pearsall. New York: Routledge Press.

___. 1989b. "The Body Politics of Julia Kristeva." *Hypatia* 3 (3) (winter): 104–117.

___. 1989c. "Sexual Ideology and Phenomenological Description: A Feminist Critique of Merleau-Ponty's *Phenomenology of Perception*." In *The Thinking Muse: Feminism and Modern French Philosophy*. Edited by Jeffner Allen and Iris Marion Young. Bloomington: Indiana University Press.

___. 1989d. "Foucault and the Paradox of Bodily Inscriptions." *The Journal of Philosophy*, LXXXVI (11) (November): 601–614.

___. 1990. *Gender Trouble: Feminism and the Subversion of Identity*. New York: Routledge Press.

___. 1991. "Imitation and Gender Insubordination." In *Inside/Out: Lesbian Theories, Gay Theories*. Edited by Diana Fuss. New York: Routledge Press.

___. 1993. *Bodies That Matter: On the Discursive Limits of "Sex."* New York: Routledge Press.

___. 1994. "Gender as Performance: An Interview with Judith Butler." *Radical Philosophy* 67 (Summer): 32–39.

___. 1997. *The Psychic Life of Power: Theories in Subjection*. Stanford: Stanford University Press.

Butler, Judith, and Biddy Martin. 1994b. "Cross-Identifications." *Diacritics* 24 (2–3) (summer/fall): 3.

Bynum, Caroline Walker. 1995. *The Resurrection of the Body in Western Christianity 200–1336*. New York: Columbia University Press.

Card, Claudia. 1995. "Gender and Moral Luck." In *Justice and Care: Essential Readings in Feminist Ethics*. Edited by Virginia Held. Boulder: Westview Press.

Casey, Edward S. 1993. *Getting Back Into Place: Toward a Renewed Understanding of the Place-World*. Bloomington: Indiana University Press.

Caskey, Noelle. 1985. "Interpreting Anorexia Nervosa." In *The Female Body in Western Cul-*

ture: Contemporary Perspectives. Edited by Susan Rubin Suleiman. Cambridge, Massachusetts: Harvard University Press.

Castro-Klaren, Sara. 1993. "What Does Cannibalism Speak? Jean de Léry and the Tupinamba Lesson." In *Carnal Knowledge: Essays on the Flesh, Sex and Sexuality in Hispanic Letters and Film.* Edited by Pamela Bacarisse. Pittsburgh: University of Pittsburgh Press.

Chanter, Tina. 1995. *Ethics of Eros: Irigaray's Rewriting of the Philosophers.* New York: Routledge Press.

Chapkis, Wendy. 1986. *Beauty Secrets: Women and the Politics of Appearance.* Boston: South End Press.

Chernin, Kim. 1981. *The Obsession: Reflections on the Tyranny of Slenderness.* New York: HarperCollins Publishers, Inc.

Cixous, Hélène. 1980. "The Laugh of The Medusa." In *New French Feminisms.* Edited by Elaine Marks and Isabelle de Courtivron. Amherst: University of Massachusetts Press. Revised from "Le Rire de la méduse." *L'arc* (1975).

___. 1990. "Castration or Decapitation?" In *Out There: Marginalization and Contemporary Cultures.* Edited by Russell Ferguson, M. Gever, T. T. Minh-ha, and C. West. Cambridge: MIT Press. (1981) *Signs* 7 (1) (autumn): 41–55. First appeared as "Le Sexe ou la Tête?" 1976. *Les Cahiers du GRIF* 13: 5–15.

Clement, Grace L. 1996. *Care, Autonomy, and Justice: Feminism and the Ethic of Care.* Boulder: Westview Press.

Cohen, Lawrence. 1995. "The Pleasure of Castration." In *Sexual Nature, Sexual Culture.* Edited by Paul R. Abramson and Steven D. Pinkerton. Chicago: University of Chicago Press.

Collins, Patricia Hill. 1990. *Black Feminist Thought: Knowledge, Consciousness, and the Politics of Empowerment.* New York: Routledge Press.

Copjec, Joan. 1994. "Sex and the Euthanasia of Reason." In *Supposing the Subject.* Edited by Joan Copjec. London: Verso.

___. 1994. *Read My Desire: Lacan against the Historicists.* Cambridge: The MIT Press.

Cornell, Drucilla. 1995. *The Imaginary Domain: Abortion, Pornography, and Sexual Harassment.* New York: Routledge Press.

Cortese, Anthony Joseph Paul. 1990. *Ethnic Ethics: The Restructuring of Moral Theory.* New York: SUNY Press.

Crosby, Christina. 1992. "Dealing With Differences." In *Feminists Theorize the Political.* Edited by Judith Butler and Joan W. Scott. New York: Routledge Press.

De Lauretis, Teresa. 1987. *Technologies of Gender: Essays on Theory, Film, and Fiction.* Bloomington: Indiana University Press.

___. 1994. *The Practice of Love: Lesbian Sexuality and Perverse Desire.* Bloomington: Indiana University Press.

Deleuze, Gilles. 1991. *Bergsonism.* Translated by Hugh Tomlinson and Barbara Habberjam. New York: Zone Books. Originally published as *Le Bergsonisme* (Paris: Presses Universitaires de France, 1966).

___. 1994. *Difference and Repetition.* Translated by Paul Patton. New York: Columbia University Press. Originally published as *Différence et Répétition* (Paris: Presses Universitaires de France, 1968).

Deleuze, Gilles, and Félix Guattari. 1983. *Anti-Oedipus: Capitalism and Schizophrenia.* Minnesota Press. Originally published as *L'anti-Oedipe* (Paris: Editions de Minuit, 1972).

___. 1987. *A Thousand Plateaus: Capitalism and Schizophrenia.* Vol. 2. Translated by Brian Massumi. Minneapolis: University of Minnesota Press. Originally published as *Mille Plateaux*, Vol. 2 of *Capitalisme et Schizophrénie.* (Paris: Editions de Minuit, 1980).

Descartes, René. [1641] 1979. *Meditations on First Philosophy.* Translated by Donald A. Cress. Cambridge: Hackett Publishing.

Douglas, Mary. [1966] 1992. *Purity and Danger: An Analysis of the Concepts of Pollution and Taboo*. New York: Routledge, Chapman & Hall, Inc..

Fanon, Franz. 1967. *Black Skin White Masks*. Translated by Charles Lam Markmann. New York: Grove Press, Inc. Originally published as *Peau Noire, Masques Blancs* (Paris: Editions du Seuil, 1952).

Farquhar, Dion. 1996. *The Other Machine: Discourse and Reproductive Technologies*. New York: Routledge Press.

Featherstone, Mike. 1991. "The Body in Consumer Culture." In *The Body: Social Process and Cultural Theory*. Edited by Mike Featherstone, M. Hepworth, B. S. Turner. London: Sage.

Fisher, Seymour. 1986. *Development and Structure of the Body Image*, Vols. I and II. New Jersey: Lawrence Erlbum Associates, Publishers.

Foucault, Michel. 1979. *Discipline and Punish: The Birth of the Prison*. Translated by Alan Sheridan. New York: Random House, Inc. Originally published as *Surveiller et Punir: Naissance de la prison* (Paris: Editions Gallimard, 1975).

_____. 1980. "Introduction." In *Herculine Barbin: Being the Recently Discovered Memoirs of a Nineteenth-Century Hermaphrodite*. Translated by Richard McDougall. New York: Pantheon Books.

_____. 1984. "Nietzsche, Genealogy, History." In *The Foucault Reader*. Edited by Paul Rabinow. New York: Pantheon Books.

_____. 1985. *The Use of Pleasure: The History of Sexuality*. Vol. 2. New York: Random House, Inc. Originally published as *L'Usage des plaisirs* (Paris: Editions Gallimard, 1984).

_____. 1990. *The History of Sexuality: An Introduction*. Vol. I. Translated by Robert Hurley. New York: Vintage Books. Originally published as *La Volenté de savoir* (Paris: Editions Gallimard, 1976).

_____. [1954] 1993. "Dream, Imagination and Existence." In *Dreams and Existence: Michel Foucault and Ludwig Binswanger*. Translated by Forrest Williams. Edited by Keith Hoeller. New Jersey: Humanities Press.

Frankenberg, Ruth. 1993. *White Women, Race Matters: The Social Construction of Whiteness*. Minneapolis: University of Minnesota Press.

Freud, Sigmund. [1914] 1957. "On Narcissism: An Introduction." In *A General Selection in the Works of Sigmund Freud*. Edited by John Rickman. Translated by Cecil M. Baines, revised by Joan Riviere. New York: Liveright Publishing Corperation.

_____. [1923] 1961. "The Ego and the Id" and "Some Psychical Consequences of the Anatomical Distinction Between the Sexes." In *The Standard Edition of the Complete Psychological Works of Sigmund Freud*. Vol. XIX. Translated by James Strachey. London: The Hogarth Press and the Institute of Psycho-analysis.

Friedman, Marilyn. 1987. "Care and Context in Moral Reasoning." In *Women and Moral Theory*. Edited by Eva Feder Kittay and Diana T. Meyers. Savage, Maryland: Rowman and Littlefield Publishers, Inc.

_____. 1995. "Beyond Caring: The De-Moralization of Gender." In *Justice and Care: Essential Readings in Feminist Ethics*. Edited by Virginia Held. Boulder: Westview Press.

Frye, Marilyn. 1989. "To See and Be Seen: The Politics of Reality." In *Women, Knowledge, and Reality: Explorations in Feminist Philosophy*. Edited by Ann Garry and Marilyn Pearsall. Boston: Unwin Hyman.

_____. 1990. "The Possibility of Feminist Theory." In *Theoretical Perspectives on Sexual Difference*. Edited by Deborah Rhode. New Haven: Yale University Press.

Fuss, Diana. 1984. "Interior Colonies: Franz Fanon and the Politics of Identification." *diacritics*, 24 (2–3) (summer/fall): 20–42.

Gallagher, Shaun. 1986. "Body Image and Body Schema: A Conceptual Clarification." *The Journal of Mind and Behavior* 7 (4): 541–554.

Galler, Roberta. 1984. "The Myth of the Perfect Body." In *Pleasure and Danger: Exploring Female Sexuality*. Edited by Carole S. Vance. Boston: Routledge and Kegan Paul.

Gatens, Moira. 1988. "Towards a Feminist Philosophy of the Body." In *Crossing Boundaries: Feminisms and the Critique of Knowledges*. Edited by Barbara Caine, E.A. Grosz, and M. de Lepervanche. Sydney, Australia: Allen and Unwin.

____. 1996. *Imaginary Bodies: Ethics, Power and Corporeality*. London: Routledge Press.

Gilbert, Sandra. 1979. "Hunger Pains." *University Publishing* (fall): 1, 11–12.

Gilligan, Carol. 1982. *In a Different Voice: Psychological Theory and Women's Development*. Cambridge: Harvard University Press.

____. 1993. "Reply to Critics." In *An Ethics of Care: Feminist and Interdisciplinary Perspectives*. Edited by Mary Jeanne Larrabee. New York: Routledge Press.

____. 1995. "Moral Orientation and Moral Development." In *Justice and Care: Essential Readings in Feminist Ethics*. Edited by Virginia Held. Boulder: Westview Press.

Gitlin, Todd. 1988. "We Build Excitement." In *Watching Television: A Pantheon Guide to Popular Culture*. Edited by Todd Gitlin. New York: Pantheon Books.

Goldberg, David Theo. 1990. "Introduction" and "The Social Formation of Racist Discourse." In *The Anatomy of Racism*. Edited by David Theo Goldberg. Minneapolis: University of Minnesota Press.

Gordon, Lewis R. 1995. *Bad Faith and Anti-Black Racism*. New Jersey: Humanities Press.

Grosz, Elizabeth. 1989. *Sexual Subversions: Three French Feminists*. Sydney, Australia: Allen and Unwin.

____. 1990a. *Jacques Lacan: A Feminist Introduction*. London: Routledge Press.

____. 1990b. "The Body of Signification." In *Abjection, Melancholia and Love: The Work of Julia Kristeva*. Edited by John Fletcher and Andrew Benjamin. New York: Routledge Press.

____. 1991. "Freaks: A Study of Human Anomalies." *Social Semiotics* 1 (2): 22–38.

____. 1992. "Bodies-Cities." In *Sexuality and Space*. Edited by Beatriz Colomina. Princeton: Princeton Architectural Press.

____. 1993. "Merleau-Ponty and Irigaray in the Flesh." *Thesis Eleven* (36): 37–59.

____. 1994a. *Volatile Bodies: Toward a Corporeal Feminism*. Bloomington: Indiana University Press.

____. 1994b. "A Thousand Tiny Sexes: Feminism and Rhizomatics." In *Gilles Deleuze and the Theater of Philosophy*. Edited by Constantin V. Boundas and Dorothea Olkowski. New York: Routledge Press.

____. [1989] 1994c. "Sexual Difference and the Problem of Essentialism." In *The Essential Difference*. Edited by Naomi Schor and Elizabeth Weed. Bloomington: Indiana University Press.

____. 1994d. "Experimental Desire: Rethinking Queer Subjectivity." In *Supposing the Subject*. Edited by Joan Copjec. London: Verso.

____. 1994e. "The Labors of Love. Analyzing Perverse Desire: An Interrogation of Teresa de Lauretis's *The Practice of Love*." *differences* 6 (2–3): 274–295.

____. 1995a. "Animal Sex: Libido as Desire and Death." In *Sexy Bodies: The Strange Carnalities of Feminism*. Edited by Elizabeth Grosz and Elspeth Probyn. London: Routledge.

____. 1995b. *Space, Time and Perversion: Essays on the Politics of Bodies*. New York: Routledge Press.

Guillamin, Collette. 1995. *Racism, Sexism, Power, and Ideology*. London: Routledge Press.

Halberstam, Judith, and Ira Livingston. 1995. "Introduction: Posthuman Bodies." In *Posthuman Bodies*. Edited by Judith Halberstam and Ira Livingston. Bloomington: Indiana University Press.

Haraway, Donna. 1991. *Simians, Cyborgs and Women: The Reinvention of Nature*. New York: Routledge Press.

Heidegger, Martin. 1962. *Being and Time*. Translated by John Macquarrie and Edward

Robinson. New York: Harper and Row. Originally published as *Sein und Zeit* (Tübingen: Max Niemeyer Verlag, 1927).

———. 1993. "Letter on Humanism." In *Martin Heidegger: Basic Writings*. Edited by David Farell Krell. Translated by Frank A. Capuzzi with J. Glenn Gray. San Francisco: Harper Collins. Originally published as *Brief über den Humanismus* (Bern: A. Francke Verlag, 1947).

Held, Virginia. 1995. "Feminist Moral Inquiry and the Feminist Future." In *Justice and Care: Essential Readings in Feminist Ethics*. Edited by Virginia Held. Boulder: Westview Press.

hooks, bell. 1990. "Marginalization as Site of Resistance." In *Out There: Marginalization and Contemporary Cultures*. Edited by Russell Ferguson, M. Gever, T. T. Minh-ha, and C. West. Cambridge: MIT Press.

Hope, Trevor. 1994. "Sexual Indifference and the Homosexual Male Imaginary." *diacritics* 24 (2–3): 169–183.

Horkheimer, Max and Theodor W. Adorno. 1996. *Dialectic of Enlightenment*. Translated by John Cumming. New York: Continuum Publishing. Originally published as *Dialektik der Aufklärung* (New York: Social Studies Association, 1944).

Hume, David. [1739] 1978. *A Treatise of Human Nature*. Edited by L.A. Selby-Bigge. Oxford: Oxford University Press.

———. [1757] 1989. "Of the Standard of Taste." In *Aesthetics: A Critical Anthology*, 2nd ed. Edited by George Dickie, R. Sclafani, and R. Roblin. New York: St. Martin's Press.

Husserl, Edmund. 1965. "Philosophy as Rigorous Science." In *Phenomenology and the Crisis of Philosophy*. Translated by Quentin Lauer. New York: Harper and Row Publishers, Inc. Originally published as "Philosophie als Strenge Wissenschaft." *Logos*, I (1910–1911): 289–341.

———. [1913] 1962. *Ideas: General Introduction to Pure Phenomenology*. Translated by W.R. Boyce Gibson. New York: Collier Books.

Irigaray, Luce. 1981. "And the One Doesn't Stir Without the Other." *Signs* 7 (1) (autumn): 60–67.

———. 1985. *This Sex Which Is Not One*. Translated by Catherine Porter with Carolyn Burke. New York: Cornell University Press. Originally published as *Ce Sexe qui n'en est pas un* (Paris: Minuit, 1977).

———. 1988. Interview in Paris (summer 1980). In *Women Analyze Women in France, England, and the U.S.* Edited by Elaine Hoffman Baruch and Lucienne J. Serrano. New York: New York University Press.

———. 1991. *Marine Lover of Friedrich Nietzsche*. Translated by Gillian Gill. New York: Columbia University Press. Originally published as *Amante Marine de Friedrich Nietzsche* (Paris: Les Editions de Minuit, 1980).

———. 1993. *An Ethics of Sexual Difference*. Translated by Carolyn Burke and Gillian C. Gill. Ithaca: Cornell University Press. Originally published as *Éthique de la difference sexuelle* (Paris: Les Editions de Minuit, 1984).

Jaggar, Alison M. 1995. "Caring as a Feminist Practice of Moral Reason." In *Justice and Care: Essential Readings in Feminist Ethics*. Edited by Virginia Held. Boulder: Westview Press.

Jay, Martin. 1993. *Downcast Eyes: The Denigration of Vision in Twentieth Century French Thought*. Berkeley: University of California Press.

Johnson, Mark. 1993. *Moral Imagination: Implications of Cognitive Science for Ethics*. Chicago: University of Chicago Press.

Kafka, Franz. 1983. "A Hunger Artist." In *The Complete Stories*. Edited by Nahum N. Glatzer. New York: Schocken Books.

Kant, Immanuel. [1785] 1964. *Groundwork of the Metaphysic of Morals*. Translated by H.J. Paton. New York: Harper and Row.

Kaschak, Ellyn. 1992. *Engendered Lives: A New Psychology of Women's Experience.* New York: Basic Books.

Kierkegaard, Søren. 1983. *Fear and Trembling.* Translated by Howard V. Hong and Edna H. Hong. Princeton: Princeton University Press. Originally published as *Frygt og bœ ven* (Copenhagen: Bianco Luno Press, 1843).

Kittay, Eva Feder. 1995. "Taking Dependency Seriously: The Family and Medical Leave Act Considered in Light of the Social Organization of Dependency Work and Gender Equality." *Hypatia* 10 (1): 8–29.

Kofman, Sarah. 1985. *The Enigma of Woman: Woman in Freud's Writings.* Translated by Catherine Porter. Ithaca: Cornell University Press. Originally published as *L'Enigma de la Femme: La Femme dans les textes de Freud* (Editions Galilée, 1980).

Kohlberg, Lawrence. 1981. *The Philosophy of Moral Development: Moral Stages and the Idea of Justice.* San Francisco: Harper and Row.

Kristeva, Julia. 1980. *Desire In Language.* Translated by Thomas Gora, A. Jardine, and L. S. Roudiez. New York: Columbia University Press. Originally published in two separate editions: *Polylogue* (Paris: Editions de Seuil, 1977) and *Recherches pour une sémanalyse* (Paris: Editions de Seuil, 1969).

———. 1982. *Powers of Horror: An Essay on Abjection.* Translated by Leon S. Roudiez. New York: Columbia University Press. Originally published as *Pouvoirs de l'horreur: Essai sur l'abjection* (Paris: Editions de Seuil, 1980).

———. 1987. *Tales of Love.* Translated by Leon S. Roudiez. New York: Columbia University Press. *Histoires d'amour* (Editions Denoël, 1983).

———. 1988. Interview in Paris (summer 1980). In *Women Analyze Women in France, England, and the U.S.* Edited by Elaine Hoffman Bruch and Lucienne J. Serrano. New York: New York University Press.

Lacan, Jaques. 1953. "Some Reflections on the Ego." *The International Journal of Psychoanalysis* 34: 11–19.

———. 1977. *Écrits: A Selection.* Translated by Alan Sheridan. London: Tavistock Publications. Originally published as *Écrits.* (Paris: Editions Seuil, 1949).

———. 1985. *Feminine Sexuality: Jacques Lacan and the École Freudienne.* Edited by Juliet Mitchell and Jacqueline Rose. Translated by Jacqueline Rose. New York: W.W. Norton & Co.

Larsen, Nella. [1929] 1986. *Quicksand and Passing.* Edited by Deborah C. McDowell. New Jersey: Rutgers University Press.

Le Doeuff, Michèle. 1989. *The Philosophical Imaginary.* Translated by Colin Gordon. Stanford: Stanford University Press. Originally published as *L'Imaginaire Philosophique* (Paris: Editions Payot, 1980).

Leys, Ruth. 1992. "The Real Miss Beauchamp: Gender and the Subject of Imitation." In *Feminists Theorize the Political.* Edited by Judith Butler and Joan W. Scott. New York: Routledge Press.

Lorde, Audre. 1990. "Age, Race, Class, and Sex: Women Redefining Difference." In *Out There: Marginalization and Contemporary Cultures.* Edited by Russell Ferguson, M. Gever, T. T. Minh-ha, and C. West. Cambridge: MIT Press.

Lugones, María. 1990. "Playfulness, 'World'-Traveling and Loving Perception." In *Lesbian Philosophies and Cultures.* Edited by Jeffner Allen. New York: SUNY Press.

Lydon, Mary. 1988. "Foucault and Feminism: A Romance of Many Dimensions." In *Feminism and Foucault: Reflections on Resistance.* Edited by Irene Diamond and Lee Quinby. Boston: Northeastern University Press.

Lykke, Nina. 1996. "Between Monsters, Goddesses and Cyborgs: Feminist Confrontations with Science." In *Between Monsters, Goddesses and Cyborgs: Feminist Confrontations with Science, Medicine, and Cyberspace.* Edited by Nina Lykke and Rosi Braidotti. London: Zed Books.

MacIntyre, Alasdair. 1981. *After Virtue.* Southbend, Indiana: University of Notre Dame Press.

MacSween, Morag. 1993. *Anorexic Bodies: A Feminist and Sociological Perspective on Anorexia Nervosa.* London: Routledge Press.

Mann, Thomas. 1945. *The Magic Mountain.* Translated by John E. Woods. New York: Vintage Books. Originally published as *Der Zauberberg* (Berlin: S. Fischer Verlag, 1924).

McNay, Lois. 1991. "The Foucauldian Body and the Exclusion of Experience." *Hypatia* 6 (3) (fall): 125–139.

Mead, George Herbert. [1934] 1962. *Mind, Self, and Society from the Standpoint of a Social Behaviorist.* Edited by Charles W. Morris. Chicago: University of Chicago Press.

Merleau-Ponty, Maurice. 1962. *Phenomenology of Perception.* Translated by Colin Smith. London: Routledge and Kegan Paul Press. Originally published as *Phenomenologie de la perception* (Paris: Editions Gallimard, 1945).

___. 1964a. "The Child's Relations With Others" and "Eye and Mind." In *The Primacy of Perception.* Edited by James Edie and Carleton Dallery. Translated by William Cobb. Evanston: Northwestern University Press. Originally published in two separate editions: "Les Relations avec autrui chez l'enfant," in *Cours de Sorbonne* (Paris, 1960) and *L'oeil et l'esprit* (Editions Gallimard, 1964).

___. 1964b. *Sense and Non-Sense.* Translated by Hubert L. Dreyfus and Patricia Allen Dreyfus. Evanston: Northwestern University Press. Originally published as *Sens et non-sens* (Les Editions Nagel, 1948).

___. 1964c. *Signs.* Translated by Richard McClearly. Evanston: Northwestern University Press. Originally published as *Signes.* (Paris: Editions Gallimard, 1960).

___. 1967. *The Structure of Behavior.* Translated by Alden L. Fisher. Boston: Beacon Press. Originally published as *Structure du Comportement.* (Paris: Presses Universitaires de France, 1942).

___. 1968. *The Visible and the Invisible.* Edited by Claude Lefort. Translated by Alphonso Lingis. Evanston: Northwestern University Press. Originally published as *Le Visible et l'invisible* (Paris: Editions Gallimard, 1964).

___. 1973a. *Consciousness and the Acquisition of Language.* Translated by Hugh J. Silverman. Originally published as "La Conscience et l'acquisition de langage." *Bulletin de psychologie,* 236, XVIII, 3–6 (1964): 226–259.

___. 1973b. *The Prose of the World.* Edited by Claude Lefort. Translated by John O'Neill. Evanston: Northwestern University Press. Originally published as *La Prose du Monde.* (Paris: Editions Gallimard, 1969).

___. 1988. *In Praise of Philosophy and Other Essays.* Translated by John Wild, J. Edie, and J. O'Neill. Originally published in two separate editions: *Éloge de la Philosophie* (Paris: Editions Gallimard, 1953) and *Résumés du cours, Collège de France* (Paris: Editions Gallimard, 1968).

___. 1993. *The Merleau-Ponty Aesthetics Reader: Philosophy and Painting.* Edited by Galen A. Johnson. Translation editor Michael Smith. Evanston: Northwestern University Press.

Meyers, Diana Tietjens. 1994. *Subjection and Subjectivity: Psychoanalytic Feminism and Moral Theory.* New York: Routledge Press.

Miles, Margaret R. 1986. "The Virgin's One Bare Breast: Female Nudity and Religious Meaning in Tuscan Early Renaissance Culture." In *The Female Body in Western Culture: Contemporary Perspectives.* Edited by Susan Rubin Suleiman. Cambridge, Massachussets: Harvard University Press.

Mishkind, Marc E. et. al. 1986. "The Embodiment of Masculinity: Cultural, Psychological, and Behavioral Dimensions." *American Behavioral Scientist,* 29 (5) (May/June): 545–562.

Morgan, Kathryn Pauly. 1991. "Women and the Knife: Cosmetic Surgery and the Coloniza-
tion of Women's Bodies." *Hypatia* 6 (3) (fall): 25–53.

Morris, Meaghan. 1988. *The Pirate's Fiancée: Feminism Reading Postmodernism*. London:
Verso.

Munter, Carol. 1984. "Fat and the Fantasy of Perfection." In *Pleasure and Danger: Exploring
Female Sexuality*. Edited by Carole S. Vance. Boston: Routledge Kegan Paul.

Murphy, Julien. 1992. "Is Pregnancy Necessary? Feminist Concerns about Ectogenesis." In
Feminist Perspectives in Medical Ethics. Edited by Helen Bequaert Holmes and Laura
Purdy. Bloomington: Indiana University Press.

Murphy, Robert. 1987. *The Body Silent*. New York: Henry Holt and Co.

Nagel, Thomas. 1979. *Mortal Questions*. Cambridge: Cambridge University Press.

Nietzsche, Friedrich. 1956. *The Birth of Tragedy and the Genealogy of Morals*. Translated by
Francis Golffing. New York: Doubleday and Company, Inc.

___. 1968. *Twilight of the Idols*. Translated by R.J. Hollingdale. Originally published as
Götzen-Dämmerung, oder: Wie man mit dan Hammer philosophirt (Leipzig: C.G. Nau-
man, 1889).

___. [1887] 1974. *The Gay Science*. Translated by Walter Kaufman. New York: Random
House.

Noddings, Nel. 1984. *Caring: A Feminine Approach to Ethics and Moral Education*. Berkeley: University of California Press.

Okin, Susan Moller. 1990. "Thinking Like a Woman." In *Theoretical Perspectives on Sexual
Difference*. Edited by Deborah Rhode. New Haven: Yale University Press.

Oliver, Kelly. 1991. "Book Review on *Throwing Like a Girl and Other Essays in Feminist Philosophy and Social Theory* by Iris Young." *Hypatia* 6 (3) (fall): 218–221.

___. 1993. *Reading Kristeva: Unraveling the Double-Bind*. Bloomington: Indiana University
Press.

___. 1995. *Womanizing Nietzsche: Philosophy's Relation to the "Feminine."* New York: Rout-
ledg Press.

Ortner, Sherry. 1974. "Is Female to Male as Nature is to Culture?" In *Woman, Culture, and
Society*. Edited by Michelle Zimbalist Rosaldo and Louise Lamphere. Stanford: Stanford University Press.

Piercy, Marge. 1976. *Woman on the Edge of Time*. New York: Knopf.

Probyn, Elspeth. 1991. "This Body Which Is Not One: Speaking an Embodied Self." *Hypatia* 6 (3) (fall): 111–124.

Purdy, Laura. 1996. *Reproducing Persons: Issues in Feminist Bioethics*. Ithaca: Cornell University Press.

Rawls, John. 1971. *A Theory of Justice*. Cambridge: Harvard University Press.

Rich, Adrienne. 1976. *Of Woman Born: Motherhood as Experience and Institution*. New
York: Bantam Books.

Richard, Patricia Bayer. 1995. "The Tailor-Made Child: Implications for Women and the
State." In *Expecting Trouble: Surrogacy, Fetal Abuse, and New Reproductive Technologies*. Edited by Patricia Bolling. Boulder: Westview Press.

Ricœur, Paul. 1991. *A Ricœur Reader: Reflection and Imagination*. Edited by Mario J.
Valdés. Toronto: University of Toronto Press.

Rivière, Joan. 1929. "Womanliness as Masquerade." *IJPA* x: 303–313.

Rodriguez, Richard. 1990. "Complexion." In *Out There: Marginalization and Contemporary
Cultures*. Edited by Russell Ferguson, M. Gever, T. T. Minh-ha, and C. West. Cam-
bridge: MIT Press. Previously published in *Hunger of Memory. The Education of Richard
Rodriguez: An Autobiography* (Boston: D.R. Godine, 1982).

Ruddick, Sara. 1989. *Maternal Thinking: Toward a Politics of Peace*. New York: Ballantine
Books.

___. 1995. "Injustice in Families: Assault and Domination." In *Justice and Care: Essential Readings in Feminist Ethics*. Edited by Virginia Held. Boulder: Westview Press.

Sartre, Jean Paul. 1955. "Dirty Hands." In *No Exit and Three Other Plays*. Translated by Lionel Abel. New York: Vintage Books. Originally published as *Les Mains Sales* (Paris: Editions Gallimard, 1948).

___. 1956. *Being and Nothingness*. Translated by Hazel E. Barnes. New York: Washington Square Press. Originally published as *L'Être et le néant* (Paris: Editions Gallimard, 1943).

Sawday, Jonathan. 1995. *The Body Emblazoned: Dissection and the Human Body in Renaissance Culture*. London: Routledge Press.

Schilder, Paul. [1935] 1950. *The Image and Appearance of the Human Body: Studies in the Constructive Energies of the Psyche*. New York: International Universities Press, Inc.

Schor, Naomi. 1994. "This Essentialism Which Is Not One: Coming to Grips with Irigaray." In *The Essential Difference*. Edited by Naomi Schor and Elizabeth Weed. Bloomington: Indiana University Press.

Seltzer, Mark. 1992. *Bodies and Machines*. New York: Routledge Press.

Sexton, Anne. 1971. *Transformations*. Boston: Houghton Mifflin Company.

Silverman, Hugh. 1993. "Cézanne's Mirror Stage." In *The Merleau-Ponty Aesthetics Reader*. Edited by Galen A. Johnson. Evanston: Northwestern University Press.

Silvers, Anita. 1995. "Reconciling Equality to Difference: Caring (F)or Justice for People with Disabilities." *Hypatia* 10 (1): 30–55.

Singer, Linda. 1993. *Erotic Welfare: Sexual Theory and Politics in the Age of Epidemic*. Edited by Judith Butler and Maureen MacGrogan. New York: Routledge Press.

Stone, Allucquère Rosanne. 1995. *The War of Desire and Technology at the Close of the Mechanical Age*. Cambridge: The MIT Press.

Tiemersma, Douwe. 1989. *Body Schema and Body Image*. Amsterdam: Swets and Zeitlinger.

Tolstoy, Leo. [1886] 1981. *The Death of Ivan Ilyich*. Translated by Lynn Solotaroff. New York: Bantam Books.

Turner, Bryan S. 1994. *Regulating Bodies: Essays in Medical Sociology*. New York: Routledge Press.

Vintges, Karen. 1996. *Philosophy as Passion: The Thinking of Simone de Beauvoir*. Bloomington: Indiana University Press.

Walker, Margaret Urban. 1992. "Feminism, Ethics, and the Question of Theory." *Hypatia* 7 (3): 23–38.

Weiss, Gail. 1995a. "Creative Agency and Fluid Images: A Review of Iris Young's *Throwing Like a Girl and Other Essays in Feminist Philosophy and Social Theory*." *Human Studies* 17: 471–478.

___. 1995b. "Ambiguity, Absurdity, and Reversibility: Responses to Indeterminacy." *Journal of the British Society for Phenomenology* 26 (1) (January): 43–52.

___. 1995c. "Sex-Selective Abortion: A Relational Approach." *Hypatia* 10 (1): 202–217.

Whitford, Margaret. 1991. *Luce Irigaray: Philosophy in the Feminine*. New York: Routledge Press.

___. 1991. "Irigaray's Body Symbolic." *Hypatia* 6 (3) (fall): 97–110.

Wiegman, Robyn. 1995. *American Anatomies: Theorizing Race and Gender*. Durham: Duke University Press.

Williams, Bernard. 1981. *Moral Luck*. New York: Cambridge University Press.

Wittig, Monique. 1986. *The Lesbian Body*. Boston: Beacon Press.

___. 1992. *The Straight Mind and Other Essays*. Boston: Beacon Press.

Wollheim, Richard. 1974. "Imagination and Identification: The Inner Structure of a Psychic Mechanism." In *Freud: A Collection of Critical Essays*. Edited by Richard Wollheim. New York: Anchor Books.

Young, Iris. 1990. *Throwing Like a Girl and Other Essays in Feminist Philosophy and Social Theory*. Bloomington: Indiana University Press.

Žižek, Slavoj. 1989. *The Sublime Object of Ideology*. London: Verso.

{index}